BEYOND DESPAIR

BEYOND DESPAIR

The Rwanda Genocide against the

Tutsi through the Eyes of Children

HÉLÈNE DUMAS

Translated by Catherine Porter

Foreword by Louisa Lombard

FORDHAM UNIVERSITY PRESS NEW YORK 2024

This book was originally published in French as Hélène Dumas, *Sans ciel ni terre: Paroles orphelines du génocide des Tutsi (1994–2006)*, Copyright © Editions La Découverte, Paris, 2020.

This work has benefited from French government funding managed by the Agence Nationale de la Recherche under the France 2030 program, reference ANR-11-LABX-0067.

Cet ouvrage a bénéficié du soutien des Programmes d'aide à la publication de l'Institut français.

This work received support for excellence in publication and translation from Albertine Translation, a program created by Villa Albertine and funded by FACE Foundation.

This book is published with the support of La Fondation pour la Mémoire de la Shoah.

Visit us online at www.fordhampress.com.

Library of Congress Cataloging-in-Publication Data available online at https://catalog.loc.gov.

Printed in the United States of America

26 25 24   5 4 3 2 1

First edition

To those who wrote their memories
of a ravaged childhood

CONTENTS

Part III   The Life of an Orphan Has No End—*Ubupfubyi ntibushira*

Photographs follow page 108

FOREWORD

June 2023

Louisa Lombard

The elderly man spoke carefully, listing the names and ages of his neighbors before the Genocide against the Tutsi in 1994. It was July 2002, and we were in Byumba, a town sixty kilometers north of the Rwandan capital, Kigali. I was observing the initial phases of the *gacaca* courts that were being set up to try those accused of genocidal crimes. An early step was to take a town census. The man trailed off—*what were they called again*? He couldn't get the details to resurface in his mind. My friend Pascal, a genocide survivor, whispered to me, "When whole families were killed, it's difficult to remember names and ages, especially of children." He shrugged. The memory lapses were both tragic and understandable.

It was in this not-long-after period of Rwandan history that more than one hundred child survivors of genocide hunched over desks and filled the pages of flimsy school notebooks with names, ages, and so much more. Their careful handwriting conveys the weightiest of recollections: their experiences of the 1994 Genocide against the Tutsi. The notebooks are now housed at the Commission nationale de lutte contre le génocide (CNLG, National Commission for the Fight against Genocide) in Kigali, Rwanda. They are one hundred versions of what genocide looks like "from the height of a child," as Hélène Dumas puts it.

Children tell us things about genocide that we would not otherwise have known. An adult who returns to her primary school will inevitably remark that the chairs are smaller than she remembered. Surely they weren't so small at the time. Though an adult can conjure back the feelings or events of childhood, the remembrances are filtered through subsequent experience in ways that inevitably alter them, and absent some special prodding (a photo, someone else's memory), many details are simply lost. Children's narrations of genocide show us truths that adults cannot remember in the same way, or have forgotten, in part because of what it takes to become an adult.

One such child-specific truth is children's experiences of family life. In response to the inevitable scrapes and bruises of growing up, parents and other elders always had a *pole* [po-lay] at the ready, a phatic word that expresses "I'm sorry you are hurt, but it will get better." Children first encountered racist ideas and discrimination in their schools. They report coming home to ask their parents what it meant to be Hutu or Tutsi and which they were. Some parents told their kids to pretend they were Hutu so they would not get bullied or refused opportunities on that basis. Others told them they were Tutsi and warned them they would be insulted because of it but must ignore the slights. Through children's words we meet parents with different styles of discipline, different ways of teaching their children, and different tactics to keep them safe amid the fear, anger, and turmoil of the years preceding the genocide. The specificity, thoughtfulness, and diversity of parenting approaches in these children's stories rarely come across so strongly in depictions of African parents provided by adults. The horror of the genocide is made all the more profound by having been granted this view into the everyday, loving family life it shattered. One thing that was lost: the wisdom and guidance of elders. "What makes me sad," wrote a girl who was thirteen during the genocide, "is that in those days I heard [my parents] give a lot of advice to my older sisters but I didn't understand its value then, and I didn't know that this would be the last of it." She could identify the nature of what they were saying but was too young to grasp its meaning and carry it with her. While the experience of understanding form but not content is not unique to children, it is nevertheless more common earlier in life.

Another topic that children report on much more extensively than older people is animals. Adults recounting their experiences of genocide let other animals make cameos: a cow that was executed, a dog that accompanied the people who were hunting their fellow humans. The children seem not to have learned to filter out other creatures and make the humans always the protagonists. They describe the ways the genocide remixed the relationships between humans and other species. Some species joined the killers, participating in the genocide in fact if not in intent. Dogs sniffed out people who were hiding, bit and chased during attacks, and desecrated corpses.[1] Small birds also seemed to conspire with the killers, because they would twitter loudly when they encountered humans hiding in the fields and swamps where they did not usually trespass, thereby alerting the hunters to where they could find their prey. Other species became victims alongside humans through the manner in which they were tortured and killed. The children write that cows "screamed" (not lowed or mooed) in agony as they bled out over several days after having their tendons slit.

The children describe how the animal metaphors that had long been used to demonize Tutsi became more literal during the genocide. *Inzoka* (snake, viper) was one such epithet. Yet snakes became comparatively friendly during the genocide, almost kin, as a girl of eight at the time wrote afterward: "You who will read this testimony, you know that during the war [the genocide], snakes were our friends. We spent time with them in the holes they had dug; we spent nights in the bush they inhabited; we gobbled down their food; we licked the earth where they had left their traces. . . . I'm talking about snakes because they knew that we were their brothers. They were good neighbors for us at a time when humans like ourselves abandoned us." The children are specific and vivid in describing how their struggle to survive genocide meant their lives became intertwined with animals, plants, and wild ecosystems. Given their agrarian lifestyles, they knew this natural world well and were able to describe precisely how the genocide changed the relationships and patterns of cohabitation among creatures.

A third trait of children's accounts of genocide is the limited role that they accord to ideology or other redemptive narrative arcs. They are focused on people—the beloved family members whom they lost—and what they actually experienced, rather than on extrapolating from that to a level of transcendent or immanent meaning. Rather than explaining the causes or the meaning or the lessons of genocide, they tell what they saw, heard, smelled, feared. Their experiences support the idea that genocide is a crime unlike others, even in the context of the high levels of political violence in the African Great Lakes region. But many of them faced enormous hardship and privation after the genocide ended, as well. Some of the combatants in the Rwandan Patriotic Forces (RPF) who fought their way to Kigali and in so doing ended the genocide stopped long enough along the way to care for the surviving children they encountered. They disinfected and bandaged wounds, washed and combed the children's insect-filled hair, clothed their naked bodies, and spoon-fed them. But other child survivors believed the fearsome stories that circulated widely about the "animal-like" RPF insurgents and fled before their approach, ending up as servants and laborers in refugee camps run by genocidaires. Still others remained abandoned after the genocide and received little to nothing from the new government, which saw itself as inherently different from the genocidal regime that preceded it but whose officials lived in bubbles of security compared to the millions whose lives had been torn asunder by the cataclysm.

It is a testament to Hélène Dumas's integrity as a historian that she does not instrumentalize and thereby distort the children's accounts on behalf of a grand takeaway message of her own. Instead, she fills in the elements of the scenes that the children leave out and explains the common themes, so that the full force of the children's experiences hits readers all the harder and more directly.

My own involvement with Rwanda began in 2002, when I spent three months in the country observing the early phases of the *gacaca* courts and talking to people about what the buzzword "reconciliation" might actually mean in practice, research that became my undergraduate thesis. That was a far less certain period, just eight years after the genocide. People did not know whether the relative lack of violence in the country would be punctured by another "hole," as Rwandans came to think of the effects of the brutality that had been recurrent since before independence.[2] Some people were worried, others hopeful, others despairing; all had to make decisions about how to go forward, and few of the options they could muster were good ones. One student leader and genocide survivor I spoke with described her practical studies as "a punishment"—she'd wanted to become a scholar, but all the elders who could have supported her had been killed.

I did not return to Rwanda until 2016, by which point Rwanda had become known for its exceedingly low levels of violent crime, brand-new convention center, and effectively one-party state. In 2017, I began a new research project exploring how the many Rwandan soldiers working abroad as peacekeepers confront moral dilemmas in their work. While my research now is not explicitly about the genocide, this history of violence is not a topic anyone working in the country can ignore, even now that Rwandans think of themselves as living, for the first time, in "ordinary times."[3]

How to talk about the genocide is a more complex issue. This book takes the stance that it is not just acceptable but valuable to listen directly to the experiences of genocide survivors, to immerse oneself in what they knew, sensed, and learned as a result of what they endured, and to do so without an excess of omniscient authorial context-mongering (for example, by appending phrases like "Of course, it's more complicated than that . . ." to what people say). Sit with the children. Read their recollections slowly. But not just before bed. It is a privilege to learn from them. Their words will change you. Theirs are not the only voices to listen to, but they deserve your full attention.

Readers less familiar with Rwandan history might appreciate an all-in-one-place summary indicating some of the tendencies and the points of contention, as well as sources for further reading.

Geography and politics have intertwined to make Rwanda distinctive, particularly compared to its surrounding region. Smaller than the island nation of Haiti, Rwanda's territory includes both savannah and tropical forest, but its stereotypical landscape is lush hills almost entirely given over to intense cultivation and (historically) livestock grazing, especially cattle. (The towering, slim eucalyptus trees so prevalent now arrived only during the colonial period.) The high altitude banished the mosquitoes and tsetse flies that ravage tropical lowlands with disease. As a result, Rwanda has long been home to far more humans, living far more closely together, than the surrounding region. In conjunction with the dense population and agriculture, there has long been a far more centralized political system and much more extensive social control.[4]

For centuries, people have farmed, raised cattle, and hunted and gathered in Rwanda. Also for centuries, Rwanda has had an intricate web of political and social institutions, some of which link residents and others of which differentiate them. Kingdoms emerged in the 1600s, but clans were more important politically and socially. In addition, pastoralists had *abatware w'umukenke* (chiefs of pastures), while farmers had *abahinza* (hereditary land chiefs) and *abatware w'ubukaka* (another kind of land chief).[5] People were also part of multiple, overlapping family groups. The *umuryango* (lineage) and *inzu* (house) groupings were organized around a shared common ancestor, while the *ubwoko* (clan) consisted of relatives whose kinship was not based on a shared ancestor. Tutsi (herders; fewer in number and higher status) and Hutu (farmers; more numerous and lower status) were permeable categories, with intermarriage.[6] There were both Tutsi and Hutu kings. Twa (indigenous hunter-gatherers) were considered more a people apart and below—though their hunting knowledge and artistry were key to court life.[7] This complex picture changed dramatically between the seventeenth and twentieth centuries with the increasing dominance of the Nyiginya royal dynasty. To give just one example: *ubugabire* was an early social institution through which farmers could be the clients of herder patrons, but over time it transformed into the system of *ubuhake*, which was more rigid in its strictures. The military also became more important as an institution that linked all spheres of public and family life.[8] The Nyiginya military was expansionist, and by the mid-1800s it covered a space larger than the country recognized as Rwanda today. Poet-historians say that the name Rwanda comes from the verb *kuaanda* (now archaic), which means "to expand" or "to gain territory." Raiders from the Swahili Coast, of whom Tippu Tip was only the most notorious, wreaked havoc on the Great Lakes region during the nineteenth century, claiming both people and ivory, but Rwandan borders were well defended by the mid-1850s, and the raiders mostly left people living in the polity alone.[9]

European colonial administrators arrived in the late 1800s and assumed that the political institutions they encountered were evidence of immutable tradition rather than the tenuous creations of visionary and despotic leaders like King Rwabugiri (who reigned from 1853 to 1895). Germany claimed Rwanda first, but after its defeat in World War I Belgium took over. Belgians noticed the great social differences between "Tutsi" (aristocrats, cattle-keepers), "Hutu" (commoners, farmers), and "Twa" (indigenous, pygmies). They understood the differences to be racial, following the most racist thinking of the time. That is, they saw them not as social categories but as fundamental and biological differences associated with differing aptitudes. The government promoted Tutsi, the high-status minority, as not just current rulers but natural and necessary rulers. They issued everyone identification cards that listed to which of the three categories they belonged.

The colonial system began to crack in the 1950s. Hutu activists who had managed to scrape together an education despite government discrimination (young, idealistic Belgian priests helped) demanded full citizenship. Since

Hutu were a large majority (somewhere between 75 and 90 percent of the population) that needed to recover from having been denied opportunities, they felt they should be the ones to rule. Of the several political parties jostling for power at the time, one, PARMEHUTU, had an ideology that was "explicitly 'racial': its goal was to fight the 'hegemony of the invading Tutsi race.'"[10] At independence in 1962, the PARMEHUTU leader and ideologue Grégoire Kayibanda became the country's first president.

The period from the 1960s to the 1980s was marked by a few opposing tendencies. One was the scapegoating of Tutsi, including recurrent bursts of violence against them, perpetrated both by state forces and by regular people, as well as quotas and other ways of limiting Tutsi access to education and skilled jobs.[11] There were also political movements that cut across the Hutu–Tutsi divide and people who rejected the categories altogether. People mobilized around regional issues; southerners felt neglected compared to the richer capital region to the north. Rwanda was very poor, but donors loved working in the country because the government was well organized—that long history of centralized-yet-differentiated political organization was palpable in the government's ability to keep track of its citizens, all the way down to the *nyumbakumi* (ten-household) level, although this did not boost anyone's economic status.[12]

A coup in 1973 brought the former minister of defense Juvénal Habyarimana to power, and he instigated one-party rule. He remained in power until the genocide. The idea that Tutsi were evil, foreign marauders bent on dispossessing the long-suffering, hard-working Hutu of what, by virtue of their greater numbers and closer connection to the land as farmers, was properly theirs continued to appear, but the importance of that thread in the overall weave of Rwandan politics varied. At moments of stress or insecurity, leaders were more likely to "burn the middle" on Hutu–Tutsi relations.

Mass killings of Tutsi were recurrent, beginning in 1959, with death tolls in particular periods of violence (such as December 1963–January 1964) reaching the thousands. The government portrayed these acts of violence as nothing but "gusts of wind," as if humans were not the perpetrators.[13] With each attack, many survivors fled to neighboring countries, where they lived as refugees. Eventually Uganda came to host over two hundred thousand Rwandans, while Zaire and Burundi each came to host some sixty thousand. The refugees made lives as best they could, but locals found a variety of ways to tell them—directly and indirectly—that they did not belong, and the land they were given was generally wild or ill-suited for the agrarian life they were used to. Some of the Rwandan Tutsi refugees discussed what it would take to make it safe for them to return home and on occasion organized discrete attacks against the Rwandan government.

Two macro trends made the 1980s a pivotal decade across the African continent. One was economic freefall due to the tanking of export-crop prices and governmental fiscal mismanagement, both of which afflicted Rwanda.[14] The other was the end of the Cold War, which led to rich countries shoving the dictatorships they had previously supported in the direction of multiparty elections, which they saw as the sine qua non of democracy and freedom. Economic decline and from-nowhere multipartyism together fanned the embers of political instability into wildfires. Ruling elites used whatever means they could to shore up their power, such as turning to ethnicity as a truer marker of solidarity and fellowship rather than alternatives like nationality.

In Uganda, north of Rwanda, Yoweri Museveni started the National Resistance Army and fought a bush war that ended with him taking the presidency in 1986. Among the fighters who trained with him and helped him claim the post were Rwandan refugees who had grown up in Uganda. Also in 1986, the Rwandan government, claiming population density was already far too high, decreed that refugees could reclaim their citizenship only on a case-by-case basis. The young Rwandan exiles built upon previous efforts to raise the consciousness of their fellow refugees and decided to form their own liberation movement to return triumphantly to the country they or their parents had fled. They called their movement the Rwandan Patriotic Front. They actively recruited among all the Rwandan exiles, regardless of ethnicity, and promoted a vision of a future Rwanda inspired by precolonial principles of unity and greatness rather than the racial divisionism promulgated by colonists and turned to new ends by the Hutu Power government.[15] But given that almost all the Rwandan refugees were Tutsi, the ethnic makeup of the RPF was lopsided.

The RPF established a military organization, the Rwandan Patriotic Army (RPA), which attacked Rwandan territory in October 1990. Its charismatic founder, Fred Rwigyema, was killed in the first battle. His adjoint, Paul Kagame, abandoned his military training course at Fort Leavenworth to lead the fighters onward. By 1993, they had forced Rwanda's President Habyarimana into peace negotiations. The two sides signed a peace agreement in Arusha, Tanzania. The United Nations sent a small peacekeeping mission to Rwanda to ensure the agreement's terms were respected. But despite these hopeful "front-stage" scenes of peacemaking, frightening "backstage" politics were only ramping up. Habyarimana and the extremists in his government increased their demonization of Tutsi and sidelined or killed anyone who voiced a more moderate view. Government officials ordered tens of thousands of machetes from China, which arrived by boat over a period of months; their plans to arm people with fresh blades were premeditated. Prominent media outlets vilified Tutsi, publishing articles and cartoons that portrayed them as subhuman, animal-like, and monstrous.[16]

On April 6, 1994, President Habyarimana's plane was shot down just before it landed in the Rwandan capital, Kigali. Everyone on board, which included the Burundian president, died. Almost thirty years later, there is no definitive answer as to who shot down the plane. The French government brought key wreckage, including the black box, to France and for many years would not let anyone access it. Critics of the RPF claim that it was the only logical perpetrator. Michela Wrong described the plane's downing as the "massive secret that squats like a giant toad at the heart of the RPF"—"ugly" and "poisonous."[17] She is probably not aware that toads feature prominently in Rwandan fairytales or that some child survivors wrote that during the genocide they lived like toads. A French judicial inquiry (the plane's crew were French) found that the plane had most likely been shot down from the Kanombe military barracks, held by the government.[18]

What is not in dispute is what happened next. Extremist government officials dispatched militias to kill moderate politicians and others who might reject their project of exterminating Tutsi. They ordered the security forces and the local militias, the Interahamwe, to begin killing all Tutsi. Local government officials and other bullies amped up the pressure on those reluctant to kill. Over about one hundred days, some eight hundred thousand people, primarily Tutsi but also people who dared refuse the madness, were killed. Most were killed by other peasants like themselves, not by professional fighters. Because the children's vivid accounts are about the genocide, I will leave its description in fuller detail to them.[19]

The RPF insurgency and the genocide were intertwined, but it is indefensible to claim that the former caused the latter or that the former made the latter more or less intense. The genocide was the creation of ideologues in the Rwandan government and other elites who lit a fire that many downtrodden

Rwandans fanned, some eagerly and others because they felt they had no choice. Absent the insurgency, would the genocide have happened? That we cannot know, but the genocidal motivations had more roots than just the civil war and branched into more aspects of Rwandan society. Pogroms long predated the RPF's creation, and vilifying Tutsi had been a political strategy since before independence. Moreover, international law clearly differentiates between war (just under certain circumstances and following certain rules) and genocide (never permissible under any circumstances). There are no mitigating factors when it comes to genocide.

The RPF's forces entered Rwanda from Uganda and battled the Rwandan Armed Forces and other genocidaires who stood in their way, in the process ending the mass killings of Tutsi. They claimed Kigali on July 4 (now celebrated as Liberation Day) and declared a unilateral ceasefire on July 19.[20] In the course of their operations, they killed people. The genocide meant that most men had mobilized with weapons—usually machetes but also any guns they had on hand—blurring the distinction between soldier and civilian.

While in Byumba in 2002, I met a shopkeeper named Félicien. Early on during the genocide, a neighbor family was killed, but two children escaped. Félicien hid them first in his sorghum fields and then, for two weeks, in his latrine. He said that he'd managed to duck scrutiny because he had stocks of beer to hand out. The children eventually made it to their aunt's house and safety. In the tense just-after months of mid-1994, the RPF forces called a meeting in Byumba. Félicien's family assembled as they were told to do. Félicien had a bad feeling and hid in the same sorghum fields where he'd sent the kids. While he hid, the meeting attendees were massacred. Everyone in Félicien's family was killed that day. He said that one man jumped a fence and escaped, but since he was focused on fleeing he had not seen who had done the killing. Félicien now lived alone. Other massacres were even more notorious; Kibeho, in April 1995, is the best known.[21] How many people were killed there and how intentional the massacre was are disputed, with the government estimating fewer than four hundred killed because of confusion and people not following orders, the UN at two thousand dead, and aid organizations claiming eight thousand killed.[22] Even the lowest of these tallies is a great tragedy.

Thirty percent of Rwandans fled the country as the genocide ended. In eastern Congo (Zaire at the time), genocidaire-refugees were effectively running the massive camps that aid organizations set up as a too-little-too-late response to the genocide.[23] The camps provided insurgents with "shelter, supplies, manpower, and a tax base,"[24] and insurgents were soon launching attacks on Rwandan territory. Genocidaires still in Rwanda—the southwestern and northwestern regions were particular trouble spots—did as well. The attackers would steal cattle and seize other sources of wealth and assassinate people who were working with the new government so that survivors would be afraid to do the same.

By 1996, there were about one hundred thousand insurgents mobilized in Zaire's North and South Kivu provinces. Senior Rwandan government officials decided to bring the refugees back to Rwanda, reasoning that if they lived in the less-concentrated yet more surveilled setting of their home country it would be harder for them to organize undetected. A massive repatriation began, and by November 1996, most Rwandans in the camps had returned. The insurgency continued, however, and the battles were intense. "Often RPA [the armed forces of the RPF] units would be heavy-handed with the predominantly Hutu population in the northwest. These human rights abuses did little to win the hearts and minds; they supported EX-FAR [former Rwandan military] claims that the RPA wanted to eliminate all Hutus."[25] With time the government approach shifted from military combat to indoctrination, generous packages to integrate ex-soldiers into the new army,[26] and development and protection initiatives in the regions where the insurgents had found willing participants. The less-violent future promised by the new government was attractive to many people exhausted by this lost decade of war. When insurgents attacked and demanded that people separate into Hutu and Tutsi groups, people refused.

But while violence decreased in Rwanda, it increased in Zaire. Until the mid-1990s, Zaire was ruled by Mobutu Sese Seko, a dictator who kept everyone else at heel. One source of his stability had been the Western donor-benefactors who saw him as an ally against communism, but with the end of the Cold War they pushed for democratic reform, and he was left isolated. Mobutu welcomed the former Rwandan government forces, which France had been supporting, and let them organize and launch raids in Rwanda between 1994 and 1996. In October 1996, the Rwandan government invaded Zaire on the pretext of definitively routing the insurgents. To give their operations a plausible Congolese revolutionary face, they enlisted Laurent Kabila, a 1960s-era Congolese revolutionary who had been living relatively quietly with some followers in Tanzania. Kabila's men and RPF forces marched west to the capital, Kinshasa. Kabila replaced the ailing Mobutu, who died a few months later, but rebellion, violence, and conflict in the country metastasized, pulling in other regional leaders and armies as well as regional and international peacekeepers. In 1997, President Kabila changed the country's name to the Democratic Republic of the Congo (DRC).

A vérité-style feature film, *The Mercy of the Jungle*,[27] depicts this period of Rwandan intervention in the Congo. An older Rwandan soldier and a new recruit who get separated from their unit must survive on their own. They traverse jungles and ingratiate themselves with locals, mostly successfully passing as Congolese. When they make it back to Rwandan territory, their fellows torture them. (Anecdotally, the ranks of the Rwandan military dipped in the 2000–2002 period, when soldiers who had been sent to the Congo finally made it home and renounced military life.) The film is a quietly powerful statement about the absurdity of war, particularly in a context like this one, where political borders are rigid but social boundaries are far more complex and overlapping and the result is a classic case of the narcissism of small differences.

The Rwandan military officially pulled out of the Congo in 2002. Senior military and government officials remained involved in economic and political matters there, just not as overtly. One of the main criticisms of Rwandan military and government elites has been the ways they have profiteered in the Congo.[28]

Back in Rwanda, people faced the reality that, given the enormity of the violence and the interdependence of peasant life, there were no perfect solutions, only different sets of tradeoffs and the hope that things might get better someday. Volunteers had done what they could to bury bodies, but human remains still filled the churches where massacres had occurred and poisoned rivers and lakes. Fierce packs of roaming dogs had become used to eating the bodies of murdered humans and cows, and the RPA was ordered to shoot them. Attaining some modicum of dignified burial for the deceased was a Herculean task in itself. Survivors received scant assistance. Thousands of children, survivors of genocide as well as children of the genocidaires, were growing up in orphanages, where some were abused. Many women were infected with HIV when they were genocidally raped. Hunger was rampant.

By 1998, about 125,000 Rwandans were in prison awaiting trial for the violence they were alleged to have perpetrated during the genocide. Many of the killers, rapists, and looters were also spouses, parents, and breadwinners. Impoverished family members on the outside sent the prisoners the best of their limited food, throwing it over the five-foot gap that separated them during the five minutes of visitation they were allotted each week.[29] The formal judicial system barely functioned. At its pace, it would take over a century to try the accused genocidaires. While they awaited trial, prisoners died of dysentery, gangrene, and even asphyxiation from the overcrowding.[30]

Survivors wanted perpetrators held to account for their genocidal crimes. Prisoners and their families did not want people to have to languish awaiting trial for longer than any eventual sentence would be. The government decided to repurpose the precolonial tradition of *gacaca* (village-level hearings to discuss disputes and decide upon consequences) as a means of trying those accused of genocide. The new *gacaca* had a two-hundred-page rulebook, so its connection to the old ways was largely symbolic. Each hillside and village would try the people accused of committing crimes there, with elected laypeople serving as judges and everyone standing in witness. *Gacaca* courts heard cases from 2002 to 2012. People's sense of satisfaction with the justice they provided varied widely, depending on the makeup of the court and dynamics in each locality.[31] Human rights organizations complained that the accused did not have all the protections they would have had in a regular government court. The government countered that the right to a speedy trial took precedence over those procedural rights. As early as 2002, prisoners were being released in large numbers, particularly those who confessed, and some were sentenced to community works projects rather than prison.[32]

A new government had been formed in July 1994, using the Arusha Accords as a starting point but with the important modifications of excluding the parties most involved in organizing the genocide and adding the post of vice president, which would be filled by the RPF and its General Paul Kagame, who was also minister of defense. The president, Pasteur Bizimungu, was also RPF. No other party received as many powerful positions.

In the decade after the genocide, uncertainty, violence, grievance, and hope all swirled in the political and social ether. From our position now, thirty years after the genocide, it seems possible to resolve the uncertainty and detect the straight lines, but that was not how people experienced life at the time. By the late 1990s, many Rwandans had become angry with their government. Elites were getting rich, while the poor remained abandoned to aid organization handouts. Ministers and high-level officers had claimed large swaths of the best land for themselves. I became friends with Bob, who worked at one of Kigali's nicest internet cafes, owned by a sportscar-driving Lebanese man. Bob spent his childhood in the Congo but returned to Rwanda in 1995. His parents sent him to Groupe scolaire in Butare, which is one of the best secondary schools. Classmates left notes on his pillow saying they would kill him, so he slept with his jeans and his shoes on in case he needed to flee. Another friend said that the real division in the country was no longer Hutu and Tutsi but people who lived in the country before and during the genocide and people who returned after. The returnees saw all Hutu as perpetrators and did not understand how awful the genocide had been for everyone, he claimed. Other people still dared to question why there should be a public remembrance of the genocide at all. "With time, the heart becomes hard," was how the survivor Géraldine Umutesi put it to me back then. "Why don't people acknowledge the magnitude of the genocide? Because they don't understand." A Rwandan Justice Department official who had lived in Canada said his great hope was that one day Rwandans would not build walls around their houses as soon as they had the money for it, or affix metal grilles on their windows, or position guards with guns outside their homes and shops. When that happens, "we will know that peace has come." (Today, the armed guards—so prevalent at that time—are indeed gone. The walls remain, though.) The children whose accounts compose this book were writing during this uncertain, liminal period.

Many accounts of Rwanda's present are actually arguments—and warnings—about the future. Revisiting old ones can show what was expected and what surprising about the present. In 1998, the noted Rwanda scholar and Human Rights Watch researcher Alison Des Forges wrote an advocacy letter to a contact in the US government. She described the genocidaires' insurgency and the RPA's harsh response. "In the end, the ordinary people, terrorized by both sides, will have nowhere to go. In such a situation of generalized fear, they will be all the more vulnerable to hate propaganda and calls for ethnic violence."[33] That was a reasonable concern then. But the government changed its counterinsurgency strategy, making reintegration its key tool rather than force, and Rwandans in Rwanda have turned away from ethnically based incitement.

At that time, as today, it was clear that the RPF was consolidating power,[34] particularly in the person of Paul Kagame, who has been president since

April 2000.[35] President Kagame can be ruthless in pursuing anyone he sees as a damaging dissenter, as a tarnisher of the image of his party and government, or as getting too self-important. He has imposed his will on the country in many striking ways. The government has shifted from French to English as its official language, to accompany the national language of Kinyarwanda,[36] which gave an advantage to returnees who had grown up in English-speaking countries (at least in the short term). Rwanda joined the Commonwealth in 2009. The government changed the administrative organization of the country, and towns and cities were renamed. While the reasons for the name changes are not as clear as the Hindification that occurred in India around the same time, they nevertheless indicate the power of a government that can get people to say "Musanze" instead of "Ruhengeri" and generally not even ask why. The last Saturday of the month is *umuganda*, a public works morning, and people who don't show up may get chastised for it, though there is no formal penalty. Some Rwandans appreciate what this social control lets their neighborhoods and country accomplish; others chafe at it. Proponents of the government's heavy-handed tactics also justify them by referencing the future: Strict, harsh policies like outlawing street peddling are necessary now in order to build the coming Rwandan development miracle.

Rwandans displaced by development projects are often disgruntled, but many others are proud of their country's transformation. From an NGOistan where aid workers drove around in monster trucks, Rwanda has become a place with almost no violent crime and many orthodontia clinics. The government also provides citizens with extensive services. Health care is offered for an annual premium of US$8, a fee waived for the poor. Regional hospitals with advanced diagnostics like radiology have been built across the country. You can tweet to government ministries and expect a helpful response within an hour or two. While Rwanda's history is as present as it is in any other place, it is striking that twenty years ago no one making predictions about Rwanda's future imagined anything like the Rwanda of 2024.

For all the government's initiatives and its interest in citizens' lives, many Rwandans have other concerns. Rwanda's growing numbers of elderly people, who were in the late prime of life during the genocide, are finding ways to contribute to the younger generations, care for one another, and prepare for a dignified death—something so many of their family and friends were denied.[37] Young people left orphans by genocide formed families to support one another. The family groups started with genocide survivors in boarding schools, but over time they have expanded and become popular even with people who did not face those particular challenges. One young person takes the role of mother, another father; still others are siblings, aunts, grandparents. While they are generally all around the same age, they agree to play these family roles for one another and to support one another, especially as they prepare for crucial life events like graduations and weddings. There is a burgeoning fine arts and music scene. Young artists are taking up traditional art forms and making them cool and modern.[38]

Up to and through the genocide, an ideology of "racial" animosity was a strong thread in Rwandan politics. In 2008, the government issued a sweeping law outlawing what it called genocidal ideology. Finding that the law was being applied too broadly, the government revised it in 2013, more precisely defining the crime and limiting its scope. The government promotes "one-Rwanda" thinking—shared language, shared culture, shared history—and hopes it will help make the old racial ideologies wither, becoming no more than a tragic history lesson, evidence of how colonialism warps public life.

One corollary of the limited space for extremist positions in Rwanda, however, has been the flourishing of those ideas outside of Rwanda, especially in the diaspora. Websites like *Jambo News* serve up multiple opinion pieces about the "double genocide" in Rwanda on their homepages.[39] Some children of former Hutu Power elites are incensed about their exclusion from the ruling class. The official name of the genocide indicates how these tensions have played out dialectically between the Rwandan government and its opponents. In the decade after 1994, most people spoke of the "Rwandan genocide." Excellent scholarship from the period uses this term. It was not an official name, just a kind of shorthand. While imprecise, it was not seen as a problem because there had only been one genocide in Rwanda. But as genocidaires and other pushed-out elites began either to deny the genocide or claim there had been two genocides, the Rwandan government worried that "the Rwandan genocide" made it seem like there had been a free-for-all of violence, rather than the calculated targeting of Tutsi that the child authors in this book recount. The government therefore insisted that the genocide be referred to as the Genocide against the Tutsi. But the *Jambo News* authors parried by promulgating their own (inaccurate) term: the "Genocide against the Hutu."

In a 1997 interview, André Sibomana, a priest, journalist, and human rights activist, gave an early version of what has become a standard critique of governance in Rwanda. He worried that "it is as if Rwandans have been handed over from one administration to another without ever acquiring the right to think for themselves. That is extremely dangerous. The country had already seen the results of a cult of authority and blind obedience to orders. The Rwandan state or Rwandan society will never recover without prior recognition of fundamental public liberties, which is far from being the case."[40] Yet elsewhere in the same interview, he described Rwandans as "like a flock of sheep without a shepherd, standing on the edge of a cliff."[41] These assessments—that Rwandans need more political liberties and that they need strong guidance—are contradictory. They might both be true, but not necessarily at the same time.

The enormity of what Rwandans have undergone supports an approach evoked by a Kinyarwanda proverb: *Ijyisho rya mukuru ntirizinduka liba ryagiye kurora*. Literally: "A mature person does not just see with the eye." Figuratively: Eyesight is not enough for insight, which requires observing in a different, more careful manner. That means listening to what people have to say, including the ideas that are contradictory or conflicted, and understanding the compromises people are making as just that—compromises. It means being hesitant to make sweeping generalizations and remembering that society is composed of individuals who are generally doing the best they can in imperfect situations. In 2015, Jean Hatzfeld interviewed members of the "*ejo* generation"[42]—people who were born around the time of the genocide, making them the connecting point between before and after, and who are now in the prime of their youth. A nineteen-year-old tailoring student, the son of a man imprisoned for genocidal crimes, said that among the five survivors and four Hutu at the workshop, "We lend each other a hand. . . . Everyone pitches in for food and takes turns preparing the meals. We watch movies on tape. . . . We never speak of the genocide." Speaking of the genocide would risk, as another nineteen-year-old put it, "a sudden awkwardness."[43] This is a country composed of people who had to pick up and go on after a kind of cataclysm the world rarely sees. Awkwardness is the least of it, and if awkwardness holds people back, it should count as progress.

Genocide squats in families, its unwanted presence persisting across generations. This is what makes it different from other instances of killing, even mass killing.[44] Managing the way it continues to infuse even the lives of the postgenocide generations therefore becomes a sensitive, necessary task. Beata Umubyeyi Mairesse's novel *All My Children Scattered* includes the character of Immaculata, a grandmother who survived genocide in Rwanda and found refuge in books later in life. As Immaculata prepared to die, she wrote an "enigmatic poem" to her beloved grandson: "All these books tell better than I ever could of the bitter-sweet smell of eternity. And if one day you feel alone, because we're all gone, you'll be able to find a certain kinship preserved here among them. Between words and the dead, there is only a breath, all you have to do is capture it with your lips and be sure every day to make up a bouquet of remembrance."[45] Often people write memoirs late in life, when they are taking stock of where they have been and want to pass it on to their descendents. Immaculata is instead encouraging her grandchild to develop a lifetime practice of composing daily "bouquets of remembrances." That is one way people can tend to and prune the continuing presence of genocide even after it has ended and also appreciate the ways life has grown up, on, and around it. The bouquets of children's remembrances that together make for the garden of this book are evidence of the pain, wisdom, and strength that all come from Immaculata's advice.

ABBREVIATIONS

ACMG   Archives du Centre mémorial Gisimba (Archives of the Gisimba Memorial Center)

ACNLG   Archives de la commission nationale de lutte contre le génocide (Archives of the National Commission for the Fight against Genocide)

ADL   Association rwandaise pour la défense des droits de la personne et des libertés publiques (Rwandan Association for the Defense of Human Rights and Public Liberties)

AERG   Association des étudiants et élèves rescapés du génocide (Association of Students and Schoolchildren Survivors of the Genocide)

APR   Armée Patriotique Rwandaise (Rwandan Patriotic Army, RPA)

AVEGA   Association des veuves du génocide d'avril (Association of the Widows of the April Genocide)

CERAI   Centre d'enseignement rural et artisanal intégré (Center of Integrated Rural and Artisinal Instruction)

CNLG   Commission nationale de lutte contre le génocide (National Commission for the Fight against Genocide)

FAR   Forces armées rwandaises (Rwandan Armed Forces)

FIDH	Fédération internationale pour les droits humains (International Federation for Human Rights)
FPR	Front patriotique du Rwanda (Rwandan Patriotic Front, RPF)
MINALOC	Ministry of Local Government
MRND	Mouvement révolutionnaire national pour le développement (National Revolutionary Movement for Development, NRMD)
NRA	National Resistance Army
NURC	National Unity and Reconciliation Commission
PSD	Parti social démocratique (Social Democratic Party)
RPA	Rwandan Patriotic Army
RTLM	Radio Télévision Libre des Mille Collines (a Rwandan radio and television channel)
SNJG	Service national des juridictions *gacaca* (National Service of Gacaca Jurisdictions)
TPIR	Tribunal pénal international pour le Rwanda (International Criminal Tribunal for Rwanda)

Forget the big words. Come with me. Follow me.

—RITHY PANH, *LA PAIX AVEC LES MORTS*

INTRODUCTION

Genocide through the Eyes of Children

"That's how I came to know death,"[1] wrote a girl with fine, confident strokes, concluding her testimony as a child survivor. These words echo a maxim inescapably attached to the experience of survivors since 1994: "*Ijoro ribara uwariraye* [Only someone who has gone through the darkness can tell the story]." The images of endless darkness summoned up in survivors' accounts reflect the last exhaustive attempt to exterminate a human group in the twentieth century: the attempt to eliminate all the Tutsi in Rwanda. In 1994, between April 7 and the middle of July, a million victims died during a horrifyingly efficient campaign bent on massacre: In less than three months, three-quarters of the Tutsi population had been murdered.[2] At the time, the Rwandan genocide was not recognized in its irreducible specificity by the international community, which remained passive, allowing the killing to go on in terrifying invisibility. Other interpretive frameworks took over: Barbaric frescoes and interethnic struggles were presented as customary in an "exotic" African continent contemplated through condescending and vaguely disgusted eyes.[3] A quarter of a century later, that thick veil of racist clichés combined with indifference still lingers, and the collective ignorance displayed in the media has even penetrated academia without arousing serious protests, providing fertile soil for negationist discourse.[4]

The survivors in Rwanda, the "living dead," as they sometimes call themselves, maintain their fragile existence in a country where they must live alongside the killers. Their voices were stilled in 1994—but are they better heard today? Really *heard*? For the survivors of the Tutsi genocide seek neither sympathy nor pity; it is too late for that. Among the groups of women who were raped and infected with HIV-AIDS, among the orphans who witnessed the massacre of their families, a particular anguish endures: that of being disbelieved, even mocked, outside the increasingly narrow circle of survivors. If our world has become blind and deaf to the spring of 1994, is it still possible today to pay attention to what the survivors have to say? Can their words be granted the dignity of becoming precious material, of telling their story in a way free from the stranglehold of racialized exoticism and fully integrated into *our* history?

To extricate the event of the genocide from the limbo of a discrediting discourse is to set out in search of the ineradicable traces it left on the bodies and psyches of the survivors: It is to embark on a quest for the seemingly imperceptible stigmata in the landscape; it is to return to the beings themselves, stride across hills and swamps, listen to the Kinyarwanda language. To enter, by these means, into brutal factuality. For a genocide is not an abstraction, and the words to tell its story are not tinged with an exoticized poetry. These words give voice to the insults, the noise of bodies and weapons, the screams of pain, the humiliations of repeated rape, the confrontation with one's family's death and with one's own. And they express infinite solitude in a world that has become irremediably foreign.

In Rwanda, my quest, initially awkward and uncomfortable, gradually became a little more confident as it was confirmed by *encounters*. The archives at the heart of this book were among those that upset not only my working timetable but my subjectivity as a researcher. The two dimensions of my encounter, simultaneously intellectual and human, are unquestionably inseparable. The register of compassionate deploring does not do justice to the richness of the works enclosed in the two thousand pages in which, twelve years after the genocide, five hundred orphans set down the memories of their ravaged childhood.[5] The bundles containing fragile school notebooks had been completely unknown to me. In Rwanda, "the interesting archives are always found in disorder," a close friend said to me one day, a friend who had spent endless hours in the tenacious dust of improbable spaces where heaps of paper lay scattered. My encounter thus took place in disorder—at least in relative disorder, in comparison with other such spaces. Accompanied by Rose, the in-house librarian, in September 2016, I undertook to classify the documentation piled up in the cabinets and boxes of the library maintained by the Commission nationale de lutte contre le génocide (CNLG: National Commission for the Fight against Genocide).[6] The first notebooks appeared in the nooks and crannies of shelving cluttered with a jumble of audiovisual archives; others, dispersed among various offices, were collected later.[7]

At first, a simple intuition directed my attention toward these texts. An intuition mixed with skepticism, I should add: a vague suspicion spurred by the fear of discovering in these pages the words of young people taking the form of a heroic gesture of resilience that would correspond to common expectations. As a team of psychologists aptly emphasized, "The notion of children's resilience could easily become a new way of denying their trauma, another means of allowing the political system to evade its responsibilities to the children traumatized by the war."[8] And the denial of suffering that I am denouncing here might well extend beyond the circle of the directly responsible political agencies, as a way of protecting our own moral comfort. Isn't the idea that children damaged in childhood recover from their wounds with the approach of adulthood a reassuring cliché? There was reason, then, to worry that these written testimonies had been influenced by such a perspective.

My initial skepticism quickly faded as I read and began to translate the first notebook. It became immediately clear that these narratives had not been sought with the intentions I had feared. Each of the young participants was asked to write his or her own story as a child survivor by a major survivors' association, accompanied by trauma counselors[9] and by a professor of clinical psychology at the National University of Rwanda. Between April 21 and April 23, 2006, the Association des veuves du génocide d'avril (Avega: Association of the Widows of the April Genocide)[10] brought together over a hundred orphans living in the eastern region of the country, an area corresponding to the old prefectures of Kibungo, Byumba, and Kigali-Ngali. Written in Kinyarwanda, in a script that was sometimes careful and fluid, sometimes choppy and almost indecipherable, the material can be seen from a perspective of psychological and testimonial catharsis. Having been solicited, the texts were thus *addressed*: to adult survivors, in the midst of a commemoration of the genocide, at a time when the *gacaca* trials (legal proceedings modeled on a form of community justice) that had just begun intensified the feeling of threat linked to the proximity of hostile surroundings. After these texts were drafted, they seem to have been lost in the meanderings of various Rwandan NGOs whose existence was precarious.

Entrusted for publication initially to the Humura Association, they were then deposited with the CNLG in 2016, after Humura closed down. Funds for their publication were no doubt lacking.[11]

Survivors must have been encouraged fairly soon after the genocide to "write it down."[12] The archives in Ibuka include around a thousand very good notebooks dating from 1998, written by survivors from the Gitarama prefecture.[13] Other witnesses' testimonies reached the stage of publication.[14] Clearly, the idea of bringing victims together to encourage them to leave written traces of their experience was neither unique nor belated. Since 1994, a veritable "survival culture" has developed on the ruins of the genocide, taking material form in the production of thousands of poems and songs, in addition to the countless testimonies spun out over the years on the occasion of local and national commemorations.[15]

The Avega corpus at the center of this book thus has its place in a context marked by an outpouring of diverse expressions of memory. One of its primary characteristics lies in its homogeneity, from the standpoint both of the age of its authors and their geographical origins. While the youngest were only five years old in 1994 and the oldest were around twenty, the average age for most of them was between eight and ten.[16] Among the 105 writers, there are more girls than boys, a proportion reflecting the gender ratio of the entire surviving population.[17] Brought together for three days, these young people were invited to write following a fairly standard chronological structure; they were to asked to describe their life "before," their life "during the genocide," and their life "after." There are even traces of more precise instructions in some notebooks, ones in which the orphans seem to have experienced difficulties in getting started and going on with their stories. These traces indicate particular attention to the world of school, both before and after the genocide, as well as to the modalities of the young people's confrontation with ethnoracial discrimination. The annotations relating to these prescriptions on the part of the organizers are precious in that they reveal their constant subversion: The writers in fact demonstrated complete autonomy as they "wrote it all down." There are many indications, in fact, that the writers truly appropriated the exercise for themselves: Some notebooks start with life "after," others end with a long poem or a prayer. Thus the very form of the narratives attests to the investment of the orphans in writing. Many included a title at the beginning of their text, like the girl who labeled hers "Story of My Life." Moreover, many referred to their notebooks as "books"; some posed with the precious objects in their hands for the photos that accompany each text. The affective charge invested in the writing is illustrated magnificently by one girl born in 1986 who wrote these lines in concluding her testimony: "I walked, I saw, and I endured so many things when I was only a little child. That suffering—I'll tell my children about it, my grandchildren, and even my great-grandchildren if I'm still alive. If I die, they'll read what I have written."[18]

While the desire to leave written traces is common to all the texts, most of the writers did not want to have their identity revealed. The challenge, then, for the transcriber and translator was to find a way to keep their stories anonymous while retaining their anchorage in quite specific places. But masking the names of the living did not turn out to be the most delicate endeavor after the question of identifying the dead arose. It proved impossible to modify the names of the dead without inflicting great symbolic violence on those who had inscribed them so carefully in their paper shrouds. This is why the excerpts reproduced here are often riddled with deliberate ellipses between square brackets: so the names will not have to be falsified while the identity of the writers will be protected. Only the names of the rescuers have been reproduced, with care taken nevertheless to make sure they were common enough that they would not risk compromising the writers' anonymity.

The texts around which this book is organized are not provided here in their original form. They are the fruit of a translation from Kinyarwanda. For more than four months in Rwanda, I worked on translating the texts with the collaboration of two survivors of the genocide, a man and a woman both old enough to have a good knowledge of Kinyarwanda and the common expressions pertaining to political life under the regime of President Juvénal Habyarimana; they were also able to point out specific features of the language that had been inflected by the massacre. It is important to acknowledge here that the intense work of translation represented a genuine psychic ordeal for them. The task was costly on the psychological level; we had to stop working from time to time, and my colleagues sometimes took turns working by my side. Most of the texts were translated with the help of my friend Émilienne Mukansoro, a survivor of the genocide and a psychotherapist who has dedicated her professional work to the survivors for some fifteen years. This affective proximity allowed Émilienne to share part of her own story with me, and that personal knowledge made me attentive to moments when the texts contained facts that she had trouble reading and translating. As for my other collaborator, Gervais Dusabemungu, he spoke of the immense fatigue and the nightmares that haunted him at the end of a workday. A certain complicity developed around the accomplishment of this shared task, an indispensable mutual trust.[19] The French version of the narratives is the result of this friendly intellectual complicity; it also reflects my own progress in Kinyarwanda. From the outset, I could not imagine leaving the task of translation to a third party without participating in it actively myself. I sought explanations, sometimes through gestures, of verbs designating the practices of putting to death. I scrutinized the sorghum fields and the banana plantations in order to see, touch, and absorb the botanical vocabulary. I drew on the topographical knowledge of people from the localities evoked in the stories in order to sketch in a previously unfamiliar landscape. The translation process turned into a patient decoding of each of the words brought to bear on the experience of dereliction.

As we gradually became familiar with the texts, we hoped naively that, once we moved beyond the stories recounting the ordeals of the genocide itself, we would feel a form of moral relief. A vain hope, for we discovered that the "life after" always opened onto an account of unfathomable despair. The expectations invested in the act of translating brought me closer, perhaps, to a better understanding of the subjective temporality of a genocide that was still being experienced in everyday life, more than a decade later. One of the great merits of this corpus is that it opens up the narrative of such a complex and painful aftermath of survival. We often had to punctuate the writing, introducing commas and periods in order to render readable texts that had been set down on the notebook pages in a single stream. The unpunctuated lines that went on and on without beginning or end doubtless reflected not only the level of language of young people whose schooling had been interrupted but also the gesture of writing itself, flowing unfiltered onto the pages. The writing of genocide thus presents itself on its fragile support structure in a singular graphic and linguistic materiality.

Throughout the reading and the translation processes, the image of the writers as *children* never left me. The cover photo showing young people in their writing workshop was quickly overshadowed by the granularity of words in which the figure of the child dominates. The translators working beside me had the same feeling. So the question arises: In this corpus written twelve years after the genocide, are we still in the presence of *children's* writing? From the texts there emanates, curiously, a form of writing studded with expressions, turns of phrase, spelling errors, and stylistic blunders that evoke the singularity of a child's language. Moreover, without exception the writers described themselves *as children*, never as young adults. At the time they were composing their texts, none of them had gone through the social and cultural rituals that mark the passage to adulthood in Rwanda, in particular marriage and the establishment of their own households. In their own eyes, they remained children; the experience of genocide seemed to have frozen them in childhood, as it were. How can we interpret, otherwise, the strange errors in dating that appear in these texts? One girl, for example, set her own birth date in 1994! It is as though, hunched over their notebooks twelve years after the event, the young writers were reliving the genocide in the present of their childhood.

The present of childhood and the present of the genocide are thus inseparable here. And the question does not lie so much in the degree of historical accuracy in the reconstructions of the past (and why would that question arise, moreover? Does one invent the rape of a mother or the beheading of a father?) as in the writers' capacity to manifest such hypermnesia twelve years later.[20] For the scenes they offer us spare none of the cruel details that accompanied the pursuit of their loved ones before the killings. For the reader, too, this compellingly brutal presence of the words and gestures of extermination fixes the writers at the heart of their own childhoods.

The texts thus allow us to see the genocide of the Tutsi from the perspective of the world of childhood, opening up the path to the elaboration of a history through the firsthand experiences of children rather than through the gaze of adults bearing upon children. Moreover, these sources sketch in the contours of an adult world that is either powerless to protect children or transformed into a deadly threat. The corpus also informs us about the diversity of attitudes adopted by the victims at the outbreak of the genocide: They are by no means depicted as passive. Discouragement, fatalism, anger, and intense fright did not prevent the development of survival strategies oscillating between two opposing behaviors: bringing the family together in order to "die together" or, on the contrary, encouraging the family to disperse in the hope that at least one of its members would survive. Rapidly deprived of the presence of their parents, the children thus built their own mix of survival tactics: lying about their genealogy, disobeying orders that struck them as perilous, then reconstructing their own families in the aftermath. They appear on these pages as social actors and autonomous subjects capable of making their own decisions and even of rebelling against the adults.

Moreover, written at the child's level, from the perspective of families under mortal threat, these narratives describe the deadly transformation of neighborhoods in detail, making it possible to analyze with great precision the lines crossed by the violence of the genocide,[21] on the scale of hillsides and even *ingos* (homes). Just as the time and space of the genocide is offered with great descriptive care, these children's stories are saturated with descriptions of cruel behaviors and racist speech, again facilitating a detailed analysis of the interactions between killers and victims. The stories expose with raw materiality the sophisticated organization of the massacres, which were decentralized and placed under the responsibility of local authorities and the Interahamwe militia, in a region of the country that has not yet been closely studied. In the east, the massacres were carried out with exceptional rapidity and efficiency. In fact, the rapid progression of Battalions 7 and 157 of the Rwandan Patriotic Front (FPR), led by General Ibingira, increased the murderous energy of the killers; the organizers of the genocide in that region engaged in a radical scorched-earth policy. In most of the communes where our young writers lived, the killings were completed between late April and mid-May, at the cost of horrifying tallies.[22]

For a long time, the words of the victims—and even more the words of child victims—have been tainted by an underlying skepticism in a certain number of studies carried out in large part within a legal perspective. Didn't the survivors owe their survival to the simple fact of having been confined to hiding places for three months, and were they not incapable of providing the slightest relevant information to researchers, here conflated with judicial investigators?[23] Poor witnesses for justice, the victims became poor witnesses for history: Their voices, supposedly corrupted by emotions and a thirst for vengeance, hardly satisfied the requirements of credibility.[24] Yet such a vision not only fails to take the advances of judicial practice into account,[25] but it also proves biased from a strictly historical standpoint. Postulated rather than proven, the argument that these victims' contributions to the writing of the overall history of the genocide was marginal at best does not hold up against the reading of the testimony. In fact, the persecuted Tutsi did not remain in hiding throughout the entire period of the massacres: On the contrary, they were in constant interaction with the killers, interaction that was all the more intense in that these men and women belonged to the same social world as their victims.[26] The discourse and gestures of cruelty and then of killing take on their full meaning in this shared universe. And this is precisely what the young writers describe. Relationships woven over a long time in the "life before" collapse under the effects of a powerful system of racist representations in which the Others, formerly close, are no longer perceived except through their irreducible alterity.

The voices of orphans constitute the essential material that served as the basis for the history of the Tutsi genocide proposed here. Its evocative power and heuristic richness have most often restrained my commentary. That is why it did not seem appropriate to speak after them; I felt that it was not my place to conclude.

PART ONE

Life Before

UBUZIMA BWA MBERE

1

THE WORLDS OF CHILDHOOD
Family and School

The notebooks open onto a world idealized owing to its disappearance. The effects of retrospective writing undoubtedly come through with a more pronounced intensity in the descriptions of unblemished familial and social harmony. The powerful filter of nostalgia nevertheless allows us to discern the contours of family structures and the constituents of life at a modest socioeconomic level, even if they are depicted as marked by abundance. The initial images of prosperity described by the young writers reflect the extent of the family circle: They all belonged to large families. This is hardly surprising, for in 1994 Rwanda had one of the highest birthrates in the world.[1] This demographic feature is translated quite concretely in the individual stories: Membership in large families multiplied the accumulation of losses during the genocide. Moreover, the set of narratives brings to light a sequence of singular affective bonds with paternal uncles (*datawacu*) and maternal aunts (*mamanwacu*), whose children are viewed as one's brothers and sisters. The cartography of family relations is relatively easy to establish, since the Kinyarwanda language offers a large and precise semantic range for designating the positions attributed to each person in the kinship structure.[2]

The vast majority of the vanished families lived in the Rwandan countryside,[3] in regions that had not been included in the economic development efforts being made in the 1980s, which were localized chiefly in the northwestern prefectures, the homelands of President Habyarimana and his kin.[4] Except for a small number of writers whose parents had risen to the status of salaried workers (as schoolteachers or employees of parastate agencies) or were involved in small businesses, they all came from families dependent on farming or livestock. Their descriptions of the universe of childhood thus focus on small details of rural life, which took on great value in the eyes of the young writers. The fact that the objects of narrative attention are precisely the ones that were destroyed during the genocide is not insignificant: "Life before" always appears in the powerful reverberations created by its annihilation. This makes it easier to understand the stubborn subversion of the instructions that were supposed to guide the chronological progression of the written testimonies: texts in which the nostalgic fresco of the child's world lacks any expression of contrast with the experience of the genocide are rare exceptions. One boy, for example, filled the first page of his notebook with lines in which the happy past bumps into the terrible memory of its abolition at every turn:

> We lived in the former commune of Rusumo, today [after the administrative reform of January 2006] it's the Kirehe district. To put it briefly, I lived with my parents. Before 1990, I hadn't yet acquired awareness. . . .
> I lived with my parents, they loved me. I came from the same womb as six other children: two boys, then me, the third, and four girls. We loved each other. We didn't have any problems among us; we shared the warmth of our homes. We had the means to meet all our needs. Our neighbors were members of our family and we were on good terms. Some of them were our grandfathers, paternal uncles, maternal aunts. We lived in the same place, which I could call *umudugudu* [in rough translation, a village]. The people I mentioned earlier all had their own homes [*ingo*, hearths or households]. Some had children my age and also older ones. Among all these families I have just mentioned, during the genocide some were left without a single child to tell what happened. But with others, God protected them and one child from the family was able to stay. In my case I was left with two siblings. Before the genocide, we had property and even houses. But today, nobody has anything left. The houses were destroyed during the genocide and the property was looted.[5]

In another text, by a writer who was about fifteen at the time of the genocide, the presentation of family members with their names and sometimes their birth dates ends with these words: "They all died in 1994, I'm the only one still alive, just me."[6] Individual genealogies are thus sketched out via a series of losses. At the heart of the decimated kinship structure, the image of the father stands out as an almost metonymic figure of the vanished world. The omnipresence of the remembered father in the writers' stories cannot be grasped without recalling the massive killings of men, who were specifically targeted as imagined combatants by virtue of a racist system of representation that assimilated *all* Tutsi to the FPR. Very few writers found their fathers alive after the genocide.[7] Quite a few of the girls depicted themselves as their father's favorite child and were quite willing to proclaim their special relationship. One girl, about thirteen years old in 1994, began her story with a depiction of her family in which past happiness is mingled with the violence of her father's disappearance; at the heart of this syncopated memoir, the father's image dominates:

Papa loved us, he asked us to respect every adult. He was really nice. Mama liked to tell us that a respectable girl should come home early. My big sister was the oldest in the family, and lots of people liked to say that she had the good looks of her maternal uncles. This also reminds me of my brothers and sisters, they used to tell us to never stop praying, and that no child had the right to change religion. What makes me sad is that in those days I heard them give a lot of advice to my older sisters but I didn't understand its value then, and I didn't know that this would be the last of it. In Kinyarwanda we say *utaganiriye na se cyangwa na sekuru ngo ntamenya icyo sekuru yasize avuze* [he who doesn't talk with his father or his grandfather can't know what his grandfather said before he died].[8] Whether it was Papa, Mama, grandmother, my big sisters, grandfather, all of them, I never saw anyone again who could give me advice. So what will I do? I haven't found a single relative to love me; up to now, I still don't have anybody to give me advice. But I'm trying to bear it. I feel that I hardly have any choice. Up to now, of the seven children, only three of us are left, and I'm the oldest. Before the genocide happened, I was in third grade. I had many paternal uncles; I had some maternal uncles; there were little children, but today there are only ruins left. I had playmates, for example Grace, Agathe, Devota, Dominique . . . and what makes me sad is that they're all dead and I'm still here. Every time I go to the Nyarubuye memorial, at the place where they've hung up the clothes of the victims of the genocide, I see Papa's trousers and the clothes of the other children. That brings back my memories. Before the genocide, I liked to go to Mass with my big sister and I walked around with her. She trimmed my fingernails; she washed my clothes; and all that meant that I was spoiled like the other children. All that is over. In particular, as for me, I loved Papa more than Mama, I liked to share meals with him, I liked it when he sent me to do little errands for him. This is why his memory never leaves me. Moreover, when he was dying, he said three things to me, we were in the Nyarubuye convent, he said: "Give me water. See what they've done to me." And he said: "My chi . . . [*Mwana wa . . .*]" but he couldn't finish, he died right then before my eyes. That too I can't forget. I can't forget either how we fled. I left Mama and my big sisters to join Papa for him to die before my eyes.[9]

In the portions of these texts devoted to the happy times, the writer's descriptive attention focuses on objects symbolizing economic prosperity and the fluidity of social relations. Thus it is no surprise to find beer and milk in this repertory, two drinks whose circulation among households (*ingo*) ensured the maintenance of neighborly relations. In this idealized picture of familial and social harmony sketched out by a young girl born in 1983, communal solidarity rests essentially on the exchange of these precious liquids:

Before the genocide I had all my relatives and we were born as eight brothers and sisters. I'm the ninth. We were all alive. Our grandfathers and grandmothers were alive too, along with many other members of our big family: everyone was alive. I didn't want for anything with this great big family. My parents raised cattle, we didn't lack anything. The members of my family had good relations with one another. Everywhere I went, I felt like I was at home. I was thriving, there were no conflicts, people worked together and got along really well. The children in our family and the neighbors spent time together, visiting back and forth, and we played together. My parents and my neighbors also got together; they shared beer and exchanged cows. When a neighbor got sick, they came together to take him to the health center and we milked our cows for him. When there was a wedding, everyone contributed something. I saw everybody as the same. We organized wakes at our place or someone else's, until morning, and this happened in every home [*rugo*] because we loved one another. When the beer was ready in one family or another, it was distributed in all the *ingo* with no distinction. Everyone participated. People were happy, they trusted one another.[10]

In this rural world, where life was no doubt much harsher than the childhood stories suggest, the consumption of milk was so important that it stands as a veritable metaphor for prosperity, as is clear from this report by a girl born in 1981:

> When I was seven, I learned that only one of our neighbors was a Tutsi. The others were called Hutu. At our house, they did whatever they wanted, they came over to eat and drink. In our home, we were rich, we had a lot of things. We were cattle raisers and farmers. . . . I couldn't imagine that anyone could drink water. I thought that everyone drank milk, as much as they wanted.[11]

Finally, to the stereotypical picture of abundance marked by the consumption of that drink, another girl, born in 1986, added the produce of the family fields:

> We were never hungry or thirsty because milk flowed abundantly just like sorghum beer [umusururu]. You can really see that we weren't short on food. We had granaries and big harvest baskets. In short, I didn't even know what a problem on this earth looked like.[12]

Small indications, reported with similar precision, give glimpses of the shape of the family dwellings. Here, too, we find meticulous descriptions of property fated for destruction. The care with which the following narrative (by a girl born in 1985) evokes the household furnishings is not without significance:

> Before the genocide, I was comfortable, happy with my parents, with my brothers and sisters, with my family and even with the neighbors. I didn't have any problems. I lived in peace this way because my father and Mama had enough to live on. We were farmers and cattle raisers. . . . Our house was big, it had seven bedrooms with a tile roof, and a kitchen. We had even brought in stones to build it solidly. The granaries were full of our harvests. In short, we had no problems.[13]

This idealized world is not portrayed in the light of economic prosperity alone. Games, long walks in the hills in search of better pastures,[14] basketwork instruction for the girls, and, above all, assiduous church attendance constituted regular markers in the stories of "life before." A special sense of childhood emanates from the following text by a girl born in 1983; she depicts a scene belonging henceforth to a remote, bygone past, as stressed here by the temporal marker *kera*:

> Once [*kera*] I lived with my parents. They loved me. I liked to go to pray with the other children: my big sisters, my little sisters, and my brothers. . . . We all lived with Papa and Mama. During the long vacations, all the children were there and in the neighborhood we played with others. Our favorite games were soccer and war games: We threw leaves from banana trees at one another.[15]

Within especially pious households, family life was organized around prayer and involvement in the activities of the parish, as one boy born in 1986 recalls, evoking the memory of his father:

> Papa was a deacon with the priests. We liked to pray in the Catholic church. He encouraged me to pray all the time, and every Sunday I sat in the first pew. Afterward, I studied to prepare for communion.[16]

In another fresco by a girl born in 1982, where idealization appears once again in contrast with annihilation, spirituality occupies a central place in the memory of childhood sociability:

> I had parents, I had families, we lacked for nothing. I never thought about running into a problem because I had someone who took care of it. I was only preoccupied with children's things, like studying in the primary school, looking after my little brother and the big cattle, playing ball and all the other children's games that we had then in primary school. In all these activities, at home, we were made to love God, we were taught to pray and devote ourselves to church work like serving at Mass. We also learned to greet our neighbors and the family members who lived a bit farther away, like the grandmothers, our mother's younger sisters. I did all that with joy when I was little, it was as if I lived in paradise. I lived well, without any problems because I was supported by the family, by my brothers and sisters and even my parents. No one died and no one was without somebody to bury him; you never lacked someone to say "*Pole*" to you [a word of consolation and encouragement]. . . . But in my childhood I remember a child who lived nearby and was my age—and I owe my life to that child even today because she taught me to pray in my life. Every time we were together, she told me to pray to God. . . . But my friend

who was like a relative did not survive the evildoers who took her life when she was still young. I will pray for her, pray to the God she always talked to me about. And He will listen to me. The children we played and studied with and who were also my neighbors were numerous. They were very dear to me. I can't list them all and finish. . . . I ask God to dry the tears they shed and to console them for the sorrow with which they died.[17]

At the heart of these stereotypical portraits of family harmony, school embodies the first stumbling block. This central site in the world of childhood constitutes the initial break in a past reconstituted under the effects of nostalgia. For the children, school in fact represented the creation of an ethnoracial othering that was tirelessly objectified by the meticulous census-taking on the part of teachers and the resulting mockery on the part of classmates. Discreetly labeled the "policy of ethnic and regional equilibrium" by the Habyarimana regime, the statistics aimed to define "the quotas established with regard to the populations of each ethnic group in the overall population of the country."[18] In other words, it was a matter of preventing the Tutsi, who were supposed to represent 10 percent of the population, from exceeding that threshold of "ethnic representativity" in secondary education. The conventional formulas served to undergird institutionalized discrimination against Tutsi pupils and, to a lesser extent, against the Hutu from the country's southern prefectures. In fact, not only were the young Tutsi squeezed into the narrow space of "ethnic equilibrium," but their exclusion was compounded by measures related to "regional equilibrium."[19]

The principle of such quotas was firmly embedded in the Hutu "social revolution" of 1959, during which the first pogroms against the Tutsi were carried out. At the end of the initial violence, the monarchy perceived as "Tutsi" was overthrown in favor of a republic dominated by Grégoire Kayibanda's Parmehutu Party. When the country achieved independence on July 1, 1962, the "people" were defined not as a political entity but as a *race*. Obsessed with racial arithmetic, the regime based its new political equation on the defense of the "people in the majority" (*rubanda nyamwinshi*) against the insidious threat of a Tutsi minority characterized as "feudal-monarchist."[20] In order to fight effectively against an influence that was deemed as pernicious as it was ungraspable, a politics of numbers relying on ever more sophisticated statistical mechanisms was reinforced under the regime of Juvénal Habyarimana, who took power in the coup d'état of July 5, 1973. Moreover, it was following violent uprisings in schools and universities that President Kayibanda was overthrown.[21] Announced as a general principle in 1971, the "policy of ethnic and regional equilibrium" was actually implemented under the Second Republic in 1973; it was among the first measures prescribed by Habyarimana to his minister of national education. Starting on August 29, 1973, the heads of secondary schools were given firm instructions: The minister required respect for "ethnic quotas" in admissions procedures: namely, 90 percent Hutu, 10 percent Tutsi.[22] In 1986, a voluminous statistical report seeking to evaluate the results of the "policy of equilibrium" was prepared by the "central committee" of the National Revolutionary Movement for Development (MRND: Mouvement révolutionaire national pour le développement).[23] The conclusions are unsurprising: While the proportion of Tutsi pupils went from 36 percent to 12.4 percent between 1962–1963 and 1980–1981, the Tutsi remained excessively "overrepresented."[24] As the authors note: "During the period 1960–1980, there was no *equilibrium between the ethnic groups* in secondary education, no matter what variable might be applied."[25] Unquestionably, such observations led to an increased hardening of discriminatory measures precisely during the decade in which the writers in our corpus were in school.

The obsession of the Habyarimana regime with these ethnomathematics went well beyond the context of schools. Indeed, the ideology of "majoritarianism"[26] on which the postcolonial political systems were founded between 1962 and 1994 could not have been maintained without recourse to a statistical apparatus that penetrated every sphere of social and private life. Through the power of numbers, objectivized via the census, the authorities maintained the idea of "democratic representativity" even as they nourished the rock-solid fear of a "minority" that had to be counted the better to be surveilled. Marriages (both "illegitimate" and "regular"),[27] births, moves from one commune to another: All such events of daily life were scrupulously noted and reported under the pertinent ethnoracial categories by the local authorities. The local archives contain an abundance of monthly counts established by the communes and reported to the prefectures. The local registers served as references for the establishment of identity cards that included the indications "Hutu" "Tutsi," or "Twa," inscribed below the photo of the holder, after the person's name, to be sure, but before the place and date of birth: The hierarchy of information reveals the importance of racial assignment in the eyes of the administrative authorities. Still, statistical sophistication did not preclude deviations and false declarations, in a society in which neither language nor religious affiliation nor property ownership constituted "objective" factors of differentiation. The artificiality of the ethnoracial categories—and, consequently, their *political* nature—is strikingly apparent when cases of "change of ethnicity" are discussed in the archives. The intolerable uncertainty that certain individuals introduce in establishing papers declaring their "Hutu" identity immediately triggered meticulous investigations.[28] Moreover, in 1978, the minister of national education himself sent a letter to his counterpart in the Interior Ministry as well as to the general director of intelligence services "with a plea to suppress the abuses regarding civil status in the communes" and the "false declarations." He called attention to the "serious anomalies of identification of students completing primary school," and he stressed the threat posed to the "politics of equilibrium" by children who modified their ethnic status in order to increase their chances of access to secondary education: "More seriously still, a student who was Tutsi the previous year becomes Hutu the following year without any corrective measure by the communal authorities."[29]

Our young writers experienced this policy of numbers concretely in their classrooms. Before they were required to answer the questions of the teacher charged with counting Hutu, Tutsi, and Twas, the majority of the children knew nothing of the "ethnicity stories" (*ibintu by'amoko*), as they called them; thus descriptions of their discovery of a new "identity" imposed by the counting proliferate in their writing. The text that follows, by a boy born in 1982, makes it possible to follow the process through which the assignment of identity is revealed step by step, from initial ignorance to mockery by the other pupils:

> When I started school, I went there with the children from my neighborhood and along the way we chatted without any problem. In the first year of primary school, our teacher asked us our ethnicity. I heard some say they were Hutu and the others Tutsi. And I stayed in my seat. The teacher told me: "Go home, ask your parents what ethnic group you belong to and come back tomorrow with the answer to that question." I went home and I asked Papa. Papa told me that I am Tutsi. The next day I went back to school and I gave my teacher the answer. He made me repeat it out loud so the others could hear. After that, I lost the respect of

my classmates, who kept telling me over and over that I was Tutsi and that was why I didn't have any strength.[30]

The revelation of a previously unknown membership in an ethnic group was repeatedly accompanied by insults and bullying—fanned, in the fall of 1990, by the start of the war with the FPR. If, according to most of the narratives, the parents had no choice but to respond to the questions the pupils were instructed by their teachers to ask, some tried to protect their children by advising them to blend in with the majority of their classmates. It was this recommendation that one boy, born in 1985, described receiving from his mother and one of his brothers:

> I remember that when I was in first grade at school in Gaseke, they made us stand up in class, saying: "Hutu, raise your hands and stand up. And Tutsi too, raise your hands and stand up." The teacher then told the Hutu to come to the front and the Tutsi stayed in their seats. Then she counted us before telling us to sit down. . . . When our teacher did this counting, it was because there was a visitor that I didn't know. One day, a man [probably a school inspector] came, he made us stand up, I didn't know him, and he said: "Have the Hutu go to one side and the Tutsi to the other." But I didn't know what group to go with. Then he told me to go ask my parents about my ethnic group. If my parents weren't there, I was supposed to look at their ID cards and read the word that is not crossed out. I looked at Mama's ID card and the words crossed out were "Hutu," "Twa." It was written like that: ~~Hutu~~, ~~Twa~~, Tutsi. Only the word "Tutsi" wasn't crossed out. And then I asked Mama and she replied: "If they ask you your ethnic group again, say that you're Hutu." When I was with Mama, it was about 5 PM, one of my brothers, named Bi, told me that when they ask the Hutu to stand, he stands up with them, that he doesn't stand up with the Tutsi; but every time, the teacher asks him to stand up with the Tutsi. . . . And Mama said: "Don't stand up with the Tutsi any more, but with the Hutu."[31]

The ploys devised by adults and older siblings hardly fooled the teachers, who were enmeshed in the social structures of the hill towns; they were well informed about the ethnoracial status of the families. Doomed to fail, these attempts at protection were nevertheless forms of disobedience in the face of the discriminatory system. They were sometimes tinged with a feeling of revolt, as is suggested in the story told by a boy who entered school at age seven in 1989:

> I remember very well when I went to primary school in Karama, in the second grade, they asked me my ethnic group and I didn't know how to answer. I said that I didn't know my ethnic group. They sent me away and told me to bring in my parents or to ask them to write what I am on a piece of paper, whether I am Tutsi or Hutu. It had to be written on our report cards, because at that time they wrote "Hutu," "Tutsi," or "Twa" on the grade sheets. I went home and when I got there I explained what I had been asked to do. My parents wrote that I am Tutsi on a piece of paper. Then it was put on my report card. Only the consequences that followed were the following: The day when the results were announced [after every quarter]—since I was intelligent and got good grades—I came home and showed my report card to everybody. And those who saw it, instead of congratulating me, said: "The children of the weaklings [*ingondeka*: gangling, weak—a common insult directed at the Tutsi] are intelligent." But I didn't understand the meaning of that word, any more than I understood the meaning of *inzoka* [snake—a common derogatory nickname for a Tutsi]. I had no explanation. But when I got home, I asked for explanations of those words. They didn't hide anything from me, and they explained that if people had said that to me, it was because they had seen that I was Tutsi since that's written on my report card. They went on to say that it was not an insult and that every time someone said that to me I had to keep quiet; that it wouldn't get to me. From time to time at school, when the school director [the visiting inspector] came to visit, he asked the Tutsi to stand up. And because I kept hearing the other children call me *inzoka*, I'd ended up taking it as an insult. So when he asked the Tutsi to stand up, I refused. But the teacher knew me well; he himself made me stand up and he thought I was disobeying him. From that day on he began to hit me without any reason, even if I was just making some little mistake. He said I was insolent.[32]

The story of confrontation with violence, in both symbolic and concrete forms, triggered by motives that the children could not decipher, led the writers to reconstitute the tangle of questions they had had at the time. Their interrogations about the assignment of an ethnic identity were all the more troubling in that this practice was in profound contradiction with what was being taught outside of school, especially in church. One girl born in 1982 shared her lack of comprehension in the face of the contradictory reasoning of adults:

> In class, we learned lots of useful and important things. But other knowledge was less important and could provoke conflicts and bad-mouthing. Why avoid mentioning these things? Because that is what overturned Rwanda: That is what makes Rwanda look bad. In class, I learned that there were three ethnic groups: Hutu, Twa, and Tutsi. As we were small children, we asked questions that came from what we had heard in church: God created two human beings, so what is the origin of these ethnic groups? They said: "You are Tutsi and the others are Hutu. Go ask your parents what your ethnic group is, they'll give you an answer." At home, they told us: "The teacher is intelligent, what he said is true." They didn't want to say anything more so as not to put themselves in danger and so they could live another day.[33]

The narratives written by the oldest girls and boys in our corpus described in detail the repeated failures they experienced when they entered secondary school, where nepotism was blended with discrimination so as to impede advancement in school. The following text by a girl born in 1977 spells this out:

> In the eighth grade of primary school, the late K.A. [the teacher] spoke in enigmatic terms, but we were old enough to understand. He would say, for example: "Why do I have to fill out your forms? Do you think you're going to succeed, you imbeciles?" He knew perfectly well that we were not idiots, that we were intelligent. But when we took the national exam [to get into secondary school], the results reflected his predictions: I don't claim to be exemplary, but I'm determined to say things the way I saw them. The child who passed the exam was at the bottom of the class, he could not even add 1 + 2. And that's true! I took the exam a second time, and that is when I observed the DIVISION. When we took the exam, there were lots of us, but the five children who came in after me in the grade rankings all failed [she gives their names and specifies that they are all Tutsi].[34]

Abolished starting in April 1992, after the courageous decision of Agathe Uwilingiyimana, the new minister of primary and secondary education in the first multiparty administration,[35] the quota system had long darkened the socioeconomic horizon of Tutsi families, as one young man born in 1982 emphasized:

> When my older brothers, one after another, finished primary school, my parents taught them a trade so they could meet their own needs in their future lives. They taught business to one of my older brothers and the tailoring trade to the other. Moreover, they bought him a sewing machine so that he wouldn't fail in life. . . . We often asked at home why our parents were looking for trades for us and Papa would answer: "My children, I know that you can't study like the others, not because you are dunces. That's why I'm looking for another way for you to learn and work that can help you advance in life, especially in the time when I won't be with you any more. I wouldn't want you to become beggars."[36]

Both the manufacturer of a previous unsuspected alterity and an instrument of economic oppression, school appears in the narratives as an efficient transmitter of racist clichés. In the following lines, a boy born in 1980 lists a first series of stereotypes attached to the Tutsi, touching on both their physical complexion and their exclusive pastoral activity:

> When I was seven, I was sent to school, I studied. I started school in 1987, in the primary school in Ntaruka. I was like a child who was starting first grade and who doesn't yet have a very well-grounded intelligence—why I'm saying that is because when I was in class, I heard them say: "Hutu, raise your hands and Tutsi too." I did what they said; then, when I was older, I found out that I was Tutsi. I knew that people who had lots of cattle were Tutsi; that people who had very long noses were Tutsi; that people who were very tall were Tutsi; all that made me understand that I was Tutsi. We continued to study that way until I finished primary school in 1993.[37]

While it is impossible to make precise distinctions in these narratives between the statements that came from the teaching dispensed in class and those that circulated on the playground, school as an institution was unfailingly associated with the evocation of commonplace racist tropes. The following physical and moral portraits related with an awkward naiveté by a girl born in 1982 illuminate the central place of the school in the propagation of racism at the heart of childhood societies:

When you denied your ethnicity at school, the teacher told you the basic features for recognizing ethnic groups. A Hutu was supposed to be short, with a big nose and a mouth that was red inside, and a sturdy build. A Tutsi was supposed to be very tall, slender, with a long nose, a very small stomach, a mouth that was black inside, without much strength, and I knew they had dark skin; many were arrogant; they didn't like to eat much but they liked to drink milk, because when you like to eat a lot, they too [the Hutu] would say that you had a big stomach like the Hutu. On the other hand, we were told that the Twa were dirty people.[38]

The vast repertory of stereotypes inevitably poisoned social relations among children, where derogatory nicknames flourished with striking creativity. One girl born in 1979 remembers them this way:

At school, we were asked what our ethnic group was, and when you said you were Tutsi, you no longer had any peace from the other children. It became something shameful, they gave you insulting nicknames like *Rusumbansika* [someone who is so tall he rises above the walls, *insika*, the inside walls of a house] or . . . *inzoka* [snake] and other nicknames that expressed how you were seen as a Tutsi, how you stood among the other children. The tallness of some lost its value because they said it was *Rusumbansika*. You lost your humanity when they called you *inzoka*, and all that paved the way for the genocide.[39]

Sometimes the teachers themselves spurred the pupils' mockery, organizing actual sessions of public humiliation around the revelation of someone's ethnicity. As the only Tutsi in his class, year after year, one boy born in 1981 had acute memories of the profound sense of shame and solitude he felt owing to his teacher's attitude.

I was going to primary school and we had cards on which our ethnic origins were written but I didn't know what mine was. The teacher told me to stand up when he called the Tutsi. I found myself standing up all alone. When I was in third grade, I stood up alone. The same thing happened in fourth grade. I was always alone, the others made fun of me. So I got to the point of refusing to stand up even though the teacher hit me and suspended me from school. Then he ordered me to come back bringing my parents' ID cards. The next day he walked by the desks and asked the other classmates: "When Hutu and Twa are crossed out on an ID card, what is left?" The others answered: "It's Tutsi." Then he asked me: "So, Ruta, what are you?" I answered: "I must be Tutsi." He shot back: "No! YOU ARE Tutsi!"[40]

Given that the bullying stopped later with a new teacher, a woman, who didn't organize any lessons around the mention of identity cards, the clarity of the boy's memory of that exchange attests to a searing impression.

For all the writers, the discovery of the "ethnicity stories" lifted the cloak of parental silence about the violence propagated in the 1960s. As the children pressed their parents about the nature of that ethnic membership, which remained obscure in their eyes, the latter agreed to talk about the massacres, looting, fires, and forced migrations that the families had suffered. Thus a girl born in 1980, from Sake, learned of the persecutions her parents had undergone when they were forcibly displaced after the pogroms of 1959:

> When I became aware of things, I was in the second grade and I began to approach my parents to listen to their discussions. They told us that Rukumberi wasn't the region they came from originally but that they had been driven out of the place where they were born. It was at that point that my father was separated from his family: It was in 1959. He was deported to Rukumberi, and the others took refuge in Burundi, Uganda, or Tanzania. Originally, they were from Mugina in Gitarama, and Mama's family was from Bufundu in Gikongoro. They were transported to Rukumberi in 1961. They spent two years in the Kibungo camp in Birenga. Rukumberi was covered with forests that were infested with the tsetse fly. They were deported there and were to be killed there later on. When they got to Rukumberi, they had a very hard life, and some of their neighbors died. In order to eat, they had to till the fields of people who lived close by.[41]

Like the hostile region of Nyamata, in the Bugesera, where thousands of displaced Tutsi from the north had gathered,[42] the Rukumberi region harbored a refugee camp for Tutsi families driven out of their birthplaces. At the end of 1961, there were 10,307 people crowded together in Nyamata, 2,838 in Bwiriri, and 754 in Gihinga.[43] The family of the girl just cited probably spent time in the Bwiriri camp. A report signed by the Belgian territorial administrator, dated July 1, 1961, and sent to the special resident, Colonel Guy Logiest, gives a picture of the refugees' situation while offering information on the political intentions of the colonial authorities: To banish the Tutsi from their native lands.[44] Budgetary and political concerns lay behind the plan for "definitive installation" set forth in these pages: A return to the original hill country was never envisioned. In the face of the refugees' resistance, the territorial administrator recommended constraint by way of hunger[45] if the new arrivals refused to clear and cultivate the new lands.

In the southern part of the country, in the Butare region, the questions raised by the school census broke the silence of one father, who had already lost a brother during the pogroms of the 1960s. This is the way the son, born in 1981, tells the story:

> When I went to school, I was asked if I was Hutu or Tutsi. And because I didn't know anything, I said I was Hutu, but they said I was Tutsi, because they knew my father. When I got back home, I told Papa and Mama that I had been asked what I was, and I told them that I had answered that I was Hutu because I didn't know what I am; and my teacher said that I was Tutsi. I asked Papa if I was Tutsi or Hutu, and Papa answered that I am a Tutsi. I asked another question: "Are the Tutsi Hutu?" And Papa said: "The Tutsi had their houses burned down in 1956 [*sic*; it was in 1959] and my older brother who was named Ka, they killed him in 1960 because he was an important person."[46]

Similar family grief cloaked in family silence was discovered by another boy, a year younger, revealed by his father in a discussion launched once again after the ethnicity issue came up in school:

> I remember that I myself was personally asked to approach him [his father] and he said: "Come here." I approached him and he began to tell me about my genealogy. When he finished, I asked him in turn: "You're the only one alive?" And he answered: "Yes, I'm the only one alive, the others are dead." I asked him another question: "All of them?" And he answered: "Yes." Then I went on: "They were sick and they died?" Because I didn't know there had been killings. At that point we had a long discussion, and he confided that he had been orphaned when he was seven, that his parents had been carried off by the war and that it was the Hutu who had killed them. He went on to say: "When I'm looking for trades for you, it is so that, when I die, you don't just stay and become dogs or go along the road begging.[47]

2

CHILDHOODS AT WAR

"For me, the genocide began in 1990."[1] A boy who had been eight years old at the time wrote this in the first pages of his notebook, signifying by this statement the shift into a new time frame marked by the emergence of war in his daily life.

On October 1, 1990, the soldiers of the Rwandan Patriotic Front (FPR) launched their first offensive at the northeast border, from the neighboring country of Uganda. A political and military organization founded in 1987, the FPR included in its ranks both descendants of the Tutsi exiled in 1960 and Hutu who opposed the ruling authorities.[2] Led by General Fred Rwigema, the troops (the Inkotanyi) were unquestionably determined but not very numerous; their equipment was rudimentary, and they were insufficiently familiar with the terrain. Rwigema, who had been part of the National Resistance Army (NRA), had contributed to Yoweri Museveni's victory in 1986.[3] The day after the assault, Museveni was killed by enemy fire, and the principal officers fell in turn; the governmental forces—the Rwandan Armed Forces (FAR)—pushed the rest of the assailants back beyond the border on October 28. This first offensive thus ended unmistakably in a searing failure. Regrouping in Uganda, the FPR was reorganized under the leadership of Paul Kagame, who took charge of the military operations at the end of October. As reinforcements for their counterattack, the FAR were able to draw on Belgian, Zairian, and especially French soldiers.[4]

The war that was beginning was immediately interpreted by the regime in terms of an ancestral antagonism opposing the "people in the majority" and the "feudal-monarchists."[5] At the heart of this system of representations, which drew on racist foundations from the 1960s, a dual process for assimilating civilians to the world of combat took shape. In the first place, all Hutu found themselves viewed as resolute defenders of the gains made in the "social revolution" of 1959; those who chose a different path were deemed traitors to their duty of *racial* solidarity. Thus the inhabitants of regions close to the fighting were urged to participate in the war efforts: The authorities provided weapons and ensured their military training.[6] Next, *all* Tutsi were viewed as "blood brothers" of the FPR, *collectively* treated as accomplices (*ibyitso*) of that party. Embodying a veritable "fifth column" within the population, they were suspected of using a legendary ruse to conceal their secret plan for winning power.[7]

If the boy quoted at the beginning of this chapter chose to begin *his* chronology nearly four years before April 1994, it is because the war offered a first powerful justification for the massacre and persecution of the Tutsi, who were henceforth perceived by the majority, as we have seen, as ontological enemies. But another motive also figures in this early chronology: As a genocide narrative, the boy's text is above all a *war story*. Another boy, born in 1984, like a girl writer of the same age, lived in the commune of Muvumba, which is located in the far northeast region of the country and was thus subjected to recurrent fighting starting in October 1990; however, the commune was conquered early in April 1994 by the FPR and was thus less affected by the genocide.[8] For the children from this part of northern Rwanda, the war burst into their lives through its noises. Both writers describe the same sonic memories:

> We heard the noise of the bombs at the border and right away we saw people running, fleeing. The director of the school prevented us from leaving so we wouldn't be separated from our parents. They said the Ugandans had attacked Rwanda. A short time later, we saw "uncle," who came to get us so we could escape. We fled, we left the place where we lived in Rwetanga and took shelter in Nyagatare. When we got to Nyagatare, we kept seeing people shot down by a helicopter.[9] We decided to go home: We had just found out that it wasn't the Ugandans who had attacked but Rwandan refugees in Uganda.[10]

> We heard the guns talking in Kagitumba, but I heard things explode without knowing what was going on. I heard my parents say that war had just broken out. . . . I was looking after the calves in the stable. When they had finished milking the cows, we were still hearing the gunfire in

Kagitumba. But I didn't understand what was happening at all, it was as though someone had told me that the sky was on fire [*ikirere gishya*: a common expression to account for an unknown, unimaginable event or action]. I remember that when we had finished milking, we fed the shepherds [herding dogs] and took the cows to the pasture. And I too went out to the pasture with the calves. I saw a lot of people all together, and they were saying: "It's serious!" While I was watching the cows with the other children, we were playing; we saw a lot of people who were carrying things on their heads and leading goats: They were coming from Kagitumba. We wondered among ourselves: "What's going on?" The older children told us: "It's the war that has just started!"[11]

Within families, concrete manifestations of the new period of war were not long in coming. The men were arrested unceremoniously; they were beaten and subjected to harsh conditions of detention. Uncles and fathers were accused of "complicity" with the enemy. The boy born in 1982 quoted earlier described regular beatings of his uncle and the young men of the neighborhood:

But things changed on October 30 1990, when the Rwandan army got the upper hand over the Inkotanyi. Then the problems started in full daylight. The genocide started to be carried out. It was on October 30, 1990, around 4 PM, but during the day there had been a lot of bullets. We couldn't go out. In addition to the bullets, there were bombs talking. When the bullets calmed down, we went out and we took the cattle to pasture, me and my uncle. But we didn't know what had happened. When we got to the pasture they caught my uncle, the one I was with, and took him away. I saw soldiers who didn't look like the soldiers I was used to seeing; I saw *local people coming with the soldiers*, they caught my maternal uncle . . . and they started beating him with sticks and stabbing him with bayonets. They also kicked him until he was seriously injured. I hid, and when I managed to get back home I saw that they had caught other people. . . . They had all been beaten with sticks, they tortured them to make them confess that they were Inkotanyi. And they saw that they didn't even know who the Inkotanyi were. . . . Things didn't stop there, I remember that one day a man called Leo came to the house. He was with soldiers who filled up his car. He had told them that we owned guns and military uniforms and that my uncle headed the Inkotanyi in Kayonza.

They came, they searched around but they didn't find anything: no guns, no uniforms. So they chose to stuff my maternal uncle and two other young men named André and Joseph into their car. They went to jail them in the place that was called "Commandement."[12] They came back from there after three days. They had to get treated again for their bruises and broken bones because they had been beaten with sticks.[13]

Another boy, born in 1986 and also from Muvumba, remembers his father's arrest for the same reasons:

I remember that, during that year and even a little earlier, my father was a teacher; he worked in the primary school in Bushara in the commune mentioned before. They came all the time to search our house. They even searched in the sand piles, and in Papa's friends' houses. They said they were looking for guns we had hidden for the Inyenzi.[14] They didn't find anything, but they were never convinced and they came back over and over. Sometimes they came looking for Papa, saying that he was an accomplice of the Inkotanyi. They searched and didn't find those guns, but without being convinced. One day, they came to the house with a car. Mama was with my little brother, they asked her: "Where is Paul, Nkotanyi [Paul the Inkotanyi]"? That was the name they'd given Papa. She answered that he had gone off to teach; they found him at the school and took him away in their car. Afterward, we learned that he was in prison in Byumba because they said he was an accomplice of the Inkotanyi.[15]

Given the seriousness of the persecutions to which he was subjected, this boy's father decided to leave the commune and move to Kinyamakara, far from the front, in the Gikongoro prefecture; he was killed there during the genocide four years later.

Arrests, detentions, and incessant searching of homes spread beyond the borders of the battlefields. Throughout the country, thousands of people were detained in municipal stadiums and dungeons on the grounds of their alleged complicity with the FPR. The vast majority was Tutsi, even if some Hutu who contested the hegemony of the authorities in place were also locked up. According to the figures of the Ministry of Justice at the time, more than 6,500 people were arrested as early as October 1990.[16] Gradually released during the months that followed, owing to the protests of Rwandan civil society and pressure from the international community, the former detainees nevertheless remained under strict surveillance.

The repression against the "accomplices" (*ibyitso*) takes on very precise contours at the level of the individual narratives. In the hill country, the accusation of complicity with the FPR opened the way to the real brutalization of social relations. Thus a girl born in 1982, from the commune of Kabarondo, remembers how her father was harassed:

> I also remember that my Papa was endlessly persecuted because he was Tutsi. He was accused of crimes as a pretext for persecuting him. One day, they lied and claimed that he had said: "The Hutu are dogs." Whereas he was someone who couldn't have said that. He spoke very little. He was not born taciturn but his economy of words came from what he had experienced. For him, speaking was equivalent to death.[17]

Not far away, in the commune of Rukara, suspicion justified ransacking the paternal *ingo*, as reported by a girl born in 1981:

> At our house they came and said to Papa: "We're looking for the Inyenzi you're hiding in your house." Papa answered: "There aren't any." They insisted: "We know you're hiding them." Papa said: "Come in and look for them. If you find them, kill me with them. But if you don't find them, I'm the one who'll kill you." He took a lance and stood at the entrance to the house and then he said to them: "If you don't find them, it's because you're looking for something else." They searched, they turned everything upside down; they searched the chest, they searched the smallest books and papers. They took papers from the chest and took them away, saying that they were letters exchanged with the Inkotanyi. But they were lying, for the papers weren't even letters. Then they went to grandpa's house, Papa's father's, and they didn't find anything there either. Then they went to our paternal uncle's house, and nothing there either, they didn't find any Inkotanyi. They went on searching in the bush, saying that we were hiding weapons there, guns; they found nothing.[18]

In those war years, intensified violence led to the articulation of ever more specific and alarming threats. In this connection, the dialogue between a farmer and a FAR soldier, as related by the farmer's son (born in 1981), reveals that a massive extermination of the Tutsi was gradually coming into focus for the soldier:

It was in those years that they came to take Papa, saying that he was an accomplice. I realized how bad it was to be Tutsi, for I remember that a soldier came to the house to arrest Papa. They used to say that that soldier was Habyarimana's driver. One day when I was standing near Papa and the soldier, the soldier said to him: "Emmanuel, offer me that field so I can grow some sweet potatoes in it, since we're going to take you away and no Tutsi taken away will ever come back home. You others, you're done for." Papa answered him: "What are my children and my wife going to eat?" The soldier responded: "For them too, there aren't many days left." I think that was in 1992, because I remember that they took Papa away five times, in 1990–1991, twice in 1992, and again in 1993.[19]

To the war, which brought anti-Tutsi racism to the boiling point, was added a period of partisan competition starting in June 1991.[20] Political violence is superimposed on the violence of war in the narratives, as a young girl from the commune of Kigarama makes clear:

The time of the [political] parties arrived, and things changed. Even someone you didn't know before, you knew him, because people changed in a remarkable way. The Hutu went to the meetings of the MRND [Juvénal Habyarimana's party, formerly the only party] and that's where they showed how malicious they were. And from that time on, they boasted that they were going to kill the Tutsi. They started to arrest people on the road, they attacked us at night, they threw stones on the roofs of houses, they looted things without being hunted down. A person could be attacked, hit, and there was nowhere to demand justice. And when someone tried to seek justice, they said he was the one who was a rebel. At school, things changed: The children hated one another, and when you played with another child, he hit you as much as he wanted or he insulted you by saying you were Inkotanyi. Those kids had just crossed the border. Every time you did some little thing, they would say: "Ah, that Inkotanyi is going to kill us!" So you were afraid to play with the other children. The Papas also were starting to come home early because sometimes they were attacked on the road or at home. And sometimes we spent the night outside. The Hutu said that the fate of the Tutsi was sealed and that they [the Hutu] were going to get revenge for what they [the Tutsi] had done to them during the time of the royalty.[21]

In such a context, it is not surprising to see how open the world of children was to violence. At school as well as in the hills, insults and blows multiplied. An early memory evoked in the texts refers to parodies of the burial of Fred Rwigema, who had fallen in combat the day after the offensive of October 1, 1990. The narrative just cited continues with a few lines describing the mocking atmosphere of these ceremonies:

> We continued to live that life until they made us bury banana tree trunks while saying that we were burying Rwigema. They did this while singing and they were very happy. I remember the song they were singing: "We will march in the Renewed Movement, in multipartyism. The accomplices who remain won't be able to do anything against us." As for me, I wonder where the other accomplices went? We continued to live that life until the beginning of the genocide.[22]

Similarly, a boy born in 1985 amalgamates in the same breath all the bullying inflicted by the other children during that period of great tension:

> The children were so persecuted by the other Hutu children. It was too much for them. For example, I myself never tried to play banana tree leaf ball [soccer] because when you played with the other children, they shoved you around and you could break your bones. And you couldn't complain. When the older children didn't go to school, you couldn't go without their protection. They didn't hesitate to throw rocks and fruit [*intobo*, inedible, very hard fruit from a wild bush] at you all the way home, yelling out war cries [*induru*]. That continued, and when Rwigema died, a big festival was decreed. We didn't study that day. We spent our time in marches. We marched carrying a banana tree trunk on our heads. Everyone carried a banana trunk on his head depending on his strength. They said we were going to bury Rwigema. Right away, the banana tree trunk became a symbol of the Tutsi. A principle was invented that claimed that cutting a Tutsi was cutting a banana tree trunk. The Tutsi became little animals. They were called *inyenzi* [cockroach], *imbeba* [mouse], and they said: "*Uwica imbeba ntababarira ihaka*" [he who kills a mouse doesn't spare the big mouse]; "*Uwica inzoka amena mutwe*" [he who kills the snake strikes or breaks its head]. At that time, you didn't have the same rights as the others. Above all, you didn't have the right to live. We felt like nonhumans. People continued to experience injustice, and

we wondered what good it was to live without life. There weren't any games among children of the same age because when you played with a Hutu child he reminded you constantly of the burial of the banana tree trunks (Rwigema, a Tutsi). They would say: "You Tutsi, you're tall and skinny, you have to make your own high jump. You have your own body shape."[23]

If the war, and then multipartyism, constituted a sequence of biographical ruptures for some of the writers, others, from the communes of Bugesera and Kibungo in the southwest, situate their own individual chronologies of the genocide at a different point in time: March 1992. Hundreds of Tutsi were in fact assassinated in these regions, their houses burned down and their cattle killed. The commune of Kanzenze was the epicenter of the violence unleashed after the National Radio, on March 3, broadcast a rumor about an alleged plot fomented by the Tutsi of the Liberal Party and the FPR against a series of bigwigs in the regime.[24] Starting on March 4 and 5, 1992, the persecuted Tutsi fled toward the church in Nyamata, an enclosure that was still inviolable and offered protection, as one young boy (birth date unknown) relates:

In the commune of Kanzenze, which has now become a district of Bugesera, when the genocide of the Tutsi began, we saw the Hutu attack. They began to burn down the houses located on the hills across from us, from our hill in Kayumba. They cut the people who lived in those hills into pieces; they looted their property. Those hills were in Maranyundo, Kanzenze. . . . The people began to flee toward the priests (in the Nyamata church). They thought that they wouldn't pursue them in the house of God. Among those who took refuge in the church, there was me and my family with our livestock: fifteen cows and seven goats. Thanks to God, those who lived on our hill in Kayumba reached the church in peace, because the Hutu feared our hill; they said it was the Tutsi grotto. That meant that the hill was inhabited by the Tutsi without any mixing (there weren't any Hutu). When we fled to the church, it was the first time I saw a person cut up by the Hutu because the person was Tutsi. And this wasn't the only person who had been cut up, there were many; the animals were killed in the same attack. How can you explain why they went after the animals? Is it because the animals were also Tutsi? As for me, I would say that it was out of hatred for the owners of these animals, plus the large stomachs with which this ethnic group is born. When that crowd of Tutsi had gathered at the church, someone sent a message to the town mayor named Rwambuka Fidèle. When he arrived, he explained, laughing heartily: "This isn't war, but the anger of the Hutu because of the attacks by your people who went to join the Inkotanyi. Go back home. That won't happen again." He said that it wasn't war, whereas it was the genocide of the Tutsi. There were countless dead people who used to live in the commune he headed. Those who were not dead were almost dead because of the Hutu's machetes. A white Italian woman called Antonia Locatelli[25] was caught by Habyarimana's army because she had made a phone call home to Italy. She had said [during the phone call] that the Tutsi of Bugesera were being killed. What is more, she was lodging us in her houses and protecting us. In short, we were at her home, in the church, and in the orphanage. But some time later, fairly quickly, Rwambuka Fidèle, the head of the commune, sent soldiers and policemen to her house to drive us out, so we would go back to our properties, which we no longer had. There were dead people but also people who had lost their homes: No one was prosecuted for that. They viewed us as idiots. But they didn't dare penetrate into the house of God because the time for the execution of their plan hadn't come yet. They didn't stay out because they respected the house of God but because it wasn't time yet. If they feared the house of God, they wouldn't kill human beings, because man was created in the image of God. We went back to our homes, there were many who found only ruins.[26]

This narrative, with intentionalist accents and tinged with a still vivid anger, depicts the intensity of the massacres and looting perpetrated at the time, with the active complicity of the local authorities. One girl, nine years old at the time, invokes divine protection to explain her survival in the Nyamata church in 1992:

The war began in 1992 and it was then that we took refuge in the church in Nyamata. There, they attacked us many times, but God put his protective arm in place and we survived. Afterward, we returned to where we lived and we saw that they had taken the roof off of our house. What really hurt me was that our neighbors were the ones who had done it. Things kept on like that and we arrived in 1994.[27]

Without reaching the same scale, violence came to the neighboring prefecture of Kibungo, where the communes of Sake and Mugesera were also subjected to killings and attacks on property in March 1992. As veritable court clerks of rumor, the local intelligence services recorded, for that period, insistent murmurs that always conveyed the threat of extermination for the Tutsi.[28] Two young girls living in the Rukumberi sector situated in Sake go back over the events that they had witnessed:

> In 1992, I was in fourth grade and I was twelve years old. There was a Hutu man who lived a little above us, his name was Havu. He had just been freed. He had burned his own house, which was like a kitchen, saying that it was the Tutsi who had set it on fire. This was the first time I saw a soldier. At that time, the soldiers came to our house, they took our brother M. E. who was called Cya. When they attacked us, Papa wasn't home. They ordered Mama: "Bring the guns you have." They hit her with the butt of their guns. They arrested our neighbors. . . . They beat them badly before laying them down in their car, and when the car left, the soldiers were standing on them. They were crying out in pain. They brought them to Kibungo, where they were jailed. Ever since I saw that, I have never stopped being afraid. There, in Rukumberi, as that area was inhabited by the Tutsi (for the most part), *they said every day that they were going to come and kill us*, especially in the days before the big festival days, like Easter, Christmas, and New Year's Day. I grew up in that "atmosphere."[29] And from time to time, we spent the night in the bush. Every time, before going off to go to bed, I passed behind the house, I closed my eyes even as I looked and listened toward the place where the Hutu lived, especially toward the house of the man who had gotten Cya jailed.[30]

With her own words, all in all not so different from the language of the administrators, this girl too returns to the searing rumors of the extermination to come. Another text, by a girl born in 1982, depicts the displacement of the violence from Bugesera even as it offers a detailed description of the acts. Marked by a rationality reconstructed after the fact, an excerpt like this brings to light a series of facts that are, similarly, quite close to the accounts produced by the local officials:[31]

> Things kept going this way and, in 1992, people were killed in Kanzenze, quite simply because they were Tutsi. They said they were accomplices

of the Inkotanyi, that they were *inyenzi*. At the place called Sholi, in Sake, on the border with Rukumberi, they killed the old people who lived in the stables and they ate their cows because they were Tutsi. Who killed them? It was the people who called themselves Hutu, supported by the ruling authorities. If I follow what happened during the *rwandais* [Rwandan][32] genocide, I would say that these killings that took place in certain regions of Rwanda were like "*un échantillonage* [a sampling],"[33] an attempt to see if the action they were preparing was going to succeed. From that time on, in Rukumberi, the adults lived in fear. Sometimes they spent the night without going to bed. Often they were warned that someone was going to come kill them. There was a priest called Michel; he lived in the parish of Rukoma; he asked the soldiers for help, saying it was to ensure security. When the soldiers arrived, they caught Tutsi people, they beat them and they put others in prison, saying that they were destabilizing security, when they had done nothing. All that happened before my eyes; no one told me about it.

When I began my story, I told you about various people, brothers, neighbors . . . of all those and their families, very few have remained. You may wonder: Where did they go? Why were they taken away? That genocide that they were trying out was triggered by the death of the head of the country, Habyarimana.[34]

Among the narratives describing a rapid and intense shift toward mass persecution following the triggering of the war, those of the writers who came from the commune of Murambi, in the Byumba prefecture, warrant special attention. Led by Jean-Baptiste Gatete from 1982 on, this commune was the theater of large-scale arrests that led to the "disappearance" of some twenty men, starting in October 1990.[35] Two of these victims are mentioned in the text of a young man (no birth date indicated) who describes in detail the violence committed in his commune:

> On October 20, 1990, that's when they started to arrest the *ibyitso*. In my family, they arrested Papa, my older brothers, and my neighbors. They put them in prison. There was a military barrier in Kiziguro. My other brothers . . . were made to spend the night in the dungeon of the commune. . . . I was looking after the cows. When I got back home, when I didn't find those family members, I didn't understand. I chose to close the entrance of the place where the cows were and to spend the night

outside (in the fields). On October 22, 1990, we saw *muzehe* [his father] return with two other people. We began to take food to those who had remained in prison. Afterward, they arrested other neighbors and put them in prison. We continued to bear that cross together. The only ones who stayed in prison were Gasen and G. Gasen; she remained in prison because she had come from Uganda and she had scarifications on her arm; they said that those marks represented the motto "Vive Kigeri."[36] That was why she was kept in prison, and also, of course because she was Tutsi. After two months in prison, they let her go. But she was supposed to go clock in at the commune. . . . But G. and the others who were with him . . . Gatete kept them in the dungeon. It didn't take long: In November 1990, Gatete put them in a car saying that he was going to take them to the prison in Byumba. I heard that they were blindfolded when they were taken away. He drove them off and threw them into a ditch in Byumba. They burned them. This was the death in store for those *imfura* [people noble in body and mind]. Remembering all that is very painful. On September 8, 1991, Gatete started the stories of meetings. The Tutsi were attacked in their homes and beaten. We spent a night in the fields, even though the Tutsi had built their own houses. What sin had the Tutsi committed? Is it that milk flows instead of blood in Tutsi veins? Don't ask me those questions. What did the Hutu who did all that gain from it?[37]

PART TWO

*Then the Time Came, and We Entered
into the Life of the Genocide*

UBWO IGIHE CYAJE KUGERA TWINJIRA

MU BUZIMA BWA JENOSIDE

3

SEPARATIONS

In most of the testimonies, the children say they saw their parents' faces darken when they learned of President Habyarimana's death in the April 6, 1994, plane crash. The four years of war and incessant persecution starting in October 1990 had made them fear the repercussions of such an event, even though a complete extermination of the Tutsi seemed inconceivable. The children perceived their parents' anxiety as a first manifestation of their powerlessness. A girl from the commune of Rusumo, who was fifteen years old in 1994, expresses it best: "I too felt that my father was afraid, whereas I had always believed him invincible. So I was frightened in turn, but I didn't imagine that I could die because I had no familiarity with death."[1] The seriousness of the news was deduced from the parents' reactions; some of them had been unable to hide their tears and terror. The children's stories of the first hours or days of the genocide tended to associate fear on the part of adults with a series of small changes experienced by families and communities. The initial manifestations of violence served as signs on the basis of which the writers interpreted the threat hanging over their families, signs that foreshadowed the first separations.

The survival strategies worked out by the adults as soon as Habyarimana's death was announced were based on knowledge derived from earlier experience: The Tutsi had been victims of persecution in the 1960s and 1970s. The children knew nothing, or very little, of this background, for the adults had cloaked the tragic history of the assassination or exile of certain family members during those pogroms in a protective silence. Kept in the dark about the violent past, the youngest knew nothing, either, about "ethnicity issues"; they often first learned that they were Tutsi from their schoolteachers, who were required to establish a scrupulous ethnic census. In their families, children thus depended entirely on the adults' interpretation of the threat, even though they themselves witnessed arbitrary arrests, brutal searches, and suspicion on the part of their schoolmates, starting with the beginning of the civil war against the Rwandan Patriotic Front (FPR) in October 1990. The few self-protective reflexes they might have acquired during those years of enormous tension were revived during the genocide, especially the practice of spending the night in the bush or in the banana plantations surrounding the family courtyards (*urugo*). The adults, especially the older ones, who had experienced the major pogroms of the 1960s, were sure they knew how to respond to the new threats. The men did not intend to stand by and watch their cattle slaughtered again: They organized protection of the herds in the courtyards when the women and children were elsewhere. The "Papas" had figured among the first victims of the earlier bands of killers (*ibitero*) rampaging through the hills in search of Tutsi homes (*ingo*). While the knowledge accumulated during decades of persecution might indeed have led the adults to forge more solid survival strategies, those same strategies were exploited by the killers—who also carried memories of the earlier violence—to increase the effectiveness of the massacres and looting. During the first hours and days of the genocide, not only were many children separated from their families, but the radically increased violence brought a sense of irremediable separation, a change in degree and nature that broke any sense of continuity between the period of persecutions in the 1960s and that of wholesale extermination in the spring of 1994.[2]

The memories of the oldest members led certain families to the churches, which had remained intact sanctuaries until then, as we see, for example, in a report by a girl born in 1985:

> And grandma said: "In 1959, we took refuge in the church and nothing happened to us in the house of God, an impenetrable place." We then set out on the path to the church in Nyarubuye (today it is called Nyamirambo [a place where there are many dead bodies] because of what happened, *yewe!* [oh my God!]), it's really incomprehensible.[3]

In a country that was 90 percent Christian and more than 63 percent Catholic, how could anyone imagine the radical desecration of places where killers and victims had worshiped together? How could one imagine the sacrilege committed by Catholic killers, moved by a faith that served to justify the extermination of the Tutsi, who were henceforth removed from the common world of the church? Taking refuge in His "house" stemmed as much from an ancient protective reflex as from an act of faith, but how could anyone conceive, finally, of abandonment by God Himself?

In some families where the memory of the earlier massacres had remained vivid, the adults nevertheless sought more reliable defenses against the new threat produced by the assassination of President Habyarimana. This was the case, for example, at Bicumbi, a commune led for nearly twenty-four years by Laurent Semanza, a mayor intimately linked to the extremist central power, which revived its murderous zeal as early as April 7. The figure of that former mayor, even though he had been replaced in 1993, continued to inspire fear in one mother who distributed wraps and money to her children in preparation for their flight. Her daughter, born in 1974, offers this account:

> April arrived and Mama—we were with her—called all the children who were at home because others lived in Kigali, the child of my maternal aunt whom my parents were raising and even the grandchildren. She told us that she had managed to overcome many deaths but that this one would not leave her in peace. And because I hadn't known any war, I raised questions from a child's perspective and I asked why she was going to die. She answered: "My child, in 1959, people died, others survived and escaped and the Hutu attacked the cattle, they ate. And I didn't die. The one who attacked was Semanza, who was the mayor of Bicumbi. But he had people carry the hot cooking pots on their heads to the Hutu. Now Habyarimana has just died, you think all that is going to leave us in peace?" I didn't understand anything because I was a child and because I had never seen war. I understood that only in history. Mama divided among us the clothes she had, like the wraps, and each child received something, even the money she had in the house.[4]

The filial attachment bound up with memories of earlier persecutions prevented another mother from Bicumbi from escaping and leaving her own mother, an elderly invalid, behind: "Mama told us she should not abandon her because during the war in 1959 she [the mother] had not abandoned her."[5] Hidden in a banana field next to the house, the little girl, seven years old at the time, watched her mother's murder. As for her grandmother, left alone and without help, she died of starvation a few days later.

If the memory of violence sometimes sharpened the perception of a new danger, it more often delayed flight by leading the adults, the men in particular, to take measures to defend their herds and their properties: These deferred departures from their own lands were fatal. The experience of the older generation was invested with such confidence that it managed to calm the alarmist judgment of the writers' parents, as we see from the following excerpt in which a boy, born in 1986, recounts hesitations about what to do:

> We were on vacation. Habyarimana's plane fell Wednesday night, April 7, 1994 [actually the night before]. But I didn't know this, I was asleep, and in the morning I was sent to watch the cows with the shepherd. I was ten years old. And when we brought the cattle back from the pasture, I did not know what was happening, but I heard them say: "We're done for." These men were neighbors. People from my home had no more hope, they saw that they couldn't do anything and that they [the Hutu] were going to kill them. Around 2:00, on the other side of Muhazi, in Murambi, the houses [were] burning. They had started to burn down the houses. Those who saw the houses being burned went to tell the other Tutsi. They said: "It's the end. Where can we go now? We're done for." And those who were older said: "It's going to stop, it's normal, this also happened in 1959." But everywhere there were Interahamwe meetings. On the evening of the 8th, the adults went to spend the night in the bush, and we, the little children and Mama, we spent the night in the house. Papa spent the night sitting in his stable. Daylight came, and those who were in the bush came back. During that day, the genocide began for us.[6]

The image of fathers and uncles organizing the watch over their cattle after finding shelter for their wives and children, thus doubling their own exposure to danger, is prevalent in a large majority of the texts. In the following excerpt, a girl born in 1986 attributes her father's refusal to flee, even though he had been warned of the imminent arrival of an *igitero*, to his determination to protect his property while she, her mother, and her younger brothers and sisters were hidden in a banana field:

> Papa refused, for he had a good deal of property, a large number of animals, and fields awaiting the harvest. He refused to flee while abandoning his calves in the stable, the goats outside where they were grazing. . . . Suddenly it was 3:00 in the afternoon, I myself, Mama, my big sister, and

the other children who were younger than me went to hide below the banana plantation. We didn't lock the door to the house or the kitchen
door. Papa had forbidden Mama to close the doors so they wouldn't destroy the house. Papa was in the place where he kept his cows, with his
sons. When he saw it was 3:00, he left the cows to the boys and he went
back inside. Immediately the *igitero* came down yelling. Where we were,
we were frightened, we abandoned Mama and ran. But she followed us.
When Papa reached the eucalyptus forest that he had planted himself and
that had spread, he heard the sounds of the *igitero*, they had started to
throw stones on the tiles. He got very angry, and he went up; when he
approached the house from below, he saw them, he was killed by fear.
He knelt down behind a banana tree (since death was already haunting
him, he didn't think to turn back and flee). The Interahamwe scattered
and arrived at the house. Some rushed inside to eat and drink milk, others
went to cut down the bananas. . . . I can't say this . . . they saw him. They
yelled out war cries [*induru*], saying they had just found him. Those who
were eating and drinking milk ran out and they all circled around him:
Some were hitting him with sticks, others with clubs. I can't say this . . .
on the head, on the back, on the face, as if they were killing a snake. They
cut him in pieces like a bunch of bananas. When night fell, they had finished him off.[7]

Beyond the obvious lure of profit, we cannot exclude the hypothesis that the
very presence of the owner on his lands was perceived by the killers as a form
of provocation that increased their murderous energy. The dynamic common to the massacre and the looting, so striking in all the texts, constitutes
one of the unprecedented threshold-crossing moments of genocidal violence; such moments had been impossible for the victims to imagine.

But the threat was not always interpreted by the yardstick of a past marked
by persecutions. It was sometimes gradually decoded on the basis of sudden unaccustomed acts or words that came to disturb the routine of social
relations. The unexpected closing of a market, gatherings in small groups,
an unusual increase in the volume of traffic on the roads, suspicious glances
from the neighbors sometimes accompanied by insults: All these disquiet-
ing small signs are reinterpreted by the young writers to describe the threatening atmosphere in the first hours following the attack. If the uneasiness
of the adults, reinforced by a powerful feeling of helplessness, marks most

of the narratives, the children for their part did not understand the brutal change in the expressions and attitudes of their parents. Most were too young to grasp the import of an event that took place far from their familiar universe in the hills. The following scene, related by a girl born in 1983, gives an account of that lack of comprehension:

> On April 6, 1994, the airplane of the former president of Rwanda Habyarimana crashed. At home, in Rubona, they found out the next morning, and I saw that the people around us were seized with fear. But I myself didn't know that Habyarimana's death could have consequences for us. I heard my big sisters say that our fate was sealed and that we were done for. For me, that didn't mean much, because I was still a young child. That day, I saw that everybody had changed. No one went to work. I saw them gather in small groups; they were listening to the radio, but it was not broadcasting any news, just *inanga* sounds [an *inanga* is a stringed instrument generally used to play slow rhythms]. I asked Papa what it was and he replied: "These are tears." Again I asked Papa: "Is it a person who's crying?" And he said: "Hush, I don't know anything about it." But I saw that he was sad and I started crying because he was not at peace.
>
> The evening of that day, it was Thursday, we had spent the day there without doing anything, but I noticed that our Hutu neighbors were observing us and pointing their fingers at us, whispering. We didn't know where to go. We spent that night at the house but no one slept because we were afraid they would come and kill us. But the killings hadn't yet started. We were lucky enough to see the sun rise without incident. In other prefectures, the grenades had started to set the tone, to speak for themselves. That Friday, the sun rose, and we spent the day in the house. Food was prepared, but my big sisters and Papa and Mama couldn't eat anything. When I saw all that, I was scared and I didn't manage to eat anything either.[8]

Sometimes, the break in familial and social routines was experienced by the children in the mode of play and joyful excitement. The noisy interplay between brothers and sisters and cousins gathered together in a *rugo* blended with the uneasy chatter of the adults.

Whether pronounced by neighbors or by parents, the same terrifying words came up in the narratives like a leitmotif of fatal import: "*akabatutsi kashobotse*" ("the fate of the Tutsi is sealed"). Translating the impotence of the future victims and the desire to intimidate on the part of their malevo-lent neighbors, that expression, used repeatedly, conveyed a rapid perception of the upheaval induced by the news of the death of the head of state. Still, the sense of danger engendered by the general situation of the country was not always transferred to local settings, where neighborly relations had not al-ways been systematically damaged by the growing violence of the 1990s.[9] The reaction of one father to a neighbor's accusation, depicted by a daughter born in 1985, attests to the absence of a local translation of the threat:

> It was in 1994, in April, I don't remember the precise dates. That day, a Hutu man who was our neighbor came and said to us: "Our *umubyeyi* [the father of the country], *you* killed him, so you no longer have the right to live either." Papa said to him: "You, you amaze me. I heard that he died in the plane; and you see perfectly well that I'm right here. You're telling me that I'm one of the people who killed him, does that mean I was in the same plane as he? Maybe it's an accident like the others? How is it possible that I could kill him?" In the next couple of days, the man came back and said to Papa: "The fate of the Tutsi is sealed. You, here, all of *you* don't understand anything, then. *You* are just one family among us. You aren't going to bother us."[10]

The charge brought by that neighbor in a *collective* mode henceforth ex-cludes the father from the familiar world of the hill neighborhood by as-signing him to a *different* group, one defined by a slanderous accusation. The future victim marks his apprehension, while his neighbor relays concretely, in the mutually familiar surroundings, the new national line imputing the responsibility for the attack to the Tutsi.

The eruption of the threat designating the Tutsi in their totality also targeted their cattle, to which the owner's fate was very often linked. The animals too were the objects of insults and intimidations, as one boy empha-sizes. A thirteen-year-old herder in 1994, intimately familiar with the hills and the best pastures and water sources prized by his animals, during the first days of the massacres reinterpreted a macabre prophecy that had been uttered by a neighbor some years earlier; at that time, the terrifying oracle had been directed at the cows:

> When I used to go look after the cows on the hillsides [*amabanga*] and in other places, I would meet people who would say to me: "Those things

there [speaking of the cows] that belong to you, we're going to eat them. You wear yourself out for nothing looking after them. We already ate them in 1959 and we're going to kill you." That was something I couldn't believe, because I had never seen a person cut any animal or even seen an animal slaughtered to be eaten like that and its owner killed. So the people who said that made me laugh. This was before 1990. . . .

The time of 1994: . . . I went to look after the cows and where I passed by some residents whose names I don't remember would say: "Your things, we're coming to gobble them up!"[11]

This threat was implemented, for the first threshold of violence crossed by the killers, as the young herder made clear, lay precisely in the slaughtering and consumption of cows looted from their Tutsi neighbors. To that sinister promise was added another transgression having to do with the way the cows were designated, reduced to "things" by the use of the expression "*bika byanyu*" ("your *things*"). Ordinarily, cows were evoked with a particularly rich vocabulary that translated the respect owed to those animals. Ultimately, the attacks on herds and the burning of neighbors' houses led the young herder to flee, and thus be separated from his family.

It was becoming clear that the threat was not brought to the hills by outsiders, by strangers in uniform, but rather by neighbors. The premises of violence were brought home to the victims through familiar figures. This initial betrayal by near neighbors marked an irremediable shift into a new order of violence. Neither moral qualities nor social capital nor the memory of mutual benefits constituted a barrier against the murderous about-face. Here is how one boy, eight years old at the time, relates the very first attack carried out against his father by a neighbor:

Papa refused to follow us; he seemed to have lost all trust in the Hutu, for many people of great goodness had just been killed because of their ethnicity. Certain Hutu whom we had thought were good people, like Nya, who was our neighbor, well, I'll never forget how he hurled his sword against Papa on the hillside, in front of Bi's house, saying "Stop him and bring him back here! His cows that went to pasture with mine are all going to come back to my place. I'm going to expand my stables and we'll have no more pasture problems!" . . . We heard Nya shout out *induru* to ask the others to come together to kill Papa, whereas the previous Wednesday, they all had uttered cries of joy while sharing beer in a big pitcher with Papa, for Mama had just given birth to the child she held in her arms, Emmanuel.[12]

The father escaped from that first assault, but he was killed the next day by an *igitero* formed by neighbors after the latter had learned of the definitive order of extermination at a meeting called by the local authorities. The mother and her newborn baby survived just a few days longer, only to be assassinated by a neighbor whose wife was a friend of the decimated family. At the moment when the mother was killed, there was a dialogue between the killer and his victim, a dialogue made possible by their sharing of a common world, nourished by great social proximity and even friendship. The nature of the links uniting the actors is even spelled out by the killer: The families seemed to be connected by a friendship doubly shared by the killer and his wife. Here is how the boy recalled that terrifying discussion:

I stayed with Mama and the little children from my house, for the others had run away. A man called Ka . . . who lived in Nkanga arrived where we were, myself and Mama. When he got there, he was taking big strides and he said to Mama: "Give me all the money you have and all your clothes, even those you have on. I don't want you to get them stained with your blood when I cut you." I was sitting discreetly aside but I saw everything. Mama gave him everything she had and Ka said to her again: "When I saw that you respected me and that you avoided giving me a hard time, I began to take pity on you. But I don't have enough pity to spare you. On the other hand, I have enough to kill you while letting you keep that dress on. And then, you were among the faithful friends of my wife and F was my great friend. But he is already dead." Ka said to Mama: "What death would you choose?" And Mama answered: "Kill me however you want but spare my child and give him to another parent if you would, to another parent who isn't going to die like me, so that parent will feed him. This child hasn't committed the crime you accuse us of because he is too young, he hasn't even begun to think." Ka responded to Mama: "I haven't understood a thing you said. Choose a weapon from those I have. Choose the one I'm going to use to kill you." And Mama replied: "Kill me with whatever you like but first let me pray." Mama bowed down to pray. From where I was, I didn't want to watch Mama being cut and dying, the one who bore me for nine months. I ran off, and that evening, when the Hutu had finished killing, they went to eat some cows and goats. I went back to see Mama; I thought they had pardoned her but they had killed her with the little child she was holding. They had thrown them onto a terraced farm field.[13]

The sudden rupture in affective relations is attested by another boy, also eight years old at the time, from the commune of Muhazi. After a night spent in the bush, terrorized by the yelling, the fires, and the dogs let loose at their heels, the family decided to beg a neighbor to hide them. Here is how the child relates the welcome in store for them: "The next day, we went to our neighbor, thinking that they would hide us. The old woman there was a great friend of Mama's and she said to her: 'Go away, go away, go home! I have no more relations with a snake!'"[14] The betrayal of neighbors left deep traces in the memory of the young writers, to the point that it gave rise to the following lines, full of anger, by a girl (birth date unknown) beginning her narration of the first hours of April 7, 1994:

> If I tell the long and the short of it, the day and the night would go by. The night is told only by the one who lived through it, for my story is too long. *They* are bad, *they* slept in our sheets, *they* ate the meat of our cows, *they* wore fine clothing for the first time in their lives, *they* had dressed in the *imishanana* [cotton garments worn like togas] of our old women saying that they wanted to resemble us. But you will never resemble us! God alone will condemn you.[15]

In many other texts, the threat does not take on the familiar form of a neighbor but is manifested in the deafening noise of weapons, shouts, whistles, hunting horns, and barking dogs. Newly started fires, particularly easy to spot on the hills, were added to the racket, convincing families to flee. Here are some images, auditory as well as visual, transcribed by one of the young boys, about eight years old at the time, observing from his courtyard:

> On the other side of our house, at Jonas's, they shouted out *induru* and got their dogs barking. They blew on *horns*. They also had lighted a fire [around which they had gathered]. We spent the night there. The next morning, we saw Jonas's boys—I no longer remember their names—they came down in front of us. They had shiny machetes, they were headed to the soccer field. They were singing: "*Umubyeyi* [the father of the nation] is dead, and he was killed by the *inyenzi* [cockroaches, but also used to designate the FPR and by extension the Tutsi as a whole]." 11:00 came,

and lots of people showed up. . . . They began to loot the small livestock: the goats, the sheep, the chickens. They brought them there, to the field; they slaughtered them and divided up the meat. They came back, went into the house and took whatever they wanted; the owner stayed outside. They would pass in front of you without any problem, saying: "Tomorrow it will be you that we're leading; you won't be able to escape us. This land is ours."[16]

Several young people depicted the first manifestations of violence as if they were describing the actual start of a hunt, mentioning the presence of dogs—spotted immediately by the children—and that of horns and shouting along with hunting weapons. In that region, in the eastern part of the country where the Akagera National Park is located, hunting practices had not disappeared under the pressures of property ownership, and the skills of hunting dogs were reinvested from the start in the extermination of the Tutsi.[17] Two young writers allude to this directly: "From that moment on, they began to chase the Tutsi with dogs and hunters," writes one boy, about seven years old at the time; "the dogs were harnessed with bells so they would hunt the Tutsi hidden in the bush as if they were hunting hares," another boy emphasizes.[18]

The appearance of members of the *ibitero*, when they were covered with banana leaves, either green or dry, increased the children's fright. Covered in makeup, screaming, bristling with weapons, they struck one nine-year-old girl as almost supernatural beings:

It was from that time on that we heard people say: "Come look, those people are green!" Looking outside, we saw banana trees, eucalyptuses: all that was covering over people. They were wearing grasses on their heads. You couldn't recognize anybody.[19]

The eruption of these colorful, noisy crowds was regularly evoked by the young writers to account for the flights from the family compound.

But it was a sudden, enigmatic phenomenon that sometimes brutally hastened the abandonment of the *rugo* for scattered hiding places. A boy from the commune of Kayonza, twelve years old at the time, recalled the event that spurred his family's flight. From April 7 on, he explained, the Tutsi in the sector spent their nights in the bush, returning home only in the early morning, for already "the bad words were spreading around." One man, a respected personality nicknamed *padiri* (priest) for his wisdom, was one of the earliest targets of the killers led by former town supervisor Célestin Senkware that day. Within the *rugo*, no one figured out at first why that neighbor was being assassinated, and the young boy's family rushed to the *padiri*'s house to try to help him. This scene clearly shows the shift into a new order of violence, sanctioned by a communal authority characterized by its duplicity:

> The next morning, it was April 8, 1994, we heard that they had killed Sagahutu. We went to see him that morning and we found him dying. A lot of people came, I remember that my older sister went to the kitchen to prepare some mush. . . . At that moment, we saw the commune's car coming, there was the former head of the commune who was called Senkware Célestin. He was with the policemen and he found us weeping. Senkware asked us to calm down and [said] that they were going to find a way to take him to the doctor. Alongside, there was a dog who was drinking the blood of that Sagahutu who had just been killed. I remember that my sister chased away the dog, because she saw that it wasn't good, she knew very well that the blood of a human being always had value, in normal times. As for me, I remember well that one of the policemen who was with the town leader named Senkware said to my sister: "Let him drink." Do you understand, he let the dog drink the blood of a human being.[20]

What struck the boy was not only the death of a respected neighbor but also the degradation represented by the image of the dog lapping up his blood, an axiological upset encouraged by the communal authorities. Shortly after the passage of the town leader and the policemen, the *ibitero* surrounded the hill, forcing the boy to leave his family behind and "go into the bush."

The presence on that scene of representatives of public authority is not without significance. It is impossible to understand the differentiated chronology of the shift to genocidal violence without examining the essential involvement of the governmental apparatus at the local level. In the communes or sectors harboring the fiefdoms of personalities deeply committed to Hutu ethnonationalism, the massacres began as early as the evening of April 6, severely reducing the possibility of establishing flight strategies for the families threatened. Rapid, precise, and massive from the outset, the killings bore the signs of meticulous preparation. Thus, for example, the commune of Kanzenze, located in the Bugesera region, already marked by a long history of persecutions against the Tutsi that began in 1959, was the theater, in March 1992, of massacres of several hundred Tutsi. On the evening of April 6, the commune was immediately overtaken by violence; the echoes of the explosion of the presidential plane even reached the ears of the residents. During the night, one ten-year-old girl's family was the object of a first attack that left little doubt about the killers' aims:

> On the date of 6 1994 [sic], we were seated in the house, in Kayumba. We heard something explode. Afterward, my brother said that a factory had caught fire. After a moment, we heard on the radio that the president was dead. Papa was gripped with fear, and he said: "This time, they're going to finish us off. Let's go to the sorghum plantation." And my older sister said to him: "Let's go to bed and sleep, we'll leave very early in the morning." Around 3 o'clock in the morning, the Interahamwe came to the house, they said to Papa: "This time you're still not accepting that your fate is sealed?" And Papa answered: "Do I have any quarrel with you?" An Interahamwe replied: "Nothing, but we don't want any more snakes in our country." Around 4 o'clock, those Interahamwe were hemming and hawing about who would kill Papa. And Papa said to them: "Let me get my jacket in the house." Then the Interahamwe struck him with a club, saying: "You no longer have anything, everything belongs to us." So we all went out, they made us sit outside and the sun came up on April 7. Very early in the morning, the mayor woke up, saying that it was necessary to exterminate the snakes, that they had to be made to cross the river [the Nyabarongo] so they would go back to their own lands. They began to work, they killed people, and each time they finished killing a person they knew well, they went to loot his property.[21]

Similarly, the young writers from the commune of Murambi, which in April 1994 was led by the fearsome Jean-Baptiste Gatete, all attest to an immediate descent into violence during the night of April 6–7. Two boys report that they had witnessed the town supervisor, his assistant, and some of the local policemen making their murderous rounds on April 7. According to the account of one young man born in 1973, these officials passed from sector to sector and cluster to cluster, exhorting the residents to go to "work," that is, to proceed with the extermination of the Tutsi:

Around 2 PM, that's when we saw an official car coming from town. There were some policemen and the assistant town supervisor inside. When they arrived, one of them was speaking on a loudspeaker. He was saying: "We're coming from Gorora, we've killed in Karake, Karagire, and in another place we've finished them off! So here, what are you waiting for? If you can't do anything, tell me, I'll do it myself!" He continued to spread the message about cutting up Tutsi, even in other clusters.[22]

Another text, written by a girl eight years old at the time who had been visiting her grandfather, also describes the zeal with which the supervisor Gatete sought to ensure a rapid and effective extermination of the Tutsi from his commune.

It was Easter vacation, the spring term holidays. At home, we got permission to go to our maternal grandfather's house. He lived in Murambi, under Gatete—you've certainly heard about him. During the night of June 6, I heard a child from the Pasteur house, grandfather's neighbor, knock on the door, around 5 AM. He told my grandfather: "Papa sent me to tell you that the president has just died." Then I saw my aunt get up full of fear, she walked shakily around and she told [the news] to the old folks. They got up in turn and I saw everybody standing: The maternal uncles were all there. They all came and we piled into grandfather's house. Then it was the 7th, the sun was shining, it was a fine day. We had heard people who were going to draw water say that a man who lived a bit above us whose name I don't remember had just been killed. They had had his bags of peanuts brought out and thrown out. We began to pester our aunt to wash our clothes. We wanted to go home so as not to die in that place. We didn't know that the whole country was involved. Gatete who was the town supervisor had the right to go into another sector besides his own and to say that it was time to go to work. To please the children, our aunt got out our clothes and started to wash them. But I heard her say, lamenting: "I'm washing them, at least we'll die clean." And I heard *muzehe* [grandfather] scold her: "Stop frightening the children." It was right then that we saw the Interahamwe arrive with machetes, lances, little hoes, and grass-cutting tools. They came in saying: "We're surprised to find what spoiled children the Tutsi are. We're wondering whether up to now they haven't known what was in store for them."[23]

Attacked starting April 7 in an area with a long history of anti-Tutsi violence, the adults had virtually no hope about the likelihood of survival. For the little girl just quoted, the early onset of the assault implied a rapid and brutal separation from the members of her family.

In the neighboring prefecture of Kibungo, an examination of the chronology of the launching of the massacres requires attention to more elaborate administrative hierarchies than that of the commune. Led by a moderate prefect, a member of the Social Democratic Party, whose national representative, Frédérique Nzamurambaho, was assassinated on April 7 in Kigali, the impulse to exterminate drew support from less official but nevertheless well-structured networks. The opposition of the prefect Godefroid Ruzindana to the killings led to his removal from office and then to his assassination, along with his entire family, on April 24. In Kibungo, Colonel Pierre-Célestin Rwagafilita, his loyal followers who had been placed in key administrative positions, and the powerful Interahamwe militias ensured the orderly pursuit of executions. The presence of the former head of the general staff of the police force, despite having been forced to retire in February 1992, "was part of the MRND's overall strategy designed to demobilize a certain number of influential higher officers and use them in their hometown prefectures to reinforce the party's position in the face of the growing opposition."[24] A representative of Hutu extremism at both the local and the national levels, Colonel Rwagafilita used his influence and his energy to build a powerful Interahamwe militia in the prefecture. The starting points of the violence thus lay in the prior existence of these networks, especially in the city of Kibungo (Birenga commune) and in the sector of Gasetsa (Kigarama commune), where the colonel was from. Analyzed on the scale of narratives of childhood, this highly decentralized organization of the genocide explains the frequent reference to resistance on the part of local populations against the incursion of "people from Gasetsa," the "Interahamwe from Birenga," or "bandits."

For several days, the identity rooted in the hill country kept neighbors, Hutu and Tutsi alike, solidly together against incursions perceived as foreign. In every case, however, the resistance was shattered by the intervention of representatives of the central government, who passed on the directives for extermination to the Hutu. In the commune of Rusumo, the parish of Nyarubuye took in refugees fleeing from the neighboring communes located farther to the west, Birenga and Rukira. Up to April 14, the relative calm drew in those being persecuted in the surrounding regions. The evening before, the residents of Nyarubuye's high plateaus spotted houses on fire in the Butezi cluster in the direction of Rukira, while refugees flooded in and conveyed alarming news, asserting that they were "fleeing from the robbers and villains who, as they came through, killed the Tutsi and destroyed their homes."[25] These statements reassured the local residents, who had been fighting together for a week against the incursions of "bandits." Here is how one girl, twelve years old at the time, recounted the common resistance and the brutal clarification by the police by way of the new watchword:

It was the 7th, Habyarimana's plane crashed, and we began to hear that the people in it were dead. It was the time when Agata [Agathe Uwilingiyimana, the prime minister, who belonged to the opposition party] died, and, for us, the war hadn't yet come. But we didn't have peace, and we didn't know that they were killing Tutsi. This went on until the 11th, and war came from the other side of our town. They were burning the houses. The residents of Nyarubuye, Nyarutunga, and Mareba [clusters in the Nayrubuye sector] came together, everybody, and the Hutu were among them. But they were pretending. They were saying: "Let's leave and fight those bandits who want to take our property and even our cattle." Many people had taken refuge in our corner; the others went to the church. Then they unified their forces and went off to fight during those three days until the 14th. That is when they knew that those who were dying were the Tutsi. The Interahamwe who were fighting against the residents of our area who had come together called the police for help, and the first person who died was called Vincent. He died on the 14th among us.

The police came, they lied by saying to the people who had come together to fight the Interahamwe: "Come on, we're coming to save you. The Interahamwe won't attack you any longer." They all piled in together there. As the residents had caught and tied up an Interahamwe thinking that he was a thief, a policeman asked: "Who tied up this man?" and Vincent answered: "I did." He didn't know that it was a problem. The policeman immediately shot him in the head and he fell over on the spot. Afterward, that policemen asked at once: "Who are the members of Vincent's family?" There was his paternal uncle who was called Bahutu who said: "I am." Then the policeman told him: "Bend down and drink the blood of your child." He drank and afterward they shot him too. The policemen said to the residents who were there: "Have the Hutu sit on one side and the Tutsi on the other." The policemen told the Hutu to cut the Tutsi into pieces. They began to cut them into pieces and the others ran toward the church, toward the bush. It was then that we learned that a single ethnic group was being killed.[26]

The descriptive acuity of the narratives makes it possible to observe from up close the shifts into genocidal violence, which were sometimes gradual, sometimes extremely rapid, during the hours and days following the April 6 coup. In all cases, the first manifestations of the murderous energy of the *ibitero* spurred flight from the familiar premises of the *rugo* and brutal separation of children from their fathers. Very often hidden in the bush, the banana plantations, the sorghum fields, and the churches, the children for the most part managed to flee with their mothers and/or maternal aunts and their siblings. Concealed in precarious hideouts, in areas constantly traversed by the killers and their dogs, they never fled very far from their compounds. In fact, one of the very first requirements of the order to pursue genocide was designed to prevent flight toward other sectors, other communes where the Tutsi could escape from the communities where they were well known. This spatial and social proximity probably explains why the vast majority of the children witnessed their family members being tortured and killed.

4

"THEIR GOD IS DEAD"

Three parishes, three churches, three "houses of God": all transformed into deadly traps for the tens of thousands of Tutsi who had taken refuge there beginning on April 7, 1994. The massacres that unfolded one after another in Rukara, Kabarondo, and Nyarubuye from April 10 to April 17 make it possible to draw up a religious map of the genocide. From north to south, along the route of the killers' retreat toward Tanzania, these three church buildings were the objects of massive attacks. The same methods were always used, intended to shatter the victims' resistance and ensure maximum efficiency in the killings. Among the refugees sheltered in these churches, six children between the ages of ten and fourteen wrote down their recollections of that period, twelve years later. Like their parents, they could not have imagined the sacrilege manifested in a massacre committed by killers who were Catholics themselves. A powerful index of the organized, systematic wrecking of the cultural and axiological foundations of an entire society, the churches were the second most important site of killings in a country that was, in 1994, nearly 90 percent Christian, 63 percent of whom were Catholic.[1]

In recalling these scenes, the children describe bloody skirmishes with an obsessive clarity that sometimes compels them to suspend their story. Such ellipses in the narration—one is tempted to speak of its respiration— organize each of the texts into a series of brutal scansions, shifting from the present of the writing to the present of the massacre. The clash of temporalities that can be detected in the materiality of the handwriting is conjugated with a patient reconstitution of the respective chronologies of the "time of the genocide." The temporal markers that are abundantly present in the narratives—even when they do not correspond exactly to the actual calendar of the massacres—are so many signposts on the basis of which the children lived the experience of extermination.

Their arrival in one of the parishes represents a first moment in the chronologies reconstituted by the children. The image of crowding is evoked by a fourteen-year-old boy who has reached Nyarubuye in his flight: "Really, we found many, many other people there, impossible to count. When you managed to observe well, you found that there were 200,000."[2] This is obviously a considerable overestimation, but it conveys the boy's perception of the crowd in which he found himself the night before the April 15 attack.[3] Trusting in the inviolability of the site, the refugees tried to organize a semblance of ordinary life. As the same boy's story indicates, "Some had even spent the night there, they had gotten used to the condition of refugees: they cooked, they ate, for we had even found help getting food." A young girl, nine years old in 1994, who had also reached the parish of Nyarubuye with her family, described the state of the premises this way: "Then we arrived at 5 PM. We met the priests who had begun to distribute porridge paste to the small children. We spread ourselves out among the rooms, the classrooms near the church, and the others did the same, in the various courtyards and in the rectory."[4] In Rukara, the persecuted crowd began to gather in the church on April 7, with their cows and small belongings. One girl, also about nine years old, reached this precarious haven thanks to the help of a neighbor who blocked the groups of killers with his car, thinking that he was shielding his protégés from harm. Here is how the girl described the situation when she arrived:

When we got there, we saw that a lot of people were coming to take shelter there, especially those who lived near the church. Others were coming from all sides. All of us had hope in this house of God where we had sought refuge: There, it was impossible that anything could happen to us. We spent several days there. A white priest gave us some crackers, but he mostly took care of the children. Masses were celebrated. Everything kept on going. Our parents, I'm talking about Papa, went with the others into the countryside to look for food for us. They brought back some bananas, but those people who lived near the church had brought everything with them; they had fled with their goods. People cooked together and we all ate, but starting with the children. Life went on this way, we spent several days, but this is how life was organized. Moreover, we were beginning to hope that we would be saved. We didn't know that our hour was near and that they were keeping us like this in order to exterminate us. They were organized in such a way that they had begun with the people in the courtyards, in the bush, in the sorghum plantations. And those who had gathered together, for example in the churches . . .[5]

The retrospective interpretation, with its evocation of the killers' duplicity, does not stand in the way of a precise description of the conditions of survival for the families within the parish complex. The "normality" observed by the girl, the routine that ensured that the refugees had food, nourished the hope that they would remain alive. The situation was radically different at Kabarondo, where the Tutsi had nothing. One twelve-year-old boy arrived at the church building on April 10, on the order of the town supervisor Octavien Ngenzi, after several days of flight from bush to bush. There, the refugees were crowded together without any resources:

We went to the Kabarondo church, where we found a lot of people. We joined them. We believed that we were no longer going to die. Among all those people, no one had even a cooking pot, a little blanket for protection against the chill, or the smallest basic utensil. There were old men and women, children, women, young men, and girls. We received no help at all. And every minute people were arriving, people who had succeeded in escaping the killers. On April 9, 2004 [sic], they began to close the roads. They took a census of the refugees who were there, and we were so numerous that they ran out of paper to write on. When they stopped writing, they said that our count was nearly 5,000. But without including those who came later. We spent three days without eating or drinking. We gave the little we could find to the small children. Even the one who had brought us there [the town supervisor Octavien Ngenzi] did not come back to see how we were doing.[6]

For the Tutsi refugees, recourse to the church was invariably tinged with a spiritual dimension. One nine-year-old girl noted that Mass was celebrated as usual in Rukara. Another girl, born in 1986, reports that in Kabarondo, Oreste Incimatata maintained a spiritual life, putting the fate of his flock in the hands of God: "The morning of the third day, the priest Incimatata celebrated Mass for us. He told us: 'Make your prayers powerful, because, in the state we are in, the strength of human children is exhausted. For the rest, let us leave it to God.' When he finished celebrating Mass, the Intera-hamwe attacked the place."[7] Thus the texts are full of prayers sent toward Heaven the night before the attacks. In Nyarubuye, priests and nuns were evacuated a few days before the April 15 assault, but the departure of the clergy in no way prevented the refugees from expressing their faith. On April 14, shortly after the town authorities and police had relayed the watchword of extermination to the populations that were still wavering and organizing collectively to push back the attacks of the killers who had come from neighboring sectors, the Tutsi men came back to the parish with these words, as reported by a young girl who was nine years old at the time: "Be calm and accept the fate that God has chosen for you because those people are with the policemen whom they have summoned."[8] Here, the de-cision of the central government, enacted by the policemen, is conflated with a divine decree. After that announcement, the girl explains, "Those who were patient began to pray, asking God to accommodate them."[9]

God, then, appears as an ambivalent figure, simultaneously decreeing the tragic end of the Tutsi and remaining unfailingly at the side of the victims. As for the killers, they did not see their actions as sacrilegious: God was sup-porting the legitimacy of the massacres, which were part of His plan. The religious justification of the extermination fed their murderous energies, as we can see from the following excerpt, in which another girl, eleven years old at the time, reports what a priest said shortly before the start of the killings in Ntarama:

> One of the Rwandan priests answered us: "The Tutsi are the ethnic group delivered by God. They must die. As God exterminated Sodom and Gomorrah by fire and exterminated the people of Noah's day by the Flood, the Tutsi have to die until a Hutu child asks what a Tutsi looked like." Those are his words, I was there and I heard them.[10]

Not only did the assailants see their actions blessed by a priest, who affirmed that they were the instruments of a divine will, but they also decreed the death of the "God of the Tutsi," successfully removing the victims' ultimate protection. The fervor of prayers was thus no longer of any use, as related by one girl, age nine, holed up in the Rukara church with her father:

The night of that miserable day, they came back around 7 PM. They were singing the well-known song: "*Tubatsembatsembe* [Let's exterminate them]. Their God is dead." When they arrived, we were praying. The priest was celebrating Mass for us. We were taking communion. They arrived, they broke the windows of the church. They ordered the priest to leave; if he did not leave, he was going to die with the Tutsi snakes. He went out. I don't know where they took him.[11]

"Abandoned by God," the victims still tried to organize themselves to resist the killers. At Rukara, at Kabarondo, at Nyarubuye, the children recounted desperate attempts led by the "Papas" to push back the deadly assaults, while the women and children gathered rocks and other makeshift defensive projectiles. At Rukara, the men even took the risk of protecting their cows, as the same girl reports:

When they arrived, they threw themselves at the cows that were there; there were so many that they filled up the ground and even the forest that surrounded the church. The men—I'm speaking about my fathers before they left us—left the church and went to confront those Interahamwe dogs so they wouldn't take the cows. They had already started to cut the cows with the machetes, and they made the decision to fight those Interahamwe. They confronted them, really, they chased them, they pursued them as far as the health center, a bit away from the church. But the Interahamwe wanted precisely to pull them away from the church so as to kill them more easily. That is how the events unfolded. When they had got them farther away, they made them turn around while cutting them to pieces, running them through with lances, tossing grenades at them. They killed them, it's too much, really. They were running back toward the church while others were plunging into the bush. And that is when I saw Papa fall to the ground: He had just arrived in front of the church.[12]

Repeated failures of attempts at self-defense preceded the deadly attacks in which neighbors, local administrative authorities, and members of militias and the armed forces were intermingled. The crushing of resistance efforts did not erode the faith of the victims, who then commended their souls to God. In the following excerpt, from the text of a then twelve-year-old boy who had survived the killings in Kabarondo, the initial scene of the attack amalgamates the clattering of weapons and the sound of a requiem chanted by the victims:

> They began to shoot around 10 AM [on April 13]. They started first with the foundations of the church, so that it would collapse. But that didn't work. Those who were in the church were chanting a hymn: "Be strong, servants of Christ." Really, the voices were mingled, numerous.[13]

Soon, the melody of the prayer was eclipsed by the noise of grenades and machine guns, and by the screams of the victims. The young writer recalls, from his position inside the church, a horrendous bloody crush, at the heart of which sonic memory occupies a central place:

> Then they threw grenades on the tile roof. The tiles were dislodged. Then they began to toss grenades through the holes in the roof. They threw them inside, among the people. They hurled grenades and *amastrim* [a type of oblong grenade]. When the grenades exploded, some people died and the others tried to escape by seeking refuge in all the corners. And when you passed by the window, you received gunshots. They threw a grenade right where I had just positioned myself and it took off my leg. A torrent of blood hindered people's movements; a great deal of blood was coming out of the corpses and flowing out the door.
>
> A huge bomb exploded; it blew up a lot of people and a lot of corpses that fell on top of me, with a lot of blood. I couldn't get out of there. They threw a new grenade which thrust us up again; some shrapnel hit me in the head and then I fell down in front of the altar. Afterward, I tried to stand up to go see the people with whom I had come to the church and my neighbors. I saw that they had preceded me in death, and grief killed me. There was a heavy side door in the middle of the church. A woman called C. had leaned against it. She held a small child in her arms. There were other people I didn't recognize, also leaning against that door. They brought in the big gun with tires and shot a huge ball into that door, and I saw everyone become like flour. So that ball blew up those people and C. came crashing down on the altar. I saw that what was left of her was only her head and one arm. She was crying out in pain and when I ran toward her to help, she had just expired. They kept on shooting,

people kept on dying, innocent people. At one point I lost consciousness and I lay down in the blood, like a dead person.

Around 3 P.M., that's when they spoke through a microphone and said: "Let everyone who is still breathing go out. We pardon them." I tried to think what we might have done for them to pardon us, but I didn't find anything. Even the one who had lost his legs dragged himself on the ground to go out. They made us sit down outside, in front of the church. I too was among them; I was wounded in my leg and somewhat in my head. They took out of our group the girls who were not yet dead. They said that they were going to make them their wives, so they would have children, and if they happened to bring boys into the world, they would kill them, because they didn't want them to be able to seek vengeance. They also said that those who had money could buy back their lives [*kwigura*: literally, "buy themselves"]. But no one among us gave any money. There was someone next to me who had lost his arm. He asked me to look in his pocket for the 10,000 Rwandan francs he had so I could give them in order for them to spare us. I took the money. I stretched out my arm to give it to them. They took the money while they were shooting a bullet into my arm. Then I saw blood flow as if it were a jug pouring out water. They began to kill again and this time they didn't use bullets. It was the Interahamwe who charged against us. They cut us into pieces with machetes. The soldiers were there, in a second line. They hit my head with machete blows and I fell on the ground. The one who had just cut me left, but another came and cut my face. He was just about to pluck out an eye. I lost consciousness and I don't know what happened next. I heard noises, the sounds of machetes cutting into shreds, as in a slaughterhouse where they cut up meat.[14]

The memory of the firearms, depicted here in the words of children, is not covered over by knowledge acquired later about the precise nature of the deadly projectiles. Machine guns, mortars, and grenades assailed the church in the sonic reanimation of the scene described by the boy as he was writing. The same descriptive clarity guides the narrative of a then nine-year-old girl who took refuge with her family in the Nyarubuye parish. Reading her story, one is struck by the care with which she patiently reconstitutes her own timetable, even if the calendar references do not correspond to the chronology of the attacks launched against the church between April 15 and April 17. She describes *her first day* by evoking the same image of a bloody mob in which the bodies of her loved ones lose their human form:

At that moment, they came and broke down the door. Mama placed her hand on each one of her children and said to them: "*Murabeho* [Adieu]!" The bullets spoke; the children cried. Right then the Interahamwe came in chopping. Before they reached me, I escaped through a door on the other side, where my brother had gone, and then I found myself in another room. When I got there, all the people threw themselves on me, I felt suffocated. It was horrible. People died like crushed ants. Above me, there were so many bodies like bananas that are put in *urwina* [holes in which bananas intended to ferment for the manufacture of beer are placed]. I felt a burn on my leg, but at that moment it was not my preoccupation. In my ears I heard a kind of buzzing; I no longer knew where I was but I tried to open my eyes and look up a little. I saw my older brother run, but they shot an arrow in his ribs, he fell and then they shredded him. *Yewe!* I'd like to stop, because this is hard to tell. I heard people going back and forth over the distribution of goods that were there. Night had fallen and they said: "We're going to stop here and we'll come back tomorrow." I heard them leave and go home. I lifted up my head and I saw that what were human beings had become tomatoes crushed by trucks. Blood was flowing like a river. I wanted to go back to the room where I was with my family and when I tried to stand up, I couldn't. Looking at what had happened to me, I saw that my legs were pierced with holes but that in the holes there were different pieces of iron. I left on my buttocks. I left passing by the bodies, seated in blood, and I arrived in the room where we had been before.

I called out: "Mama! Grandma! Mukanda!" and the same for all those I knew. When I called my older brother, I heard "Ho!" It was like the sound of an owl. And little by little I kept moving forward on my buttocks and I went to the back of the room. I sat there and kept quiet. I didn't sleep; I spent a sleepless night and then I heard the birds sing. The people who weren't dead yet began to budge. . . . I moved closer among them and looking to the side I saw Mama, I called her and I set out to see Mama's face. I got there by pushing aside the bodies that were next to Mama then I arrived up close to Mama. When I put my hand on Mama's head, I saw that she had been cut. Then I also saw my little brother who was dead: They had cut out his Adam's apple and had put it on his shoulder. All the people I knew were dead.[15]

At this stage of the narrative, the girl describes waking up among bodies, the birds warning her that with dawn the threat of the killers' return was imminent. As soon as the sun rose, the killers returned, prowling around the parish complex. The din was tremendous:

> At 6 in the morning, I heard the whistles and some chants: "*Tubatsembatsembe!* [We're going to exterminate them!]" They came into the rectory. And when they arrived where I was, they asked one another: "Is it really necessary to verify that someone is still alive?" They went on: "Let it go. We're going to throw a grenade." The others said: "No, that would be a waste of a grenade, we need to use our hands, they're in good shape!" They began with my maternal aunt, who raised her head, and they struck her right away with several blows from a hammer and her head was crushed. Then they looked at my older brother, the one just ahead of me in age, he's the one I had called out to during the night and who responded like an owl. They had cut him on the neck (during the night, he wanted to show that he was still alive so they would come finish him off). They said: "If it's that one, let him alone, the little ants will kill him." When he tried to swallow his saliva, it [the saliva] came out [through the neck wound]. They pushed him away. My youngest brother, who was there, it was like he was in a coma. They reached the point where I was with my sister-in-law and her child, my older brother from my maternal aunt's house, and others. My older brother from my maternal aunt's house, they hit him with a hammer on his head. Me, I closed my eyes. They jumped over my body and arrived at my sister-in-law and her child who was still nursing; they cut off the child's legs. Me, God protected me. They went all around the room, but my littlest brother who looked like a person in a coma, they didn't see him.

On that second day, the process of tracking down the survivors from the night before was accompanied by a systematic looting of the bodies. Nothing escaped the killers' greed, not even the intimacy of the clothing covering the bloody corpses. In the enclosure of the parish, women took care of that task. When one of the scavengers expressed a religious scruple, it was quickly rejected: The "God of the Tutsi" was dead.

Among those who were killing the others, there were women who undressed the dead people. *Yewe!* Even the clothes full of blood, which was so frightening: They took them and said they were going to wash them. They continued to loot, raising up the bodies to strip them. But me, they didn't come to me, for I was covered with so much blood, I had passed through a torrent of blood, like torrents that happen when it has rained a lot. One of those women said: "What are we doing here in the house of God?" And another retorted: "The house of God is what? Their God is dead. We have to start over, verifying that they're really dead. For when you kill the snake, you have to smash his head."

After the departure of the killers and looters, sanctioned by the satisfaction of the "great task" accomplished, the little girl raised her aching head and counted the family losses. Her father was missing from that macabre enumeration, for she hadn't seen either his assassination or his body. Missing also was her little brother, gravely wounded and suffering thirst from the loss of blood. The third day at dawn, the whistles sounded again around the parish, and a single preoccupation stirred her: to quench her little brother's thirst. In vain:

> Afterward, around 3 PM, a woman married to a Hutu came in with water in a little pitcher. I said to my little brother: "Get up and go ask for water." He asked for water while holding out his hands. The woman went out and the child followed her, moving on his buttocks. She stayed at the door without coming in. I too, moving on my buttocks, couldn't help my brother to stand up to follow the woman. That evening, it rained and the rain fell on him. In the morning, I saw that he was no longer alive. That third day, I thought I was alone in all of Rwanda. I remember what happened during those days: I saw people cut, people killed by hammers, guns, pestles, machetes, arrows. Where I was, the bad smell had become unbearable. That is too much for me, my God. Only the power of God was with me.

This patient reconstitution of the chronology is doubtless illuminated by a harsher light in what follows in the text, when, stretched to infinity, the little girl's universe was invaded by the terrible smell of decomposing bodies and the sight of necrophagous insects. The narrative shifts into another temporality, no longer marked by the threatening approach of the killers, who too were repelled by the diabolical odor, but by the search for food in a space saturated with rot.

Two boys rummaged through the charnel houses looking for survivors before bringing them together in the convent's kitchen:

> Those boys came where I was and said: "They're all already dead." And I said: "I'm alive, I hear you." They came to see me, they walked around me, in that unbearable bad smell. The buildings were full of bodies, some being gnawed on by worms, especially in the places where there were wounds. They walked around the room and came to the nuns' kitchen, and they found flour for porridge, casseroles, and matches. God alone manifested himself through that. Those two boys also bore machete wounds on their heads. They came to lift me up and take me into that kitchen. They started to cook, with wood for cooking, and we ate. The bad smell continued to prevail, for when you wanted to leave the room you had to pass by the bodies being eaten by worms to get into the kitchen. The next morning, the two boys found another child who was moving on his buttocks and another girl alive. That evening, they found an old Mama whose neck had been cut, worms were falling from her wound, but she was still breathing. They brought those along too. Then they found yet another girl whose ears were oozing pus. They also found a little girl who had her fingers cut off and who had received machete blows on one leg. They brought her in. And one more girl, cut under her ear, they brought her in too. There were eleven of us.

Soon, water and food had run out, while the murderers made their rounds, fewer of them but still just as threatening, continuing to terrorize the survivors. The only way out available to them was to hide among the rotting bodies, owing to the repugnance these inspired in the killers. A boy, fourteen years old at the time, a companion in misery to the little girl in Nyarubuye, tells how the corpses served as hiding places: "After, when those Interahamwe came in to loot, a bird came and told us, so we hid in the corpses. We took hold of them and covered ourselves with them."[16] A terrifying protection that intensifies a little more the memory of the physical and psychic degradation amid the invasive rot. Spreading into all the corners of the precarious hiding places, it ends up eroding the determination to survive, as the girl says again:

In the whole rectory, you saw only the worms, there weren't even any more bodies. We walked around in that place as if there was an ordinary path there. In the kitchen where we were, the worms had found us. Even the bananas called *kayinja* [for making banana juice] surrounded by worms, we ate them. The nuns were already gone and those bananas were alongside their house. The nuns left those bananas, which were starting to rot. But we ate them. It was a place where many people had been killed. But with those worms, we ate those bananas. I remember well, *Mana we* [My God]! We ate them for several days, and we finished them. Then we didn't have anything more to eat, and we prayed to God that we would find death. The lice incrusted in our clothes, in our hair, in our finger-nails began to run around on our bodies. We asked God for death. Among us there were people who looked like the dead; me, because of the blood soaked into my clothes and the lice in my hair, I started to give off a bad smell: from my nails, from my entire body. I wanted to find someone who would kill me quickly. I told myself that I was powerless.

Only the absence of her father among the corpses and the hope that he might still be alive suspended her deep discouragement for a moment. But at that point in the narrative, the girl summons up another figure who would in turn lessen her despair. Getting past the atrocious stink that reigned over the parish and the danger of the *ibitero*, a helpful man on two occasions brought some squash and a little sweetened liquid to the survivors holed up in the convent kitchen:

We heard the noise of a person who wanted to open the door. And we saw that it was the man who had brought us the squash. He told us: "The people with whom we were before were Interahamwe and they wanted to kill you. But I refused. Afterward, they told me not to bring you any more food. And that if I brought food I would come back alone, because they would have killed you first. But up to now I haven't seen those men again, I don't know where they went to work [to kill]. I know that you're here, and I'm bringing you something to eat: a bit of food and juice." He poured some juice in a goblet, and he helped the people who couldn't drink on their own. He told us: "If I have another opportunity, I'll bring you food again, but for now stay with that." (God alone knows the good-ness of that man.) What troubles me a lot is that he came and told us that his name is Rudahunga; his good deed, when he didn't know us, touched my heart; but those who knew us, those who were our neighbors, those are the ones who killed our families even though we had no problems with them. . . . Killing people wasn't a problem for them, really. Killing Tutsi was like killing little snakes.

The memory of that man's gesture of help is present in all the narratives written by the children who took refuge in Nyarubuye, attesting to the traces left by the generous attitude of a stranger, while those close to them participated in the murderous assaults against the church.

Across the entire set of children's texts, the constant presence of a totally different figure appears: God stays unfailingly at the side of the victims. For them, "their" God is not dead. He removes the fatal danger with "His protective arm."[17] For the young writers, there is no doubt about it: They owe their survival to divine protection. It could hardly be expressed more clearly than by the six-year-old girl who took shelter in the Ntarama church and then in the nearby swamps: "If I was saved, it is thanks to the Eternal. He protected me, and He continues to protect me today."[18] As we saw in the words of the girl who survived at Nyarubuye, God suspended for an instant the imminence of the fatal outcome. Not only did He move the killers away at the moment of the massacre and breathe His strength into the young girl so she could overcome the stink of the bodies, but He caused food and cooking utensils to appear when hunger threatened in its turn to finish off the few survivors of the killings. The little girl in Nyarubuye is not the only one to account for her survival by invoking divine protection. Hidden among the leaves of an avocado tree, an older girl (age twenty at the time) escaped from the meticulous looting of the *ibitero*. She explains: "Luckily, they didn't find us even though they were seated at the foot of that tree. God closed their eyes and they didn't see us."[19] Sometimes God distracted the exterminators' attention, betting on the killers' thirst for profit, as we hear from a boy born in 1983 who was trapped in the snares of his hostile neighborhood: "They programmed a date to come kill us, but God gave us one more day. Every time they programmed a day to kill us, they found a cow that they slaughtered and they shared the meat. We spent one more day: God turned them away."[20]

The fact that that divine presence—always intervening in the moments when the threat is most powerful—might appear as the product of a retrospective interpretation does not mean it can be ignored. The faith of the young victims was not shaken by the ordeals they went through. And that trust in God was far from being blind, as we can tell from several narratives in which the young writers express their doubts, even their mistrust, sometimes engaging in veritable indictments against the Heavens. Let us go back for a moment to the narrative by the young girl in Nyarubuye when she and her companions in misery noted that the unbearable stink of the decomposing bodies did not protect them against threatening intrusions. Discouraged, they doubted the infallibility of divine protection. Here is how she describes their anguished questioning:

> We opened the door, they came in but they were holding their hands over their noses to protect themselves from the bad smell. Those people, where did they come from? Maybe they've gone off to call the others, and then we'll die, in spite of God's protection. Maybe he has withdrawn his protecting arm? Some said: "We have to find a way to escape from those people." The others said: "No." No peace was left for us (escape, but where?).

At the height of despair, powerless to find a little food for his young brothers and sisters, whose impatient cries threatened to reveal their hiding place in the bush, a boy thirteen years old at the time confesses his angry doubts about divine beneficence:

> The next morning, it started raining on the bush where we were; I can't say it was raining on our doorstep because I no longer had a house. It wasn't ordinary rain, it was mixed with hail. The children cried a lot, grief was killing us. We began to regret that God had created us.
>
> When there was nothing else we could do, we put Heaven on trial. We asked the rain to soak us and to spare the children. Me, who was I? A child too. It hurts to tell this part of my story. These memories gnaw away at my heart.[21]

Similarly, a nine-year-old boy hunkered down with his family in a sorghum field did not understand the terrible fate that had befallen him. He entered into a dialogue with his father, questioning the presence of God at their side:

> I kept asking Papa: "What have the Tutsi done to make the Hutu hunt them like partridges and make them sleep in the cold?" He tried to console me by saying: "In a short time, all that will be over." I kept pestering him with my questions. I asked him if they had killed God before killing

the Tutsi. Then, he said to me: "*Humura* [take comfort], God will save us. If he doesn't save us and he allows us to die, we will go to Heaven, where people don't stab others, where people don't cry, where hunger doesn't exist." These words restored my hope. I continued to pray, saying: "God, give us at least Heaven." I thought that being saved or actually surviving was impossible.[22]

More than doubt, it was anger that permeated the reproaches of a girl the same age who was left alone in the world after the massacres:

Another thing I can say, is that, in my grief, during those three years [after the genocide], I hated God. I said that He did not exist and that if He did exist, He was an unjust God. I addressed him with anger because he had made things so I was left alone, but I nevertheless asked him for a miracle, saying: "If you are really God, You will bring the dead back to life." I had gotten it in my head that He had to bring back my older sister Christine because I hadn't seen her body. I thought they had thrown her into the Akagera [a river] and that she wasn't dead, that someone had pulled her out of the water alive. I thought that she might be in one of the areas that the Akagera crosses through. Thanks to my prayers and the words I addressed to God, it seemed possible to me that a brother or a sister might still be alive.[23]

The revolt she expressed against God did not prevent the fervent prayer that led her to face new dangers in the quest not for her older sister, whom she was never to find, but for a younger sister who had been kept in the camp for displaced Hutu in Gikongoro. Having become Mama to that child, as she herself asserted, her solitude and her anger were calmed, although only for a time. She ends her story with this *nota bene*: "The last day I was happy was April 4, 1994 [Easter Day, celebrated with her family]. Since then I'm no longer happy; even when I laugh, I'm lying."[24]

The expressions of faith so visible in these texts do not stem solely from the need to account for survival in the aftermath. Not only is the faith of the young writers sometimes tinged with an accusatory nuance, evidence of the real test to which it was being put, but it also clarifies the meaning of entire passages that are written as so many prayers. We could not read otherwise the following excerpt, written by a young girl nine years old at the time, sheltering in the Rukara church with her father:

I waited for them to pull me out in turn, but nothing. Papa kept crying out in pain. He told me that the bullet was burning his intestines, his heart. He kept on agonizing. He asked me to say goodbye to people for him and he said their names. He went on, saying to me: "My daughter, my child, look, I'm dying. If you have the luck to live, be honorable and be good." He ended his last words by saying: "Rather than being a dog, become a tomb." May God help me carry out his last words. Papa, *humura* [have no fear, take comfort], I'll never forget you. I am alive, and the words you left me as a legacy, I'm keeping them in my heart. Today I'm alive, I'm a young girl, I still have all the wounds. I still have headaches and toothaches . . . they're always there. But I hope that one day we'll find each other again. May God give you eternal peace.[25]

This promise in the form of the child's prayer, addressed to the father who had died in her arms, embodies the confusion between the temporality of the writing and that of the massacre. The prayer freezes time for her. In the present, that of the "grasp of writing,"[26] the genocide and its atrocious scenes are relived, they too, *in the present*. How else could we understand that two boys who had survived the Nyarubuye and Kabarondo massacres place the entirety of their narratives in 2004 and not 1994? It would be wrong to conclude that these were mere mistakes in dating, when everything points to the extreme proximity of a past that is so close and so painful.

5

THEATERS OF CRUELTY

At the heart of the children's stories, the narration of massacres—scenes *always* accompanied by the exercise of unheard-of cruelty—reveals the entire political project of the genocide.[1] The assassination of elders and infants alike for the purpose of cutting off lines of descent was coupled with a brutality that amounted to wiping out the Tutsi as a group, the enactment of a racist imaginary that controlled the very form of the attacks on bodies. The murderous overturning of the social world in which neighbors and former friends became the principal actors in the hunting and executions enacted a powerful exterminating utopia that nourished the murderous energy of the killers. For the children, the genocide triggered a profound disturbance of their relation to time and space, which, despite the extreme contraction of both, were experienced as stretching to infinity. Subjected to the same violence and cruelty that was exercised against their loved ones, the children recount their own deaths, as it were: The statement *baratwishe*, "they have killed us," becomes almost a commonplace punctuating the stories of mass deaths in Rwanda.

Nevertheless, the decision to offer readers these narratives in which children face the "reality of death"[2] was not an easy one. Drafted with a striking economy of language, almost without affect, the texts organize an unmediated return to the heart of the scenes of massacre. The descriptive meticulousness of the "theaters of cruelty" inevitably brings to the surface, for the reader, unbearable images of scenes capable of paralyzing any form of critical analysis. Does one have the right to lift the curtain on such scenes? Does one have the right to add a comment, to exercise one's trade as a historian? To these questions of an ethical order, the young writers themselves bring the answer. Most of them took up their pens so that their stories would be known. It could not be better expressed than by one boy, left alone in the world at the age of eight after the genocide, who titled his text as follows: "1994: My truth and my testimony for the great-grandchildren, the great-great-grandchildren and the whole earth."[3] To hear their voices, to take in the intensity of their words, is to return *with them* to the materiality of the genocide, to the logic of its execution and of its terrifying effectiveness.

As victims and direct witnesses of the extreme violence of the killings, the children saw the collapse of all the protective ramparts of the adult world, a world that had become powerless to defend them and had instead been turned into a deadly menace. Of this radical overturning of the "time before," one boy offers a description imbued with a strength and an acuity that my own words could never match:

> You saw a day like a week because of your pain, hunger, and thirst, for you had just spent several days without eating; cries of pain filled the air, the whistles of the Interahamwe; lots of corpses encountered in the banana plantations, on the hills, in the ruins, on the paths, at the river, everywhere you could go: Your heart wandered. You wondered if night was finally going to fall. Here I want to add that when night fell, you felt a bit of respite and you could get something like rest even if you found nothing to appease your hunger.

> Meanwhile, the Tutsi had become the enemy, he was hunted down in a very meticulous way, without stopping, with great precision. Even if you went to your Hutu neighbor to ask him to open his door for you, he couldn't open it for you, but he yelled out war cries [*induru*] against you: "Get away from my house, I don't need serpents in my house." Whereas you got along well together before, you shared fresh and cooked food, you asked each other for matches, salt, and gas. But when the time came, he drove you off, he left you in your misery. Those wretches, we milked our cows for them, we fed them, and it became like what the proverb says: *Abo Umwami Yahaye amata nibo bamwimye amatwi* [Those to whom the king has given milk are the same ones who have refused to listen to him].[4]

The terms used by the children about their experiences hold such an evocative power that I have chosen to efface myself here, reducing the exercise of commentary to a minimum, in order to privilege the voices borne by the texts.

Perpetrated in a highly reduced space-time, the massacres unfolded in the intimacy of neighborhood borders, on hillsides, without any desire to hide the *spectacle* of the killings from the sight of onlookers and of the other victims. This public and collective dimension was part of the "program of cruelty"[5] worked out by the killers, with the aim of inflicting maximum suffering. Children thus witnessed not only their parents' humiliation but also their assassination. The scenes reported, in their extreme violence and their cruel refinement, seem frozen in the present of the moment in which they were experienced. A girl from the commune of Rusumo, who was eight years old in 1994, recounts the assassination of "her Mamas": she puts before us such precise images, one after another, that she gives the feeling of reliving them as she writes:

I left with Mama and I kept asking her why we were spending the night on the hill when we had a house. When I heard someone speak, I wanted to reply. Mama told me: "Hush. The people aren't the same any more, they've become animals." She tried to explain to me that they wanted to kill us. But I didn't understand at all.

The next morning, they ferreted us out where we were hiding. I was with Mama, my younger sister, Mama's younger sister and her two children, as well as four neighbors. They were shouting *induru* against us; they made us sit down and they formed a circle around us so that no snake could escape them.

They began with Mama's younger sister; she begged their pardon but they refused to pardon her; when she heard that refusal, she reminded them of all the good things we had done for them and then she said: "Let me at least pray for the last time." I think she thought that they were going to change their minds. They answered her: "Pray fast, you're making us late, when we want to clean up all the filth!" When she had finished praying, they told her: "Lie down." And she lay down; they told her: "Face the sky!" And she obeyed. Then they took her neck and they slit her throat like an animal.[6] She expired right away. They reached Mama and she too died like cattle; they cut her head off. In short, all the parents we were with died the same way. We children were terrified. We no longer counted on their pardon. We saw that humanity had left them. We died at the very moment we witnessed the death of those who had brought us into the world. Some of them [the killers] had stripped off their clothes, searching for money.

At that moment, they turned on us, saying "We aren't finding their necks so as to cut them. Let whoever can hit these little child snakes do it! Let whoever can cut cut the one closest to him!" It happened this way: they started to toss the babies [*utwana tw'impinja*]⁷ who were with us into the air; they threw them up and they landed on the machete. They were cut in two.

They came to me and hit me on the head several times with the machete; they cut my arm but my arm didn't come off, it stayed. But the bones were broken. My younger sister received a machete stroke on the nose that took off her jaw and a small part of an eye.

All of us, we were like dead people and they left. But one of them stayed to verify that there was no one left that they could finish off. We spent two days not knowing where we were. The third day, I regained consciousness. Then I started to feel what was on the ground, around me. When I opened my eyes, I saw above me a man armed with a spear. I fell back again into the void. The evening of that day, he had just told himself that everyone was really dead, that there was not a single survivor. Around 5 PM, I came back to life and I stood up among the corpses. In my whole life I had never seen a dead person. From that moment on, I knew what death was. I started to put the cut-off heads with the bodies they belonged to. I took the wraps that we still had and that we had brought with us when we fled. I covered them [the bodies] with them. And then I touched them to see if any of them were still breathing. I found my younger sister and another child who was our neighbor; they still had a bit of breath. They started to ask me for something to eat and then for water, but I didn't know what to do. I thought of going to ask for water from the people who had just done that to us, but I didn't manage to make that decision.

I pulled together all my courage and went to a neighbor's house. When he saw us, he started yelling out cries for help, saying: "Save me from the evil spirits and the Satans that are attacking me." That was because our whole bodies were covered in blood, our fingers were hanging loose, on the point of falling off; another had an eye that could no longer see; still another, whose head had been sliced open and who no longer had ears.⁸

The social interconnections between the killers and the aunt who was the first one assassinated made it possible for there to be a dialogue that drew on a common past nourished by acts of generosity; however, this in no way lessened the determination of the members of the *igitero*. Similarly, the request for a final prayer had little impact on the religious feelings of the killers, as the young girl noticed. Finally, we find here, as in many other texts, the material greed concerning the clothing that had given the bodies some privacy.

The girl notes that the victims found themselves reduced to the status of animals, cut down like cattle. The vocabulary of butchery is mobilized almost constantly in the writers' texts, attesting to the degree to which the animalization was internalized by the victims themselves: The verb *kubaga* (slaughter) is used to describe the sites of massacre. The mobilization of the semantic field of butchery stems from a deliberate choice, to the extent that the Kinyarwanda language establishes a very sharp distinction between the animal and human lexicons. The girl just cited ultimately recounts her own death, expressing it with particular clarity: "We died at the very moment when we witnessed the death of those who had brought us into the world." In many of the texts, the young writers told the story of the abolition of the border between life and death. The little girl came back from the kingdom of the dead, and she expresses it, here too, with striking transparency. "At 5 PM, I came back to life." This double passage from life to death and back is in a sense "objectivized" by the reaction of the neighbor to whose house she went in search of water, the loss of blood having spurred the victims' thirst. The neighbor, seized with panic, believes he is seeing ghosts even though he had witnessed the massacre. This terrible story is obviously not unique; it attests to a collective experience, as is shown by the results of a survey conducted by UNICEF in 1995: 90 percent of the three thousand children questioned at the time had believed that they were going to die.[9]

Another girl, six years old in 1994, allows us to see and hear the successive assassinations of her brother and her mother, sparing none of the details that attest to the perversity and cruelty of the staging:

The Interahamwe had become like crazy people. Excuse me, I don't know the dates because I was too little. They went to the house, they looted, they cut down the bunches of bananas that were there. See how Hutu stomachs will kill them. When they came, they rushed into the house and they saw Mama, my brother, and my baby sister. I hid under a bed. They took them away, hitting them. They hit my brother on the head with a *ntampongano* [a club studded with nails, baptized "no pity for the enemy"]; he fell to the ground and lost consciousness. He stayed there, and while he was still lying on the ground, they said: "Look at the *inyenzi*'s trick!" Then they hit him a second time with the club and he screamed in pain. They then dragged him on the ground until he died. They left him there. The dogs and the crows had a feast.

They continued with Mama and my little sister. When they reached a place where there was an agricultural terrace, they asked Mama to lie down below that terrace and nurse her child. Mama obeyed, she lay down and the baby nursed. Then the Interahamwe who was the husband of the woman who was hiding us told her to follow him. Mama got up from there and they left. When they arrived at the place where they were to kill her, they first inflicted *ibyamfurambi* [rape] on her. There were eight of them and they all had a turn. When they were done, one began on one side and another on the other: One cut off an arm, another a breast, another a finger. After the breast was cut off, the finger came off with the arm. Then they told her to dig her own grave even though she no longer had arms. She couldn't. They grabbed a hoe and dug the grave. They told her to lie down and nurse her child. They covered them with dirt. Mama was still alive. You see what savagery!? They started to dance around the grave. They were hitting the grave with rebar, saying: "For the snakes to die, you have to hit their heads."[10]

Twelve years after she witnessed the atrocities inflicted on her mother, the girl characterized the husband of the woman who was hiding her as Interahamwe, marking the great distance from a man who was in reality a neighbor living very close to her own *rugo*. In the testimonies, as a general rule, the killers were designated with the same epithet even though they were not all formally members of the militia.

This terrible story lifts the curtain on the practices of cruelty exercised on the bodies of Tutsi women, aiming not only to ensure a definitive break in filiation but even more to organize the devastation. The presence of the nursing baby constitutes, from this standpoint, a powerful indication of the goal of radical extirpation. At the two extremes of the generational chain, through the specific fate reserved for the elderly as well as for the youngest children, the singularity of every genocidal policy can be read: The eradication of the past and the future of the group destined to disappear. The systematic rapes, very often accompanied by specific brutality concerning the reproductive organs, fall within this logic of extermination. For the children, the first confrontation with sexuality occurs in an inverted mode: Supposed to give life, the act of intercourse becomes an instrument of humiliation and death. Young boys and girls were direct witnesses of the exercise of sexual violence on their mothers, their aunts, their sisters.

In his frenzied flight along the winding paths of a forest in the Kinyamakara commune (Gikongoro), an eight-year-old boy lost track of his mother for a moment. Worried, convinced that she had been killed, he found her nevertheless after "a long path" in the company of another woman he had met as he raced along. Here is how he described his mother's physical appearance:

> We saw Mama coming, she was wearing only a little dress, she was losing blood near her knee, she had been struck by a machete when she was struggling with them. She was crying. She said to the wife of that man (whom they had also called) that those Interahamwe had done *ibyamfurambi* [rape] to her, all of them, and there were three. They passed her around in turn, and when she tried to defend herself they struck her with a machete above the knee (this is where she was losing blood). When they had finished inflicting that atrocious evil on her, they struck her with the back of their machetes, telling her: "Follow your worthless filthy children [*ibyana byawe*]."[11] Then when Mama left, they were raining blows on the husband of that woman [who was accompanying him in his flight]. And I think it was at that place that Mama caught the HIV that I will tell you about later. I would like to tell you that speaking about these things or rather writing about them is very painful for the one who is telling or writing it.[12]

This boy, this "orphan without an address," as he called himself before signing his text, saw his mother die of AIDS in 2000, adding a new grief to the immense family losses. Often infected intentionally, the women didn't stop living with the genocide after the massacres ended. In other cases, the sexual violence was accompanied by bodily attacks specifically aimed at the womb: The killers chose to double the killing by a gesture ensuring the reproductive incapacity of the victims. They killed them twice. This is hinted at in another excerpt, by a boy who escaped the massacre in the Rukara parish; he was ten years old in 1994:

> I remember, before forgetting, the death of one girl: The Interahamwe took her, they took turns on her, they did it again and again without stopping. When they were done, she was still alive. Then they impaled her on a stick in her sex organ and the stick came out of her mouth. Afterward, they crucified her in front of the church, on the trees that were there. The other death I shall never forget is that of my sister, whom they raped [*baviyoye*, a Kinyarwandization of the French *violer*]. They impaled her with sticks, too, and when they had finished, they killed her. What causes me pain still today is that the ones who killed her were freed, and they are here, walking carefree in the countryside. In the *gacaca* trials they joked, they ridiculed her as they told how they killed her. But *I* know that I'm going to do something because there is no one left to help her [an indirect evocation of vengeance].[13]

The atrocity of this description must not lead to a reading in terms of psychopathological deviance: The Rukara killers were not crazy—as was demonstrated, moreover, by their attitude during the *gacaca* trials. Such practices could be spotted throughout the whole country; they attested to a shared will to inflict the worst possible suffering, in order to signify to the victims their exclusion from common humanity. Another boy from Kayonza, twelve years old at the time, witnessed identical brutality. He transcribed the memory with obvious difficulty:

> We found an old woman who had also been arrested. They made her sit down, and they heard the others who had gone to bring back the children of that woman. They brought us to a place where there were holes from which minerals were extracted. They brought us there to kill us and throw us into the holes. When we arrived at those holes, they made us sit down and when we had finishing sitting down an Interahamwe said: "That old woman and you"—I'm saying old lady but they said "the wife of the Tutsi,"[14] "How pretty the wife of the Tutsi is," they said that they had to kill her by hitting her with a stick. Right away, they looked for trees—it's terrible—they took her right away—ahaha!!!—what I saw, friends, it's something else. You have to understand it yourself. What was her sex organ became something else. I can't describe it and you yourself you

understand it. As for us, while they were watching how they were running sticks through her, they forgot about us. We escaped and when they turned around, they saw that we had left.[15]

While boys and girls alike were subjected without distinction to the *spectacle* of rape,[16] only the latter recounted their own rapes. Adolescents and very young girls revealed their terrible experiences. One girl, fourteen years old at the time, wrote this:

He immediately took me to the rear courtyard, and when I remembered what had happened before, I was afraid that it would start again [she had already been raped once]. I left and, being very frightened, I begged for pardon and I asked them to kill me. They refused. He said to me: "Where are the older girls in your family? Where are they hiding? If you tell me where they are, I'll do it to them." I didn't know where they were, and he got angry. I wanted to run but I slipped on a fallen banana tree trunk and I fell on a tree branch in that back yard. I looked like a dead person. He pulled me up but I felt I had a painful strain in my ribs. And even today, there is one side [of her ribcage] that doesn't work. When he pulled me up, I stood up and when I opened my eyes, I saw a person posted at each pillar of the *urugo* [the killers had surrounded the family courtyard]; I didn't recognize their faces, for they were not the ordinary ones. Their plan was well prepared, because the three men were all there. Byi said to me: "Guess what brings you here?" And I said: "It's to kill me, so kill me." He pushed me down and he raped me for the second time. That time it was in broad daylight, before my parents, before the grandparents, before my paternal uncles.[17] I read a great sadness in their eyes, but they remained powerless. At one point, he said: "I can't make it any more. She's too small, it's hard." I regained hope that they would leave me alone because it really was hard. That man, V, who had a wife [she thought she would be spared because the man was married, and it was impossible for her to imagine a married man raping]: "Give her to me if you can't do it any more." And Byi: "OK, but I'm going to try again afterward." They said that that V had AIDS. He too did those things, but very nastily. As soon as I tried to move, the others held me, and at one point they held machetes on both arms and spears on my feet. But it was impossible not to move. So the one who held one of my feet pushed his spear in. Then they did everything they wanted to do and I stopped struggling. What saved me from the others [other rapists] is that they decided to bring the rest of my family up to the hedge surrounding the *rugo*. There, the advisor gave the order to kill them. They brought them back to the house, in the dense banana trees, and they began to divide up the cows. Those who were on top of me left me so no one would grab the best pieces of meat from them. Because I was suffering so much, I asked the son of the pastor, M. A., if he too was going to dare. And then he answered that he was just looking. I kept that in my heart. I thought that if I ever spoke, it would just attract the mockery of the others. I reached a point when I was reflecting on that all by myself and I felt that I was going to go crazy. When the *gacaca* began, that young man, M. A., spoke about it in public solely to make me a laughingstock. He had just been asked what had happened with us. I wanted to run but without finding anywhere I could stop. And that caused all the grief that filled me to explode.[18]

Haunted by the fear that she had been infected with AIDS, the girl confided at the end of her testimony that she had been unable to get tested; she lived constantly with the memory of her rape. Twelve years afterward, she wrote: "Sometimes, I think about marriage, but I give up the idea at once, for every time the memory of what happened rushes back. It pursues me relentlessly, without anyone to console me."[19]

If the gratuitous cruelties practiced in the context of rape underline the intention to eradicate the victims, the discourses addressed to them by their killers shed light on the racist fantasies that fed into the exterminating utopia. The narratives offer an account of the will to display the imagined bodily specificities of Tutsi women. Rape was justified in the name of a "difference" sought even inside the body, as attested, for example, by this passage from a text by a boy born in 1982: "A man named Ntamu said at once: 'Go on, take all these women, take them away and make them your wives!' The Interahamwe responded right away: 'Let's take them away and let's *taste* the Tutsi women.'"[20] Representations of otherness that conjugate gender and race this way make it easier to grasp the attacks focused on the *wombs* of the Tutsi women. Similarly, the rape of very young girls is legitimized by the killers in the name of a racism structured by a biological vision: The girls will give birth to Hutu and will no longer belong either to a Tutsi family or to a Tutsi parcel of land. Barely twelve years old in 1994, one girl recounts the threats she faced:

> Those from Rura went back the way they came and those from Ruyo began to judge me and condemn me to death. They all said: "Let's kill her!" But Munya said: "Why not leave her, for at her house there is no one left and since she's a girl, she can't inherit anything. You could very well make her your wife." Those words will never leave me, because if they pardoned [spared] me then, it was to decree my powerlessness. They knew they had killed my whole family, that they were going to take me as a wife and that in that way my family would be wiped out.[21]

While the girl ultimately escaped rape through the intervention of a member of the *igitero*, the killers nevertheless made explicit their intention to break her connection to a family lineage forever.

The extirpatory dimension proper to genocide was doubtless marked by a particular intensity toward the bodies of pregnant women. The ferocity directed against maternal bellies as well as against fetuses, which were racialized and animalized even before birth, simultaneously manifests the frenetic search for bodily differences and the determination to destroy the bodies forever. Hiding out in a sorghum field, one girl recounts the scene she witnessed as a ten-year-old:

> After a moment, the Interahamwe arrived where I was, but they didn't see me and they said: "The little snakes [*utwana tw'inzoka*] are done for, let's divide up their lands among us." A little before they arrived, they met a lady who was pregnant; they asked her: "You too, are you *inyenzi* [cockroach, i.e., Tutsi]?" She didn't answer. They asked her for her ID card, and they threw her medical card back in her face. They caught her, they led her quite close to where I was, and one of the killers said: "Give me the sword, we're going to cut her open to see what a baby *inyenzi* looks like." First they cut her so she would fall to the ground; they slaughtered her; they took the child out of her belly; they saw that it was a little girl. Then they said: "We got ourselves tired out for nothing." And another said: "No, for she too was going to grow up and poison us because we killed her family."[22]

The haunting thirst for vengeance evoked here by the killers was principally aimed at male infants, since boys were perceived as so many future combatants. The memory of Paul Kagame fleeing, as a child, from the violence in 1959 before returning three decades later to attack the country as the head of the FPR offered a justification for putting men and male children to death. In the case recalled here, the massacre of girls was also legitimized in the name of that same siege mentality.

The relentless focus on women's wombs, capable of giving birth to future enemies, can also be explained by the imaginary of war. How else can we understand the following excerpt from a text by a young girl, about six years old at the time, who witnessed the massacre of two neighbor women?

> They dragged them, hitting them on their heads with machetes, their brains were spurting up with the scarves they wore on their heads. They jumped enthusiastically on *their bellies*, saying that snakes were puncture-proof. Those two women were already dead but those guys said that snakes spent their time pretending to die when they weren't dead.[23]

Targeting the reproductive organs and fetuses, the ravaging of filiation also came about through the cruelty inflicted on very young children and the elderly. Once again the obsessional imaginary of a threat, conjugated with a powerful racialized vision of the Other, justified the assassination of one young girl's baby brother:

> The woman who had hidden us was sterile, so she said right away to that Interahamwe: "Can you give me that child [that of her maternal aunt, who was thus viewed as her brother]? I'm going to raise him because his mother has just died." He gave him to her and she took it away. When she was halfway home, that Interahamwe said to her: "Bring the child back! No *inyenzi* must remain alive because he would grow up." They grabbed the child and hit it with a nail-studded club. Before he was hit, the child said to that Interahamwe: "Papa!" And the other replied: "You're saying Papa? Me, I'm no *inyenzi*!" And he killed him at once. When I saw all that, I went crazy, I ran and he chased me, he struck me on the head with the club. I fell down immediately below the earthen wall.[24]

If, in the psychic economy of a young child, the image of an adult man looks like a father figure, the killer sees the child only as a potential fighter, a repulsive insect (*inyenzi*) to whom he expresses his repugnance before killing him. We find in the assassin's language the full ambiguity of the term *inyenzi*, which designates a cockroach, an FPR soldier, and/or a Tutsi. Here the imaginary of war must undoubtedly be conjugated with that of animalization. Another indication of the power of the racist belief system is found in the fate reserved for children born to couples in which the mother is Hutu and the father Tutsi. Registered officially as Tutsi, the children of such couples are identified as such and pursued on that basis.[25] One boy, about eleven years old at the time, was protected by his mother, who used both prudence and trickery to deter the threat coming from members of her own family. The boy reports what one neighbor said:

> I remember that one time Mama brought us to her paternal uncle in B. We met a person called Ki whom I've already spoken about. He said to Mama: "See how much time we've spent looking for your children without finding them. Now that I've just found them, they aren't going to get away from me. I'm going to kill them. Have a look at their brothers, the *inyenzi*, see what they're doing to us!" He had a spear and a sword. He said to Mama: "Sit down here! I'm taking your children and nothing will keep me from killing them. *Keep calm, you will have other children who won't be* inyenzi."[26]

In this way the man thought he was consoling the mother by assuring her that she would have "pure" descendants after having been relieved of the "*inyenzi*."

When the difference was not sought inside the body, phantasmatically particular body parts were the object of the cruel attention of the killers. Nose, ribs, stretch marks, skull size and shape, teeth: All these constituted bodily signs manifesting the foreignness of the Other and justifying the slaughter. A privileged space of ideological inscription, the Tutsi body was attacked precisely in those places where its difference was supposed to be manifested. On the RTLM airwaves, journalists revealed the register of these corporeal markers. The killers thus were provided with an efficient method of verification: The body was substituted for ID cards. Here is an excerpt from the testimony of one female survivor:

> How to distinguish a cockroach from a Hutu? You have several means at your disposal. The cockroach has widely spaced incisors. The cockroach has narrow heels. The cockroach has eight pairs of ribs. The female cockroach has stretch marks on her hips, near the buttocks. The cockroach has a slender nose. The cockroach has less kinky hair.

The cockroach's cranium is long in back, with a slanted forehead. The cockroach is tall, and there is arrogance in its gaze. The cockroach has a pronounced Adam's apple.[27]

The texts of the young writers are full of references to this racialized representation of their own bodies; they tried sometimes desperately to enlarge their nostrils to bring their appearance into conformity with the Hutu's somatic stereotypes. Here is an example of the internalization by the victims themselves of this racist repertory regarding physical appearance, written by a man born in 1973:

> When I arrived among them, they began to separate us and to kill the tall people. As for us, we put sticks in our nostrils to widen them, so as to be confused with the Hutu and to be saved. But we didn't succeed, they tore off our clothes, we stayed in our underpants and they made us transport the bodies. . . . The Interahamwe made me stand up, and he struck me in the ribs with the side of his machete; he said: "Look at how your ribs are, they're Tutsi!"[28]

The vast majority of the children were too young to have the ID cards that contained racial information. When they managed to escape the tight netting of social interconnections and could invent a "Hutu" genealogy as a ruse, the killers scrutinized their bodies:

> They asked me to take off my clothes to scrutinize my ribs. When they had looked, they asked me if I wasn't a Tutsi. I said no and they hit me on the head with clubs then I fell to the ground. They kept on asking me: "Your father isn't a Tutsi?!" And I answered: "No. But for Mama, I don't know her ethnicity."[29]

Attributing the supposed bodily particularities that the killers found suspicious to an uncertain heredity on his mother's side, the thirteen-year-old boy nevertheless did not escape the force of the racist projection on his own body.

Sometimes the cruelty consisted in suspending the murderous gesture, especially in the case of practices targeting babies and the elderly. Too weak and deprived of support, they were destined to certain death. A fatal outcome was intended for the younger sister of one six-year-old girl, abandoned near the corpse of her father in the Bugesera swamp; nevertheless, she survived. This is what her mother told her, counting up the family's losses two years after the end of the massacre:

> I asked her if others had been able to survive, and she told me that my older sister and my very young sister [*akararumuna kanjye gato*][30] were alive, the one that was with Papa [in the swamp]. They had refused to kill her, saying that she would continue to pester her father for food and that in any case she would die of hunger.[31]

The elderly, first forced to witness the murder of their children, were abandoned, helpless and racked with pain; the killers were ensuring a slow and painful death. One seven-year-old girl learned of her grandmother's disappearance, "dead from sorrow and hunger," from a brother who had managed to join her in her hiding place.[32] The killers had forced her to watch the murder of her own daughter even though she had begged them to kill her first so she would escape the terrible spectacle.

Invoking a proverb, the members of the *igitero* thus foresaw death by starvation for the grandmother of that boy, after she had lost all the children who were expected to provide for her well-being in her old age, as her grandson, born in 1986, relates:

> Around 7 PM, we went out and rejoined our grandmother. When she saw us, she wept, saying: "I thought you were dead." . . . Around 4 PM, we had begun to hear *induru*. We got up, and the old woman hid us somewhere further down in the compound. They came looking and found no one. *They addressed the old woman, not as a human being, but they said to her*: "Mukecuru, *in principle, when a hare is old, his children nurse him, otherwise he dies. As soon as you no longer have them, go ahead and kill yourself.*" We were listening to them from our hiding place, further down in the compound. They left right away.[33]

In a society where, in 1994, life expectancy scarcely went beyond age fifty, with an age pyramid very wide at the bottom and very narrow on top, people over sixty-five represented barely 3 percent of the population.[34] According to a census of the victims of the genocide published in 2004 by the Rwandan government, more than forty thousand people over age sixty-five perished during the genocide: The proportion was thus considerable.[35] The programmed death of the elderly aimed to eradicate the past and break the transmission of family memories in a country marked by a largely oral culture.

The destruction of family lineages was thus organized at the two extremes of the generational chain, depriving the Tutsi, destined to disappear, of both past and future. Other practices of cruelty introduced a different but equally radical type of rupture. Acts of anthropophagy and the pornographic staging of corpses touch on the axiological foundations of a society by provoking a systematic inversion. Several young writers, including a couple of girls who were seven or eight years old at the time, say that they were forced to eat human flesh, that of murdered Tutsi.[36] Others report the ultimate humiliation inflicted on the bodies of the victims when they were placed in grotesque positions mimicking the sex act. One girl born in 1981 provided this description:

> When we arrived at a barrier, we saw two corpses, one of a woman and the other of a man. . . . We then asked the children with us and they replied that they were the corpses of a woman and a man and that after killing them, they had laid the body of the man on top of that of the woman to see how the Tutsi made love.[37]

Another boy, eight years old at the time, could not keep from sobbing after watching his mother's murder, revealing his hiding place to the killers by way of his tears. Here is how he described the reaction of the members of the *igitero* when he was discovered:

> They said: "Look at this other snake! *Sha*, we were going to forget him! He was going to hide under that tree and escape us!" The leader of that *igitero* said: "Bring over that snake so that we can put him on top of that woman [his own mother] because he hasn't had the chance to have sex." They greeted me with clubs, they hit me on my head.[38]

To the scorn displayed toward the victim's body was added an unconcealed incestuous staging, doubling the scope of the transgression. Once again, the multiplication of such spectacles makes it impossible to read them in terms of individual deviance: The meticulous search for the most degrading stagings aimed to make the victims suffer *for a long time*. In the order of radical axiological inversions, we find what struck one twelve-year-old girl as an act of anthropophagy, when the *ibitero* forced the Tutsi to ingest the meat of their own cows: "They killed the cows belonging to Mama's family before our eyes, they cut them up with their skins and gave us their meat so we could be forced to eat it; we refused, and they spit in our faces."[39]

Another boy, age thirteen at the time, attested to the recurrence of such practices, whose transgressive import the killers understood perfectly well: "They began to humiliate and torture Papa. They ordered him to grill the meat and then eat it, but he couldn't."[40] It was impossible for that father to eat the flesh of his cow, which the *igitero* members feasted on nevertheless after having decapitated him.

The "theaters of cruelty" were not organized exclusively by men. Women, female neighbors, also manifested cruel refinement. By denying refuge in their domestic spaces, they were refusing a maternal protection that was counted on by children born to families with which they had ties. Thus it was to an old friend of her mother that the injured eleven-year-old girl went to beg for a little water. At the threshold of her *rugo*, the woman declared to the girl that she "would not find a cup to give to a Tutsi."[41] After having forced her to drink from a banana tree leaf, like an animal, the woman then led her with a perverse joy to the place where the nude body of her mother lay. Numerous occasions of women refusing asylum or water to children are reported in the texts. Some women turned the young victims over to the *ibitero*, as in this case of an eleven-year-old girl:

> When they didn't find Papa, they asked us where he was. We answered that we didn't know. Then that man's wife said to them: "These are vipers' children [*impiri*],[42] and vipers' children are vipers themselves. Have pity on me and clear my house of this filth, take this filth to the garbage pit." They took us out; they led us to the pit to kill us.[43]

Reduced to the status of trash, the lost, wounded children were the objects of the ferocious mockery put out by choruses of neighbors, in which women's voices were invariably included, as in this report by a thirteen-year-old girl:

> A woman married to the president of the Interahamwe took us to her house, where we found a child whose head, ears, and his whole body were covered with blood because he had remained among the corpses. When he went to the neighbors in search of help, they said: "Where is that thing going? Filth, where are you going? Go back to the corpses of your father and your mother!"[44]

At the end of a chaotic narrative marked by a series of unconnected images without any chronological progression, one girl, who had been twelve years old at the time, went back over the traumatic scenes of her experience. Among them, this description:

> Ours knew atrocities in their death; they inflicted immense suffering on them because they saw everything, even their own death; it was given to them by those they had fed, by those they had helped in various ways. The Hutu did us such evil that it cannot be told. I can't forget one old woman who was our neighbor: They had cut her into pieces, and as she was dying she asked a neighbor who was passing by (a Hutu woman) for water; she, instead of giving her water, she pissed in her mouth. You understand well that we saw so many things that we could detest all of humanity.[45]

Terrible images like these long haunted the memory of the young survivors, inscribing forever at the core of their existence the recollection of cruelty and of the humiliation of their loved ones, when they themselves were not the victims. Of these obsessive visions, one young girl, seven years old at the time, supplied an account, describing the long night of the genocide saturated by an accumulation of cruelties in words and deeds:

> In Kinyarwanda we say: "*Ijoro ribara uwaribonye*" [the one who recounts the night is the one who saw it].[46] *I saw* what the Interahamwe did to us: *I saw* humans kill other humans. I am talking about *how* the Interahamwe killed us. *I saw* the Interahamwe disembowel women; *I saw* the Interahamwe slaughter men like cattle, and to observe the degree of intelligence of the Tutsi, they opened up their skulls; *I saw* the Interahamwe cut off women's breasts, supposedly to see if Tutsi children drank their mothers' milk like the others; *I saw* the Interahamwe turn infants upside down and smash their heads; *I saw* the Interahamwe attack people who weren't dead to finish them off, and they slaughtered them like cattle, to make them understand that they had never been human beings like the others.[47]

6

ECOSYSTEMS OF SURVIVAL

For the victims, the rupture triggered by a sudden eruption of radical violence profoundly modified their relations not only to time but also to their spatial environment and to their own bodies. Their entire sensorial systems were shaken by the killings, as the familiar hills and well-known neighborhoods turned into sources of danger. The need to find food was coupled with the need to quench a thirst sharpened by the bleeding of the first wounds. Confronted with so many overlapping physiological disturbances and the perception of an ongoing threat, the children had to adapt quickly and nimbly if they were to survive. The shift in their relation to space led them to specific hiding places: Their familiarity with the local topography thus took on capital importance. The undulations of the hills and the density of the population considerably reduced the possibilities for concealment, all the more so in that the killers—who also were entirely familiar with the local terrain—deployed their energies in ferreting out the victims in the places that were the hardest to reach. So the big swamps surrounding the Nyabarongo and Akagera riverbeds became natural refuges that were immediately invaded by the *ibitero*. In reconstituting the ecosystems of survival in their diversity, I have sought to describe as precisely as possible the various types of places where the victims sought shelter, for the possibilities of finding food and the ways of moving about varied considerably in relation to the local ecology: A sugarcane swamp, for example, offered more possibilities for quenching one's thirst and appeasing one's hunger than a papyrus swamp or a sorghum field.

Moreover, certain spaces were less exposed to the killers' surveillance: The swamps, stretching out over long distances, were not always surrounded by high hills forming promontories from which to spot the victims' movements. Conversely, other spaces turned into veritable traps, for staying there meant being readily noticed. As for the forests, which were too sparse to provide secure shelter for the refugees, they were sometimes used as places for regrouping.

Some of the survivors' narratives provide an account of intense feelings of animalization, which were reinforced by survival in such places. The various forms of spatial shelter produced unprecedented physiological and psychic experiences. Surviving in a swamp or a forest led the children to identify with animals, plunging into a latrine constituted total degradation, and hiding among corpses increased the sense of porosity between life and death.

Trapped at the heart of the terrain of genocide, the victims tried to find food, quench their thirst, take care of their injuries, and protect themselves from the cold, all while fending off vultures and dogs. In their narratives, the young writers described in detail the types of spaces in which they found an always precarious refuge, the meager food sources they were able to draw from these sites, and the animals that populated them. Their voices unveil a veritable bestiary of the genocide, in which some ordinarily wild and dangerous animals became allies and others that had been part of the harmless familiarity of daily life became auxiliaries to the killers. At the height of the genocide, the children's relations to wilderness and domesticity were radically reversed. The familiar places traversed by children, who often had a perfect mastery of local geography, were transformed into unknown spaces, producing a total disorientation that increased their terror.

Examining the ecosystems of survival leads to a precise depiction of the microlocal organizations of the massacres. From this standpoint, the topographic "competencies" of the killers seem just as essential to the effectiveness of the genocide as the interrelationships, the social and spatial intimacies that came together to increase their murderous energy. In Rwanda, there were no deportations to faraway places. On the contrary, a single imperative reigned: to keep the victims within the tight borders of the neighborhood, in order to make them easier to track down and identify by those who had lived close to them. Beyond the data presented in the young writers' texts, one statistic from a Rwandan government survey gives a clear image of the killers' determination to carry out the massacres within the intimacy of neighborhood borders: Three-fifths of the victims were murdered on the hills—on *their own* hills, one might add.[1] Thus several young writers from the communes bordering Tanzania attested to the meticulous control of the Akagera River and of the nearby lakes by spotters in dugout canoes.[2]

Full possession of the territory by the very mobile *ibitero* pushed the victims to run frantically, always within a limited space. This becomes clear if one follows the itineraries of flight patiently spelled out by many of the children.[3] Here is one girl's report on the intensity of the chase:

> They had us followed while telling us to leave that place. We went back to the rocks without knowing where we were going because we passed through the bush and not on the paths, for *the paths all belonged to them, as if we others were not human beings.* Were we really human beings? No. They flushed you out the way they would have flushed out a rabbit. There were so many war cries [*induru*]. Everything had become like the bush, and they flushed you out everyplace where you were sitting down. The clubs spoke.[4]

The passage through the bush and the need to hide out there are interpreted as a form of dehumanization; the topography itself was an accomplice of the massacre. A powerful feeling of disorientation seized the young girl, lost, here too, in a perimeter quite close to the family compound but which she no longer recognized. Bumping into the barricades that had been set up on the hills, her wandering hinders her flight and thus her chances of survival:

> Other men and boys told them that they were going to a meeting and that the girls, women, and children should go home. Did we really have a place to go home to? The houses had been completely destroyed, from roof to foundation. So where could we go? *Ahi! Mana we* [my God]! They hit us so we would go home as if we were cows that they were leading to the drinking trough. We took the path and went back. At 11 AM, we arrived at a place where there was a swamp. We were exhausted. We found a barricade where there were educated men . . . around 6:30 PM, it was already dark, we escaped from them. We fled so they wouldn't kill us. But toward what were we fleeing? Even when everything is over, life pinches you to call you back. That night was full of pain and tears, the small children floundered in their Mama's blood; there were rivers of blood; the vultures had found meat to eat, they were tearing off pieces of the corpses and pulling out the intestines. What misery! We kept

on walking, and we arrived at the same barricade that we had crossed before.[5]

In another text, a boy about twelve years old also recounts what he perceived as the deadly turn of the very landscape:

Me, I kept going, and when I arrived on the hill, fleeing, I saw people on the other hill. When they saw me, they started shouting [*induru*] against me. They yelled: "*Nguwo, nguwo, nguwo!* There he is, there he is, there he is!" I felt it was over for me, but I kept on persevering in my flight. I arrived in the valley, and there I met three boys who were my comrades; we fled together, we kept on running, but *all the hills were sending up* induru *against us*.[6]

The feeling of betrayal by the places themselves was probably the more intensely felt in that his flight had not taken him very far from his *rugo*: These were *his* hills that were raging against him.

In many cases, though, the children, alone or with their families, went into spaces whose topography was unfamiliar. The swamps were among the sites most frequently mentioned. Whether they surrounded the bends in the Nyabarongo River in the Bugesera region, the banks of Lake Mugesera and Lake Muhazi, or the webbing of the Akagera River in the eastern part of the country, they appeared to the children as particularly hostile places. One needs to have visited these immense stretches of stifling stuffiness, crackling with a multitude of unfamiliar sounds, to grasp part of the anguish felt by the victims forced to immerse themselves in such spaces. We can imagine the intense fright of the children and their feeling of extreme suffocation in these swamplands, where papyrus plants and sugarcane can grow several meters high. In the texts that follow, the victims plunged into the Bugesera swamp in the wake of the massacre in the Ntarama church on April 15. Those who escaped fled; some were seriously wounded and very weakened physically. Especially difficult survival conditions awaited them in a place where edible resources were rare and the possibilities of tending to wounds nonexistent. Hidden in the putrid water of the swamps, human bodies weakened rapidly, and malaria crises multiplied. Three young survivors, six or seven years old at the time, wrote about the physical ordeals they endured, insisting on the unhealthiness of the scant food they had managed to find on the nearby hills:

When you were thirsty, you took water from the marsh to drink. And we often drank the blood of our own people because they were hunting them and killing them there. You went up to a dead person, you took some water and you drank because you had no other choice.[7]

We lived in that papyrus marsh, in the water mixed with the blood of our older brothers and other loved ones whom they had killed there. We used that water mixed with blood; we drank it. We ate little, only when we found some manioc. That manioc was only *igitamisi* [inedible manioc full of cyanide]. When we didn't find any manioc, we just drank that water.[8]

We went back into the papyrus marsh and there, rain drenched us every day, relentlessly, but we had no other choice. We had nothing to cover ourselves with. We had lice because we couldn't bathe. Every time you thought about washing yourself, you heard the cries of the Interahamwe, and you had to run. One day, we were seated at the entrance to the marsh warming ourselves in the sun. It was morning and the vultures were eating the bodies of our loved ones.[9]

If children, like the adults hiding with them, had no choice but to quench their thirst with filthy water, to calm their hunger with inedible tubers, and to endure being bitten by lice, it was because the killers allowed them no respite that could have allowed them to ward off starvation. The young writers who had escaped from the Bugesera swamp described the organization of the massacres in minute detail, for the *ibitero* did not hesitate to penetrate into the bogs in search of Tutsi refugees. One six-year-old girl had been taken out of the swamp by a man who planned to make her his household slave; her account sheds light on the discipline that governed the killing process:

> When we had advanced a little farther, that man flushed out another child, whom he cut into pieces before my eyes. As soon as he had finished, we heard whistles. It was like a signal to go back. We left the papyrus marsh. As soon as we reached the exit from the marsh, they got together to boast of the way they had exterminated us. They also said that the next day they would go sweep up the filth. . . . They had just discussed the plans for the next day: "We'll finish them all off."[10]

Described like real work, governed by hourly schedules, the massacres were carried out according to an invariable ritual that sometimes allowed the victims to crisscross the nearby hills in search of food or to warm up their bodies chilled by the low nighttime temperatures. Here is one girl's account: A seven-year-old survivor, she had profited from the intervals between attacks to run off looking for sugared water to help "her Mamas," who were suffering from a malaria crisis:

> Another day, they were late in coming to kill, for ordinarily they came at 6 in the morning and, that day, they arrived at 10. Usually we knew when they were arriving, but that day we remained calm, thinking that they had given themselves a day off—since they were working, and there is no work without time off. My brother and I had gone to buy some juice from a man who was our neighbor, but I don't remember his name. The Mamas had asked us to go buy some because they were sick.[11]

Alas, that "little respite" was only a ploy, foreshadowing a large-scale assault: In mid-May 1994,[12] the FPR troops were approaching. To throw off the vigilance of the Tutsi men posted at the top of the hill overlooking the marsh, the killers set up a ruse designed to dissimulate their advance:

> There were men watching to see where the *igitero* was coming from. Then the *igitero* was on its way, it reached the banana plantation and they cut down all the banana trees. Then they dressed the banana trees in their own white shirts and we thought they were still far away [in the banana plantation], whereas they had already moved on. We saw only their white shirts. We didn't know it, but the terrible miseries had already landed on us. The last *igitero* came and took away lots of people, too many to count. The Inkotanyi [the FPR] were coming very close, and the GP [soldiers of the Presidential Guard] who had come brought a vehicle bearing ammunition [a machine gun], and they fired just as the others were cutting. But God did a great thing, because there was water and when they fired enormous bombs to burn down the marsh with all of us inside, that bomb fell into the water and died [failed to explode]. We kept on walking into the marsh, and behind us the Interahamwe were killing people.[13]

This ambush with the help of banana trees was attested in another text, this one written by a girl who had been eleven years old at the time:

> The next morning, another *igitero* came to pursue us. We took refuge in Kimpiri. They followed us there. They cut down the banana trees, which

they clothed in their own shirts. Looking at those banana trees, we thought that the *ibitero* had stayed in that spot. They came down, bare-chested, and when they came close they began to shoot at us. We ran down the hill; they chased us and we plunged into the papyrus marsh. Before entering into the marsh, they had already killed a lot of people. We came close to the river, where we found another *igitero* that had come from Mugina of Gitarama.[14]

Caught in the trap, the girl's family members tried three times to throw themselves into the Nyabarongo, but the river "refused" them, and its current carried them onto the banks. The attack she encountered here left an exceptional mark on the young girl, who saw many of her companions in misfortune killed before her eyes, shortly before her own father also succumbed.

The immense swamps surrounding the Akagera or the lakes of that eastern region did not escape meticulous combing by the killers, either. That other major river of the country, forming a natural border with Tanzania, even became a weapon. In the territory as a whole, an estimated 45,000 people were drowned in the river or the lakes.[15] One girl attested to the murderous use of hydrography, having been thrust into the Akagera herself as a twelve-year-old, along with many other victims:

> That day, we were with other people, about seventy-six in all. There were people from our family, women with their children and neighbors. When we arrived at the Akagera, they tied some of us up, attaching our hands behind our backs. Among those people, some were adults whose heads had been cut open. They were losing their blood. . . . We were five children in our family, and they threw us, too, into the water. Everyone, they threw all of us into the water. That night, before dark, I felt that I was a prisoner of the grasses, my head above the water. The child we called Mati grabbed me, but we didn't say a word. Then she let go of me and she was carried off by the water. I stayed there and I saw before me a dead person that looked like a white man, he was so close to me that he cut off my view. I didn't know what to do, I grabbed onto the papyruses and I managed to get out of the water. But before we reached that point, they had beaten us with the papyruses they had cut, for they thought that we could swim and get out of the water. When we passed them [carried along by the current], they looked for a dugout to follow us so that we would stay

under the water. But they didn't find the dugout. When I reached the papyrus marsh, I spent the night there, and I saw no one else who had been able to get out of the water, I was the only one, all the others were dead. The next morning, I tried to find the path we had taken. The papyruses were scraping me and big flies were biting me. I spent the whole day in the swamp. That night, I heard them insulting the dugout owners, asking them where they had gone. I was afraid that someone had seen me, but I kept on. I was looking for a way out of the swamp. The second day, around 5 PM, I found the path, and it started to rain hard. They brought other people to the river whom I didn't recognize because I couldn't see them well, I was hidden in the swamp. . . . I managed to get out of the swamp that night, around 7 PM. I went up by a narrow path and I passed by a place where there was a dog.[16]

Here we can see how much energy the killers put into ensuring that the victims would drown: tying up the strongest ones, beating the youngest with sharp-edged papyrus leaves, and scouring the river in search of eventual survivors. The atmosphere of the marsh disoriented the young girl. Plunged into a hostile place, she struggled to find a way out, even though she was just a few kilometers away from home.[17] She recalled "the big flies that were biting her" in the stifling swamp; other children also mentioned insects, batrachians, and reptiles. One can imagine the terror of another girl barely six years old, wandering alone when she went into a swamp near Lake Mugesera. In her text she manifested her childhood fears centered on the unknown animals featured in fairy tales: "I kept on going, I passed through a swamp; I was afraid of the frogs that were croaking and of other sorts of terrifying birds that I had never heard. But I was lucky and I got through that place."[18] Similarly, one boy who had been about twelve at the time invokes the disturbing figure of a toad to describe his own state, hidden in the dank universe of the Akagera swamps: "Then I went down to escape the barricade and I crossed through the valley; I went into the papyrus marshes and I lived in the water like a toad. I too spent the whole day there. And Monday, in the evening, I continued on the trek I had begun."[19]

If certain animals living in the swamps intensified the children's terror, others were, on the contrary, perceived as protective allies. Repulsive and frightening snakes—and among them the most dangerous species—nevertheless appeared in a positive light to an eight-year-old girl:

You who will read this testimony, you know that during the war [the genocide], snakes were our friends. We spent time with them in the holes they had dug; we spent nights in the bush they inhabited; we gobbled down their food; we licked the earth where they had left their traces. We dug up sweet potatoes like moles. . . . I'm talking about snakes because they knew that we were their brothers. They were good neighbors for us at a time when humans like ourselves abandoned us [*abantu nkawe bari badukuyeho amaboko*].[20]

In another excerpt, a snake that was ordinarily alarming shared the terror of the young victims hedged in by bullets:

In that bush, I lay down on a snake: I was afraid of the bullets but it too was afraid. Actually, if it bit me, I don't know. It was my big sister who showed me the snake I was lying on. I felt something sliding without knowing what it was. In any case I was going to die.[21]

The writer, a girl about seven years old, explains that she first hid in "a bush" after the attack on the Mabare (Bicumbi) mosque where the Muslim population had joined the refugees to resist the assaults of the *ibitero* between April 7 and April 13; she then related her moves from one hiding place to the next.[22] One area in particular retained her attention, one that came up quite often in many of the texts: the sorghum fields. In the middle of the rainy season, the plants in these fields were especially tall, so much so that to a seven-year-old boy they "resembled a forest."[23] While they offered possibilities of concealment and some food resources, the sorghum fields were nevertheless perceived as particularly hostile places, as the same little girl indicated:

Among those Interahamwe, there was a young man to whom Mama had been generous. He chased away the Interahamwe he was leading and he asked us to follow him so he could show us where we could hide. The next day, at 3 o'clock in the morning . . . Oh! We ran into so many problems! What happened with the Rwandans is so serious! It was April 13, 1994, we were in the sorghum field, rain was falling on our heads, we had nothing to eat, we were dying of hunger and thirst. I raised my head toward the sky so the rain would fall in my mouth. Hunger was killing me, and I went to the Interahamwe to ask for something to eat.[24]

The interpolated exclamations and the presence of an exact date are signs of the vivid imprint left by that terrible night in the sorghum field, with no water or food, after an exhausting run.

Sometimes, hiding along with adults in the sorghum fields, the children managed to draw on the meager food resources available, without reducing the danger from the *ibitero*, who were paying close attention to the undulations of the plants in order to locate their victims. A boy, about nine years old at the time, writes:

> Right away we went to the place where we had some land and we hid there. We spent the night and the day in the sorghum plantation. At the point when we were being tortured by hunger, Papa cut some sorghum stalks and stems [*inopfu*, sorghum ears that will not mature and that give off a black powder], and that's what he gave us to eat. Then they began to guess that people were hiding in the sorghum plantation. They started to post watchers on the hill, and when the sorghum plants moved, they yelled *induru*, and you ran out fast. Then eating sorghum stalks and *inopfu* was over. Then we began to eat *imyeyo* [a grass normally used to make small brooms] that contained a little water.[25]

If the rapidity with which the Tutsi genocide was carried out does not immediately bring to mind the picture of intense hunger, as is the case with the other genocides of the twentieth century, hunger is nevertheless at the heart of the young writers' preoccupations. Spending several days without food or water while constantly on the run is inevitably an ordeal for the human body. In many of the narratives, the search for food increased the risk of crossing the killers' path. In addition, the initial wounds and the bleeding they spurred kindled thirst, as recounted by one young woman who was about twenty at the time:

> As I was running I bumped into a stone and twisted my legs. The stone gave me a big gash on one leg. I also hurt my head, and they caught up with me. I was still lying down and I looked like a dead person, but I was listening a bit. And then I was weakened by hunger, since from Thursday to Monday we only ate sweet potatoes that we dug up like moles and gobbled down to feel at least a bit of liquid in our mouths. Then they hit me with clubs on the back and they said: "Ah, she's dead, let's go. Let's

follow that boy." They left because they saw me losing blood through my nose and they also saw the wound caused by the stone, which they took for a machete blow. Ten minutes after they left, I tried to get up, but I didn't succeed because of the hunger and thirst. The wounds were still hot [fresh]. I started to walk slowly, but I was losing blood. I took a sweater, twisted it, and tied it around my leg to make the bleeding stop. And then I went on, staggering into the woods.[26]

Inside all these spaces, whether sorghum fields or "bush," the children were also confronted with animals. Ordinarily harmless, birds were perceived as sources of danger, even as being actual accomplices of the killers.

During this time . . . little birds called *ubukwiti* came. They began to fly in circles overhead, and they didn't stop chirping. We said to these little birds: "Pardon us. *Mwo kabyara mwe* ['May your descendants be numerous'—a wish one formulates in speaking to a person]. You too, you want us to get killed." We took leaves and threw them at them. Then we drove them off, saying: "Shhhh," but very softly so they wouldn't hear us and come to kill us. From 3 to 5 PM, those little birds didn't stop agitating so they would come kill us.[27]

While this particular boy, about thirteen at the time, recollected his intense feelings about the "malice of the little birds," the principal animal figures dominating the texts overall were dogs and cows. The dogs are consistently described as animal extensions of the killers, whereas the cows, for their part, are seen to be among the victims.

The recurring dog-related vocabulary is by no means metaphorical: The young writers recounted literal hunting parties. Launched into the bush, swamps, and sorghum fields, dogs flushed out the victims, who were relegated to the status of game; the dogs signaled the presence of refugees by barking and then hunted them down relentlessly. One boy, about seven years old at the time, described the hunt this way:

We went to hide in the sorghum plantation, and when we got there we found lots of other people: they were all Tutsi who had been hunted. We lived there, we spent three days there, and the fourth day they became like madmen. They attacked the entire sorghum plantation, and, during that period, the field resembled a forest. They hunted with their dogs, and when the dogs reached us they barked. We had just gotten used to that, for every time they found people, they barked. As for us, we left and started to run. They came after us.[28]

In a text by a twelve-year-old boy, the tracking was described in minute detail. The killers flushed out their prey with stones:

They came, they hunted, they threw stones into the bush so that the stones would hit someone, he would cry out and give his presence away, or else so that someone would get scared, go out of the bush, and be killed. But at the time when they were throwing stones at us, we were lucky and the stones didn't fall on us. Sometimes they came very close, and you thanked God. And when a stone fell on you, you stifled your cries because there was no one who could take pity on you. *Yewe!* What torment to see the people whose cows we had milked for them who can't even give you a drink of water! They yell *induru* at you, they destroy your house, they kill you and do all sorts of other nasty things to you.[29]

There is a striking congruence between these descriptions and descriptions of hunting as it was practiced in Rwanda before democratic pressures reduced the land available and led to its marginalization. By 1992–1993, hunting seems to have disappeared from social and cultural practice, since one had to turn to elderly informants for descriptions of it.[30] In the Rwanda of the past, there were two types of hunting. One type, hunting with bells and dogs, resembled the Western model of fox hunting, using hounds. The other type involved three groups of hunters: trackers, charged with flushing out game with a lot of shouting and bell ringing; a group charged with leaving silently and taking up shooting positions on the circumference of the hunting area; and shooters spread out in the area between the other two groups.[31] Although it is hard to evaluate the place of hunting practices for Rwanda in 1994 with any precision, an abundant and refined corpus praising the exploits of the best hunters ensures the cultural presence of hunting.[32]

The reader will have noticed the frequent use of the term *induru*, which has been rendered imperfectly by "war cries" or "cries for help." The term refers to a triple register: help among neighbors, war, and hunting. Consisting in an attack cry launched by covering and uncovering the mouth with a hand, it is raised during a hunt to flush out the game.[33] The sonic universe of the genocide as it is evoked in the texts consistently refers to that of a hunt.

Real assistants to the killers, dogs participated in the humiliation of the corpses; they are often evoked by the young writers as gorging on human flesh. Testimonies on the need to slaughter them by the hundreds after the massacres ended are frequent, for, saturated with human blood, they became particularly aggressive, attacking humans fearlessly from then on.

At the heart of the domestic ecosystem, an animal whose fate is depicted in quite different terms dominates the text. Anthropomorphized as much by the killers as by the victims, cows shared the tragic fate of the Tutsi during the genocide. These animals have long nourished the fascination of European anthropologists, who have documented political and social systems based on the circulation of cattle. At the heart of Rwandan literary and historical culture, its rich and delicate pastoral poetry, powerful bovine armies and multiple taboos connected with the practice of cattle breeding speak to the centrality of the place granted the animals in the regions where the monarchy left its mark, literally, with its branding irons.[34] Still, by 1994 the rights to extensive pasture lands, the *ibikingi*, had long since been lost, after a thoroughgoing rearrangement of the landscape begun in the 1930s by the Belgian colonial administration. The bare hillsides seen in early-twentieth-century photographs were gradually shaded over by eucalyptus trees, which were planted in massive numbers to meet the need for firewood and replenished later by the owners of coffee and banana plantations.[35] The struggle against erosion, the culture of land exploitation, and the search for food self-sufficiency deeply transformed the landscape. The portion of space devoted to pasturing was thus considerably reduced. If the social, political, and economic prestige of cows was seriously damaged in the upheavals of Rwandan history after the 1950s, the affective attachment invested in the animal was by no means eroded. Families knew the value of owning a cow: It produced milk and provided manure for growing crops.

Far from their ordinary place in the domestic economy, the cattle of the old days, those featured in royal parades, reappeared in the racist propaganda making the *inyambo* (cow) the metonymic figure of the conquering Tutsi, thirsty for power and spurred by a desire for revenge against the "people in the majority," the Hutu. Instruments of a reviled power, cattle were presented as a millennial weapon of servitude, as the extremist newspaper *Kangura* insisted in an article published in March 1993:

The history of Rwanda shows us clearly that the Tutsi have remained the same as always; they have never changed. The maliciousness, the evildoing, are those we know in the history of our country. When the Tutsi were still on the throne, they governed by two things: women and cows. These two things reigned over the Hutu for four hundred years. When the Tutsi were overturned by the people's revolution in 1959, they never slept again. They did everything to restore the monarchy by using their *bizungerezi* women and money, which seemed to have replaced cows. As we know, the cow was once a sign of wealth.[36]

It is impossible to understand the systematic slaughtering of the animals, their devouring on the occasion of meat-eating orgies during the genocide, without keeping in mind that ideological background. The system of racist representations based on a homology between cows and their owners found a concrete translation in the hills. The violence exercised on these creatures was inscribed in a grammar of cruelty shared by killers and victims alike, centered on an anthropomorphized vision of cows.

Describing the first desperate flights into the hills, one girl born in 1986 attests at the same time to the frightened running of the family cows, before writing, a few lines later: "They cut the cows into pieces, saying that they too were *inyenzi*; that they too were Tutsi, since they belonged to Tutsi."[37] Even more precisely, another girl a year younger noted the assimilation of a bovid to the figure of her paternal uncle: "They chased a cow, saying that this cow *was* our paternal uncle; they said that *he* was really the one they were chasing."[38] The assimilation between Tutsi and cows was so powerful that it guided the replication of the practices of cruelty we have already seen. In the following excerpt by a boy born in 1986, a heifer undergoes the same attacks as those reserved for eviscerating pregnant women: "At the entrance to the compound, they were sharing the meat from our cow, which they had just cut open in order to take out the calf. The calf was just about to be born, that day or the next. After dividing up the meat, they moved on ahead."[39]

The collapse of the human–animal border in the practices of killing was so radical that it marked the auditory memory of the young survivors in a lasting way. The sonic landscape of the genocide cannot be imagined without the noise of the cows being slaughtered, whose "screams of pain" united them with the hunted humans. One young cowherd, about thirteen at the time, was particularly attentive in describing what had happened to the animals he knew—and loved—so well: "The cows uttered cries of pain [*ziboroga*] because they were in the process of cutting their tendons."[40] Not only did the cows "scream out their suffering" as the human victims did, but they were subjected to the same bodily attacks as their owners. The young cowherd chose his words: He used the term *kuboroga* (to scream in pain), which is normally limited to the description of human cries. For him, cows didn't moo (*kwabira*); they expressed their suffering *the same way* human beings did. A similar affective attachment can be read in the following lines, written by another cowherd (a young man of twenty-two at the time) evoking the fate of one of his animals:

> Something else that hurt me was seeing *musengo yacu* [the name of his cow, referring to the coloring of its coat] that we milked for them and for their children, which, in recompense for her benefits, was cut up by them mercilessly. *Ayiwe!* Why was she subjected to that? Her owner was subjected to all that because of what he was, and I say that perhaps she too [the cow] was taken away because of her benefits, because she fed them, because she fed their family at a time when they had tiny shoulders [at a time when they were weak] because of illness, because of kwashiorkor [a syndrome of malnutrition owing to a protein deficiency].[41]

The massacre of the writer's beloved cow, she too a victim of the reversibility of social and affective bonds, was in response to no economic reality or even to a need to take nourishment from its meat. The killers never established herds that would ensure a reserve for consumption. On the contrary, the cattle were immediately butchered and literally devoured, apart from any economic or financial logic: As metonyms for the Tutsi fated to disappear, cattle were executed as part of the same exterminating utopia. Equally anthropomorphized by the victims, cows counted among the immense losses of the *rugo*. The overwhelming joy expressed by the young escapees when one of the cows managed to survive attests to the intensity of their affection and, between the lines, to the tragedy of their disappearance.

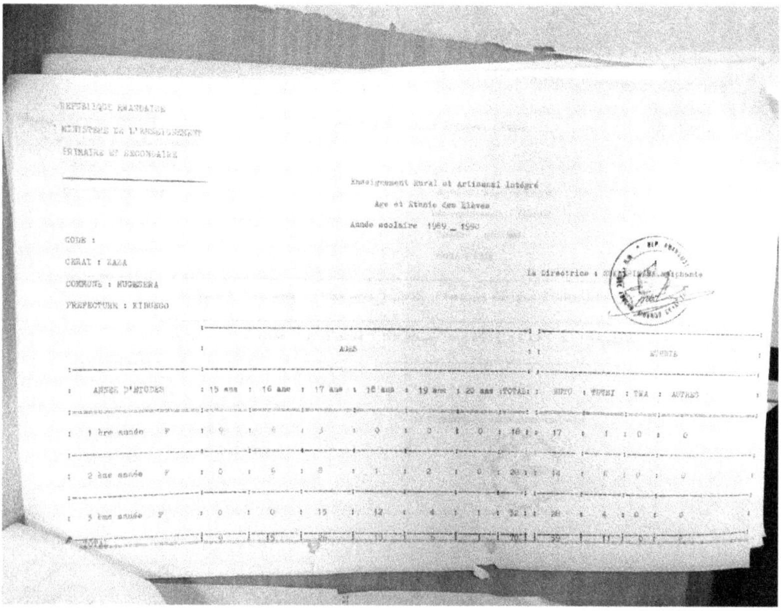

REPUBLIQUE RWANDAISE
MINISTERE DE L'ENSEIGNEMENT
PRIMAIRE ET SECONDAIRE

Enseignement Rural et Artisanal Intégré
Age et Ethnie des Elèves
Année scolaire 1989 _ 1990

CODE :
CERAI : ZAZA
COMMUNE : MUGESERA
PREFECTURE : KIBUNGO

La Directrice : [illegible]

	AGES							ETHNIE			
ANNEE D'ETUDES	15 ans	16 ans	17 ans	18 ans	19 ans	20 ans	TOTAL	HUTU	TUTSI	TWA	AUTRES
1 ère année F	9	6	3	0	0	0	18	17	1	0	0
2 ème année F	0	6	8	1	2	0	20	14	6	0	0
3 ème année F	0	0	15	12	4	1	32	28	4	0	0
TOTAL	9	15	26	13	[illegible]	1	70	59	11	0	[illegible]

FIGURE 1. Ethnic statistics from the Centre d'enseignement rural et artisanal intégré (CERA) in Zaza (Kibungo) for the year 1989–1990. © Archives de la commission nationale de lutte contre la génocide (ACNLG).

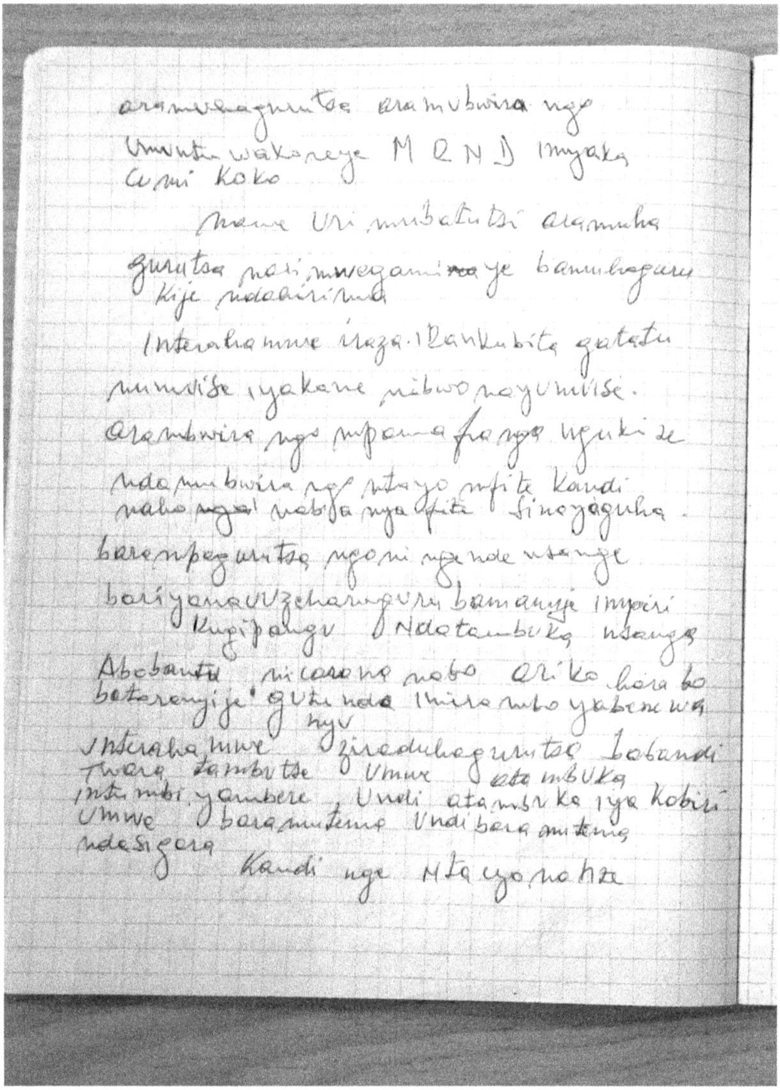

FIGURE 2. Pages from the notebook of a male born in 1973, written April 21–23, 2006. © ACNLG.

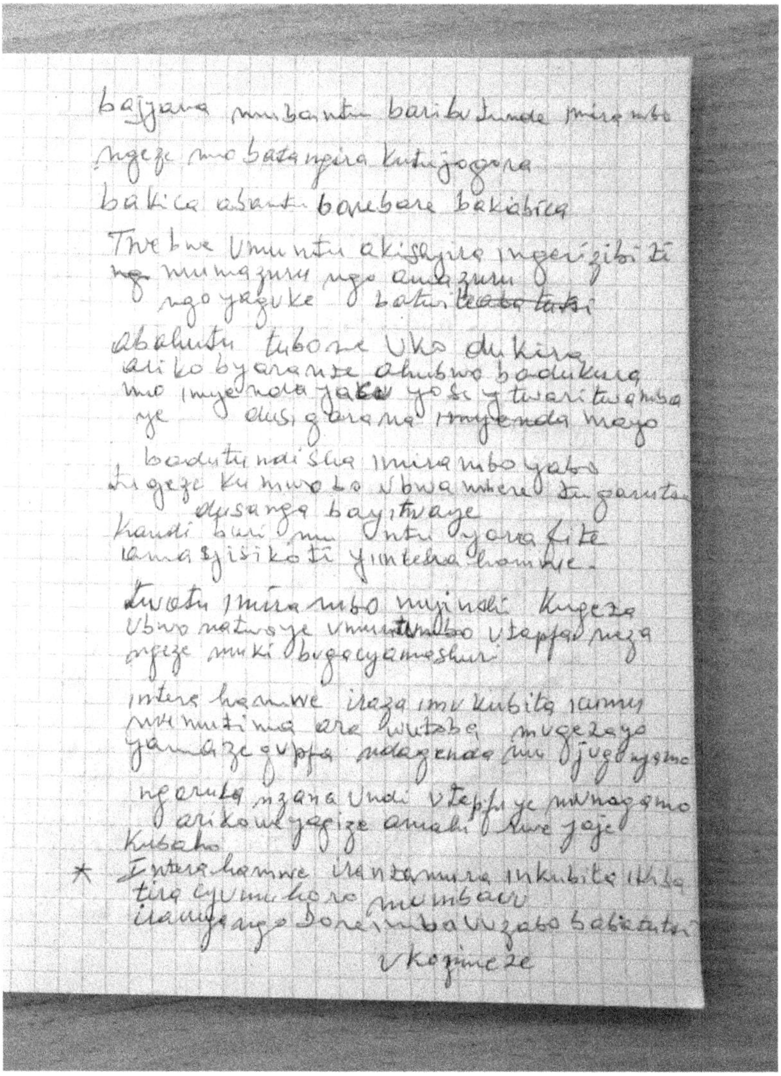

FIGURE 2. (*continued*)

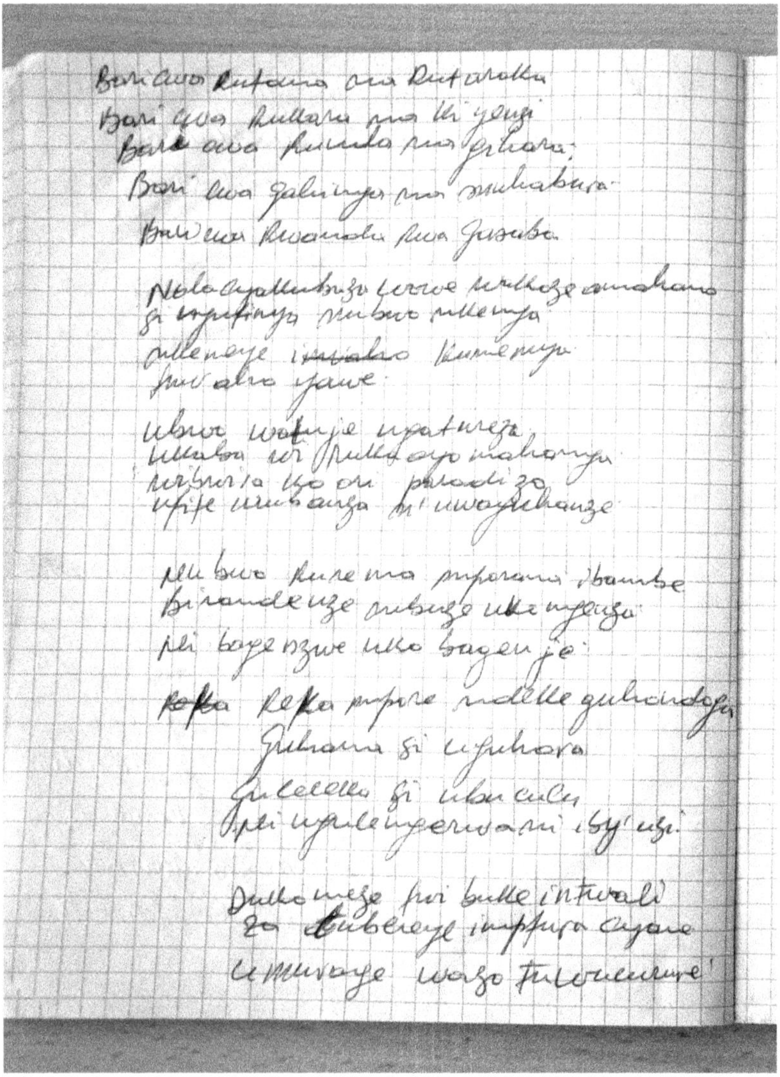

FIGURE 3. Excerpt from a poem written at the end of the notebook by a male born in 1979; the poem is titled "I sing my address to Wisdom." Written April 21–23, 2006. © ACNLG.

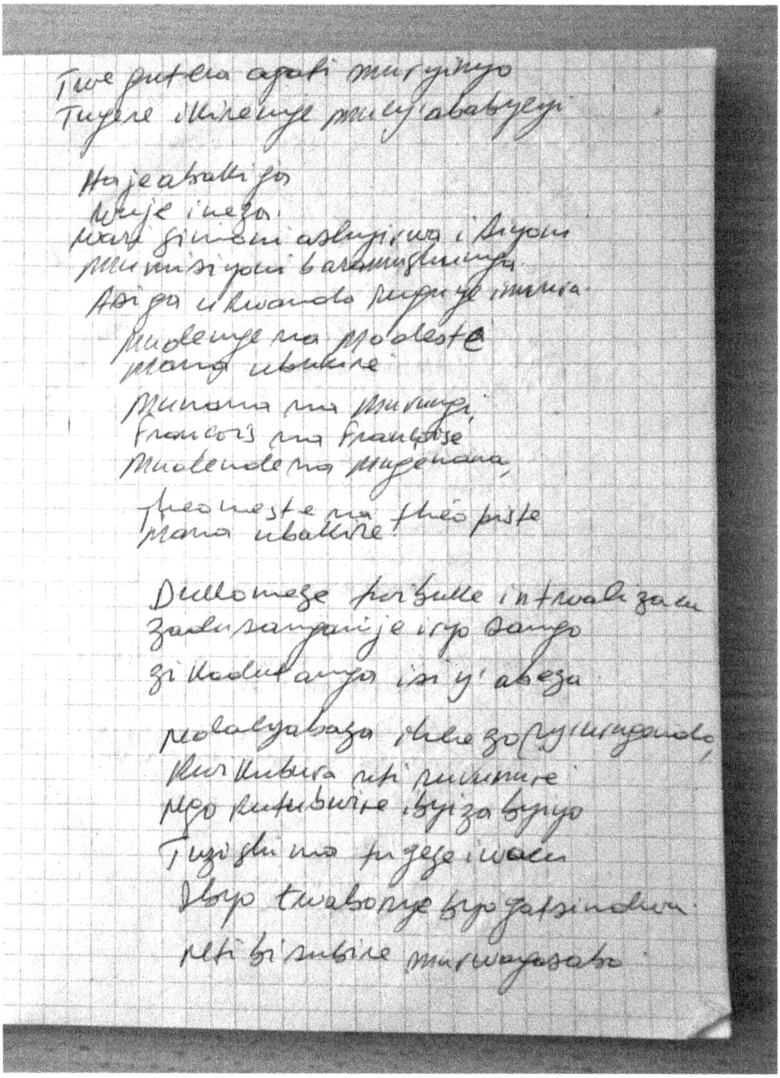

FIGURE 3. (*continued*)

CONFIDENTIEL   REF ....

DOCUMENTATION DES ENFANTS SÉPARÉS DE LEURS PARENTS

A: Biographie de l'enfant

Nom

Prénoms

Surnoms

Sexe   M   Nationalité *RWA*

D de N   Âge *≃ 2ans*

Lieu de naissance   —

Signes particuliers

2ans
Centre MASAKA
le 22-2-95

B:Situation Actuelle: (où l'enfant habite maintenAnt et si en transit, où va-t-il?)

1   centre des enfants *V*   en famille   seul   autre

2. Adresse   Préfecture *Kigali Nral*   Commune *Kanombe*

     Secteur *MASAKA*   Cellule *Binyogo*

3. Date d'arrivée de l'enfant *Avril* —

4. Lien avec la personne qui s'occupe de l'enfant *Centre d'accueil MASAKA*

5. L'enfant a-t-il des frères ou soeurs avec lui/elle?   oui   non *V*   (inscrire noms et âges)

6. Nom & adresse d'adultes et d'autres enfants en contact avec l'enfant et qui peuvent donner des informations sur la famille.

         personne

FIGURES 4 & 5. Example of an information form pertaining to "unaccompanied children," February 22, 1995. © Archives du Centre mémorial Gisimba (ACMG).

D: Histoire de la séparation

Dernier Adresse permanent _____ Situation Actuelle

Cherchez toutes les informations entre les deux

1. De qui l'enfant était separé?   2. Quand cela s'est-il passé?

3. Où cela s'est-il passé?   4. Où sont-ils allés?

5. Comment est ce que la séparation s'est passée?

Laissez l'enfant dire l'histoire de comment il s'est separé de ses parents/famille. Ecrivez ce qu'il dit.

L'enfant a été ramassé par un autre enfant, orphelin de 14 ans. Ce dernier a vu qu'il reste seul et a jugé bon de prendre cet enfant de 2 ans comme son petit-frère. Cet enfant qui tient soin de ce petit s'appelle NYARIMANA chantal. Donc l'histoire de séparation de l'enfant n'est pas connue

Y a t'il une personne que l'enfant voudrait rechercher particulierement?

Donnez le nom et adressse. _____

_____

Date de l'interview 21.2.95 Place de l'interview Centre MAJAKA

Nom de l'enqueteur K. Rosine Nom de l'organisation SCF (UK)

FIGURES 4 & 5. (continued)

FIGURE 6. Common burial pits in the Kabuga district (an eastern suburb of Kigali), discovered under homes in April 2018. The clothes seen hanging belonged to the victims. © Hélène Dumas, September 2018.

7

RESCUES

From a minuscule gesture of help to an actual rescue, sometimes collective, the specter of benevolent acts across the entire course of the genocide proves to be particularly broad. This fact warrants emphasis for at least two reasons. Contrary to the tenacious clichés presenting the extermination of the Tutsi as a vast "interethnic war" in which the Hutu and the Tutsi are reduced to the basics, in the form of two categories propelled by ethnic antagonism alone, the charitable acts offered to the victims attest to the simplistic nature of such a perception. They make visible the refusal of some to adhere to a *political* project structured around a racist vision that is not shared unanimously. Then, too, located in the margins of the event, acts of assistance and rescue reveal the constituents of the norm that prevailed during the genocide. To offer shelter or food, to quench someone's thirst, to extract an infant from among the corpses, to lie, is always to act *against*: against the order to exterminate, of course, but also against one's neighbors, even against one's own family. For the acts of rescue draw on the same relations as those of the massacre: neighborhood, religion, family. The accounts by the young writers and the rare studies devoted to the question of rescues suggest that the marginality of rescuing behaviors during the massacres also corresponds to forms of marginality on the social level. A sterile woman, a hirsute and misanthropic old man, residents versed in sorcery, believers adhering to minority spiritual movements: All these count among the "profiles" that contravene the norm, among the savior figures, too. This list is neither exhaustive nor definitive; indeed, other personalities could mobilize diverse resources, on the contrary, owing to their perfect institutional integration, and succeed in actions of rescue, as did, for example, some priests and nuns.[1]

At the heart of the children's stories, the relation of acts of rescue occupies an equally exceptional place. An effect of the source, no doubt, but reflecting nevertheless an effect of reality. Rare though they may be, where they appear in the texts they are transcribed with care.

When the massacres began in her sector of Shyanda (Kabarondo), one girl about eight years old initially saw Hutu and Tutsi neighbors unify against the "bandits" who were attacking their hillsides from Murama, a bordering sector belonging to the Rukira commune. The first assaults of the "bandits," who had taken the name Simba Battalion, were staved off, but resistance on the part of the populations quickly led the attackers to meet in an effort to clarify their intended targets. At that point, the girl became aware of the extermination order relayed by the local authorities via the neighbor in whose home she was hidden:

> They [the members of the Simba Battalion and the local Hutu populations] spent the night in a meeting that aimed to exterminate the Tutsi. They also decided that the Hutu had to separate themselves from the Tutsi. That night we fled and spent the night there, in the banana plantation, in a place called *mu gikombe* at our neighbor Niyi's house. In the middle of the night we went to Niyi's. When we got there, his wife prepared places for us to sleep, and we went to bed. But only the children went to bed. Toward sunrise, her husband arrived. We were lying in the living room, on a mat. When he came in, he said: "It smells like Tutsi blood in here." He came closer, and when he understood that it was us, he was ashamed, and then he told us that he had just come from a meeting that was preparing the killing of the Tutsi, and that no Hutu was authorized to hide Tutsi, and that if we were found in his home they were going to kill him. He went on to tell us to look for a place to hide other than in his house.[2]

The initial protective welcome did not hold up against the new injunctions or against the threats proffered toward those who might take the risk of hiding Tutsi. Driven out of her shelter, the little girl rejoined her family group wandering on the hillsides. A second neighbor then undertook to guide their flight:

> There was a man who was a friend of my maternal uncle who was called Valens. He was standing on the hill and informing us about the places

where the Interahamwe had arrived. In short, he was spying for us, and we fled. I remember that one Saturday, he stood up below our house and he said: "You people in Ruka's home [the name of the maternal grandfather who had raised him], the *igitero* has arrived in the place called *kuri muvandimwe*, and you're the first on the list of those who are being sought." We ran off and fled right away. We could hear the *induru* [war cries], the drums were speaking, whistles were being blown here and there. The day dawned and then night came.[3]

The help brought by this friend of the family delayed only by a few moments the murder of the girl's grandfather: He was decapitated by a man who boasted of having killed "Rwabugiri,"[4] in a clear reference to the despised monarchic past.

Help for those being persecuted takes a different form in another text, one by a male writer who was twelve years old at the time. After saying his final goodbyes to his parents—elderly and ill, they had refused to flee from their *rugo*—he found refuge in a Pentecostal church whose pastor had procured a bit of food and offered precious comfort:

We kept on going together and we arrived at the ADEPR temple [Association of the Pentecostal Churches of Rwanda] in Nyamirama [a commune of Kayonza]. This was still on Saturday, April 8, 1994. When we got there, we found a lot of other people who were hiding there. From that day until Wednesday, April 12, 1994 . . . during those three days that we spent in the temple—because we arrived there on Saturday—the day after that Saturday, Sunday, we expected that people would come in to pray but we didn't see them.

Sunday night and the next morning, we heard someone knocking on the window of the temple, and we were very frightened, believing that it was the people who were coming to kill us. The person who was knocking on the window called out to us and said: "Hey, you! Open up, it's me, Pastor Gapfizi." Then we opened up to him, it was around four o'clock in the morning, he wept and then he said to us: "How did I know that there were people in the temple? I had gone to bed Sunday night and I had dreams. In my dreams, I saw people lying down somewhere and I saw that they were starving. That is why I got up early to look into the temple. And here I've found you!" Since that day, he told us that outside, the situation was bad, but he added that he would use all possible means to bring us something to eat. That, truly, really, he did. He had a little bag in which he carried around his books, and inside it he put a dish full of food (rice). He brought us that food secretly so that people wouldn't notice (may God give him His blessing). You understand that he did that Monday night and early Tuesday morning. But those two times when he brought us food [*kugemura*][5] in the temple, the killers (the Hutu) were watching him. So on Tuesday, April 11, 1994, we spent the day in the temple, and that night the pastor didn't come back. We wondered about it, but we thought that the Interahamwe had caught him and prevented him from coming. Then we spent that night in the temple.[6]

The "disappearance" of the helpful pastor was a sign of the imminence of the massacre, which was carried out at dawn the following day, April 12.

A gift of food or medicinal herbs and a warning about the movements of the *ibitero* are associated again in the following description, from a text by another young man who was also twelve years old in 1994. In order to avoid revealing the presence of the refugees by going in and out multiple times (as was the case with the pastor in the previous account), one man and his protégés established strategies for concealing food:

On my side, when I returned there, to the sector [of Kaburemera, in the commune of Runyinya, Butare prefecture], I met the people with whom I shared the same problems who were not yet dead. They had been helped by a certain Hutu who lived on the other side of us and who was called Kabuke. He was an old man who had seen them together and had recognized them when he was watching his cows. He approached them, calmed them down, and gave them some indications about safety. He asked them to stay securely in hiding because the killers' plan was to no longer leave a single one of their people behind. He promised them to bring food without their having to do their own cooking. We stayed in hiding and went to seek food at that man's place, but getting there was a problem. We trusted him; he even gave us flour for porridge and medicines for wounds. . . . We pointed out to that Hutu man the hangar where we met in the evenings. If ever we didn't find a way to get to his place, he needed to send a child to that hangar to deposit the food there. From time to time, I was the one who brought the food in the dark.[7]

Nevertheless, one day the man was not able to give them root vegetables and cooked beans, as he customarily did:

> Bad luck had come for us. Once, when we went to seek food at the man's place, instead of giving us the usual food, they gave us raw things so that we would cook them ourselves (sweet potatoes, beans, flour for porridge, and penicillin). So we left with the food and matches to light the fire.[8]

Relaxing their vigilance, as the writer himself said, the boy and his companions in misery lit a fire in the middle of the night to prepare to cook: They were immediately located and attacked.

Other gestures of help, however fragile and fleeting, were always emphasized by the young writers. Thus one writer, a young woman born in 1974, recounts the rescue of a very young child who had been wounded and, unless cared for, was certain to die:

> My little sister and I kept on running and when Saturday came, in the evening, that was when a woman named Fevarie with whom we had had neighborly relations came to the house to cover up the Mamas and the others [who had just been assassinated]. And she found the small child who was still breathing. She covered Mama with a mat and other clothing that was scattered around the place where they had been killed. She took the child and ran, hiding him so that they wouldn't recognize him and wouldn't kill her along with the child. She took him to her house, and because his jaws had been smashed he was vomiting blood and he was bleeding through his nose and mouth. She continued to hide that child.[9]

In addition to helping the child, the woman performed another benevolent act with regard to the bodies of her murdered neighbors, covering them respectfully, while the common rule required, on the contrary, the systematic humiliation of the corpses.

Sometimes the attempt at protection consisted in developing a false genealogy in order to escape from the control facilitated by the social interconnections. In this way a woman encountered at an exit from the Akagera swamp gave detailed instructions to a girl about twelve years old so the child could explain to the killers she might meet why she was on the path:

> I went up and I met a woman I didn't know because I didn't know the place where I was. She asked me a lot of questions, but I didn't answer

her. She asked me where I was coming from, where I was going, and she asserted that I had just left the Akagera [swamp]. Then I finally said yes, that was true. She told me: "Don't say that you come from the Akagera, otherwise they'll make you go back there. One child called Ruti, son of Nta, they made him go back three times and the fourth time they killed him with a spear and he is dead. You must say that you are going to your older sister's place and that her child who was with us is dead." She went on to tell me that Papa was from now on a certain Samuel from Gasenyi. When we separated, on the path leading to my house, I met a young man; he had a sword. He asked me: "Where are you from?" I answered: "From Gasenyi," as the woman had recommended.[10]

This lie did not convince the killers, who nevertheless let the little girl go, replying: "Go on, you'll be killed by the others anyway." The child finally found refuge with another woman who agreed to hide her in the company of two nieces who had been seriously "cut" on their arms and faces. Given the advance of the FPR, whose approach made itself heard through the "noise of the bullets," the protective family prepared to flee to Tanzania. The care provided by the woman ended up being badly received by the rest of the family: "They started to say that they were going to kill us; they said that we were bad spirits, for they wondered how we had been able to survive."[11]

The motives guiding the search for a protective refuge obviously have to do with the nature of the relations that had been maintained between parents and neighbors. If the memory of former solidarity could lead toward compounds perceived as friendly, in other cases, the recollection of earlier violence paradoxically led the exhausted children's steps toward a household (*rugo*) whose head had been prominent in the looting and killing. Tired of the ceaseless running, ravaged by hunger and thirst, haunted by the sorrow of her loved ones' deaths, one nineteen- or twenty-year-old girl confessed her desire to "die quickly." It was in these terms that she advised the younger children in her charge: "Let's go see those people whom Papa said had exterminated people in 1990 and the others who ate our cows in 1973, those whom the Bicumbi town supervisor had asked to pour the pots of hot meat on their heads. Perhaps those people will kill us faster." She decided to go to the home of a man with a disturbing reputation, a neighbor who was a former looter. Her meticulous description of the appearance of the "head of the family" and of the miserable living conditions of that man and his wife provides a relatively nuanced portrait of those "benefactors":

> When we arrived, we went into his *rugo*, but what led us to go there is that he was known to be a very dirty person, who had a beard like the Muslims: in short, a person that everyone feared. When he saw us, he asked us where we were going, and we answered that we could go no farther because of hunger. We went on to ask: "If you would kill us and do it quickly because we've had enough running when we know that our only end is death." He answered at once: "God has cured me of killing, so come on in the house." We went in so he would do it [kill us] quickly, and we waited for death without finding it. And when his wife saw us, she cried a lot. She came into the house and she took millet and then she started to grind it rapidly to see if she could keep us [alive] before we died. When she finished, she put some water on the fire and then the flour. When the porridge was starting to be ready, scarcely hot, she served it to us, for she thought that by the time the porridge was entirely cooked we would already be dead. As she was very poor, she broke her gourds to make bowls. She poured the porridge into these makeshift bowls and served us. We drank, but we thought that in fact it was in order to kill us with full stomachs. We waited to die, but we didn't find death. We spent the night there. I was with my nursling [her baby brother]. We continued to talk with the woman, who asked us if there were, among our people, any people who were still alive. She sent someone there where there were people named Rug and Sim with their children: They were still alive. She brought them in, and they stayed with us there. She watched over us. But her oldest son went into the *ibitero* and he told us whom they had killed and whom they hadn't killed yet.[12]

The couple may have agreed about protecting children, going so far as to increase the number of their small protégés, but their son was crisscrossing the hills with the bands of killers. In a domestic space that appeared to be very poor, few hiding places were available: It was thus impossible for them to conceal the presence of the children. The haven was on the point of turning into a trap. The writer does not specify whether they were discovered by the Interahamwe as the result of an indiscretion or a denunciation by the son. The old man then tried to conceal his protégés among the fodder. And when an *igitero* burst into his *rugo* in search of Tutsi, he exclaimed to the killers: "If you're thinking of coming back here to look for Tutsi, you'll have to start by cutting me down!"[13] As soon as the old man left, when the FPR troops were on their way, the children he left behind were immediately threatened.

That *muzehe* (old man) thus acted *against* his son and *against* his neighbors, who did not hesitate to search his compound thoroughly. The success of his and his wife's rescue efforts seems to have been all the less certain given that there existed unbreachable solidarity among family members. The large diversity of behaviors can be seen even more clearly in another text written by a girl from the Rutonde commune. She had just survived a massacre carried out in a school when she desperately sought refuge in the surrounding *ingo*. One man gave her a curious piece of advice: She should seek asylum in the home of the "head of the *ibitero*," since his home was never searched. The girl and her companions in misery reached the killer's compound:

> Finally, A's wife [A was the head of the *ibitero*], called Muka, came out and she said nastily: "Get out! We don't need you!" And she was speaking loudly when she said to us: "People really have a lot of nerve!" Her mother-in-law, Marguerite, came out and met us on the path leading to the house, and she asked Muka: "Where do you want them to go?" (That old lady was the one who had chased us away when we were coming from Rutonde and they were very close friends *pe*!)[14]

Driven away from the *rugo*, the children set out again when they met Marguerite's daughter, Josépha, a sister of the *ibitero* leader. She manifested a very different attitude, despite her mother's warnings:

> We were on the path again and we met Marguerite's daughter, and she started to ask us: "Where are you going, so I can bring you some food?" Her mother, Marguerite, called out to her right then in a loud voice: "Josépha, you, Josépha! Come down, please, and let those children leave. Do you prefer to get killed along with them?" Her mother was calling in a loud voice with the intention of attracting those who were hunting the Tutsi. Then Marguerite's daughter told us to look for somewhere to hide in the bush and where she could bring us something to eat. She went running down, and she came back up bringing us something to eat in dried banana leaves. I didn't know what path she had taken to come back because, *in her home, her act was regarded with disapproval.* When she finished giving us the food, she left right away.[15]

At that point the children left the bush to take refuge with a woman who had already hidden them several times. The danger was still lurking, for there, too, the men of the house belonged to the *ibitero*:

> When that woman saw us, she was alone, for her husband and other killers had left with the *ibitero*. She brought us into the house quickly, and she gave us something to eat; she advised us to stay cloistered in the house, above all not to go outside. At nightfall, her husband came back with two of his brothers-in-law. They found us there but didn't say anything. We thought that, in the whole country, we were the only ones left. We lived in that place for almost three days, but we thought it was a whole year because of the bad life we were leading.[16]

When the FPR soldiers approached, the first family attempted to salvage their collective behavior, whereas one of its members—Josépha, Marguerite's daughter—had actually shown herself to be helpful:

> The old woman Marguerite sent her daughter Josépha and her son A., the very one who led the *igitero*, to make it known that the Inkotanyi [the FPR] had arrived and that a person who had hidden people would have nothing to fear from them. They told us that the family of Rwa [the one that was hiding the girl] was poor and had nothing to eat and no place to stay because they didn't have a house. They added that we had to leave Rwa's place and leave with her [Marguerite] because there were supplies there. They all had the intention of getting us to testify in their favor with the Inkotanyi so that their lives would be saved.[17]

No doubt the crudeness of the maneuver is commensurable with the crimes committed by the son, who is cited throughout the girl's narrative as one of the main leaders of the murderous gangs. The inexorable advance of the front in late April in Rutonde precipitated such attempts; the argument of material corruption was slipped in when Marguerite tried to attract the girl into her more prosperous compound.

One text warrants particular attention as a narrative of rescue: that of a girl recounting her "adoption" (as an eight- or nine-year-old) by the woman who had protected her until the massacres were over. The girl expresses her gratitude at the end of her testimony: "If you can publish this, include all the names that Papa and Mama gave me . . . and those given me by the relative who hid me during the war [the genocide]."[18] At the heart of this notebook we find descriptions of the atrocious deaths of the girl's parents and brothers alongside a detailed account of the series of helpful actions that allowed her to survive. Only through the thickness of the narrative can we grasp not only the extreme complexity of the situation but also the value that those actions took on in the eyes of the twenty-year-old survivor who was relating them twelve years after the fact.

After a few days, not "more than a week," the family, enlarged by the presence of paternal uncles, their spouses, and their children, was forced to leave its hiding places, as the killers had "started to kill during the day." The murder of a first neighbor from their sector of Gihara, located in the Runda commune on the border between the prefectures of Kigali and Gitarama, led the persecuted family to take refuge in the forest, where the father distributed the hiding places: "He led us into the forest and said: 'Separate yourselves. Let the adults take one space and the little ones another.' We children stayed with Mama and we hid together. Papa and my brothers went off separately."[19] We have no information about how long this period of hiding lasted; it was probably limited to a few days, but it was experienced as infinitely extended. The calendar days abolished by the experience of being hunted gave way to other temporal markers: first, the death of the father, pierced by sharpened sticks. The girl was a direct witness: "We were very close by, in the bush consisting of cypresses and other trees but *we saw very clearly and we also heard very clearly* what they were saying."[20] This visual and also auditory memory was soon followed by another murderous sequence:

> They left right away, they went up saying that they had just killed a great *inyenzi* [her father]. They said that his sons and his wife remained and that they were going to follow up with the others. So they went up, they left. The next morning, they came back into the forest, and this time they had brought dogs, and they said that the dogs were going to find the ones who were in the holes, and that way they wouldn't tire themselves out too much. They came with their dogs, they hunted with those dogs, and when the dogs came close to us they barked very loudly. And then they came and caught us.

The little group of women was rejoined by two brothers "from the same womb" and two other brothers from "[her] paternal uncle's house." They were all led "like cattle" to a latrine located in the compound of the godfather of the eldest in her family. The Interahamwe leader had ordered them, she said, to "get rid of the filth." Once again she witnessed a massacre, that of the four boys:

They brought all four, and I was the fifth. They took my oldest brother, they put a rope around his neck and hung him. He remained hanging and they struck him with machetes until he stopped breathing. We were standing, some behind others, in the line of people to be killed, and I was the last. My two brothers on my paternal uncle's side followed; one was named Nda. And the other Ruda. When they had finished dying, it was [a brother] who followed, but before they killed him he asked them: "Excuse me, can you tell me the cause of our death?" And they answered: "The cause is that you're Tutsi." And he said again: "Excuse me, I won't start being Tutsi again." They dragged him off, saying: "Bring yourself back!" He said to an Interahamwe named Ruta: "Ruta! Can you pardon me because I'm sick?" And Ruta replied: "Who takes pity on you?" And he stopped talking. With him, too, they put a rope around his neck and hanged him. I was watching; I saw everything that was happening with my own eyes. Every time they killed someone, they threw him into the latrine. He too was thrown into the latrine, before my eyes.

At the moment when the girl herself was seized by the killers, one of them said that it was not yet time to kill the girls and the women. Set free, she then rejoined her mother and two of her sisters, whom she informed of her brothers' deaths. At this point in the story, the writer relates the intervention of a first essential actor in the rescue, "a Hutu child whose godfather was my father." She confided in him the atrocities she had just witnessed and described his reaction in these terms: "I saw that young man [Kobizaba] cry and wipe his face with his hand. We went back to where my mother was and the young man told the story, he said to Mama and the others: 'It's over. I'm going to take this one (it was me) to hide her. If we're lucky, she'll live.'"

An initial precaution: The boy removes his protégée from the direct perimeter of the neighborhood so as to keep her from being connected with her "Tutsi" genealogy.[21] On the path leading to his *rugo*, where he thought he could keep her safe, he delivered a first lie to a man who had been responsible for murdering a girl from the family by striking her multiple times with a studded cudgel in the forest:

We continued on the path, and we met the man who had hit her on the head with the cudgel. He said hello to us, but I was trembling. He asked Kobizaba: "Who is that child whom I don't know?" And Kobizaba answered that I was his sister on the side of his paternal uncle. The other went on to ask: "What's going on? Why is she afraid of me?" Then Kobizaba answered that I lived in Kigali. That man came from the *ibitero* of Mubuyange, from a place called Mumugera. He [the man] took me by the arm and we went on our way. When we arrived at his house, he announced to me that we had just arrived at his house. And he said: "I'm the neighbor of the place where you're going [Kobizaba's]. You'll visit me." And I said yes. Then he said to Kobizaba: "But this child looks like a snake [*inzoka*] . . ." And Kobizaba replied: "Her maternal grandmother was Tutsi." The man acquiesced and at that moment we were already at Kobizaba's place. It was nighttime.

The proximity of the killer was not the only danger; the neighborhood extended its menacing shadow even within the boy's compound. And it was against the will of his own mother that he now had to ensure his protégée's safety:

But when we got there, his Mama told him to send me away so that her only cow wouldn't be taken from her. Then Kobizaba said to his mother: "Forgive me, but all her family members have been exterminated. Let her spend at least one night here. Tomorrow I'll take her somewhere else." But his Mama didn't accept that, and she went to round up the killers. The old woman went out to send someone to say that her son had brought in an *inyenzi* child. The person she sent went to give the message, and he also told them the time at which I would be in the house, in bed. The messenger came back and told us, he said to the boy Kobizaba, that the killers would come kill him along with me that night. They [the messenger and Kobizaba] went to hide me in a spot in the bush that they covered over with leaves. When the killers came, they claimed that another *igitero* had already come to take me away. They went back where they came from, but they remained suspicious all night, and they searched the whole house and the whole banana plantation as well as the little forest that was there. From where I was, I saw them with their flashlights. They swept everywhere. They didn't find me and said they would come back the next day.

The boy didn't wait for the first light of dawn to go look for his protégée, although she believed at that point that he was calling out in the dark *to turn her in*, after yielding to his mother's pressure. To prepare for the new trek he was getting ready to make, he disguised the girl: "I left with him, he gave me water to wash with, he also gave me a pair of his outgrown pants, and then he put a watch on my wrist and a hat on my head." Thus outfitted with these meager garments, the little girl no longer looked like a fugitive and could even pass for one of the boy's playmates. Still, more cautious than ever, the two children took side paths, avoiding at all costs the paved road, studded with "big blockades" where people who knew the girl would undoubtedly be found. The obsession remained the same: avoid social contacts. Then, at a point when they could no longer avoid the road, they had to develop a new ploy:

> We came very close to my house, and there were no more side paths. We had to go on the road. And there we ran into the blockade. There were people I knew; there was a man who was our neighbor called Mi, with another Uwi. Kobizaba went toward the barrier, he distracted them, and I went through. They didn't see anything, since they were busy telling what they had done. When I could see that I was far enough away from them, I took a side path and stopped a moment to wait for Kobizaba.

Despite their extreme vigilance, the children encountered a young neighbor who quickly started shouting *induru*! to signal the girl's presence. This time, the boy used bribery to put a stop to the racket. Then, passing in front of another neighbor's compound, the girl recognized one of the cows belonging to her family: "In that place there was a man and I saw on his property a cow tied up that had six scarifications on her forehead: You can understand very well that I could not fail to recognize her." Retraced on a map, their flight marks a major detour toward the north of the Gihara sector before going back down to the south toward the Ruyenzi sector: Between the two areas, the national highway connecting Kigali to Gitarama wended its way, studded with numerous daunting roadblocks.

The objective of that exhausting trek was to reach the home of a woman who had befriended the boy. Childless and married to a Zairian, she welcomed the boy in the absence of her husband, who was in Zaire. Here is the girl's account of the woman's very first recommendations:

The Mama took me in but warned me that she would say that I am Zairian because her husband was Zairian. And I agreed. They had hit me so that I didn't hear very well [she had been beaten by the men who had killed her brothers], and then it was hard for me to call her Mama. The lady asked me to change my names so that people wouldn't recognize me. And she called me Muja F.

In a country where patronymics are very rare,[22] this change of identity might appear curious. It was doubtless intended to mask the girl's origins more securely and reinforce her fictive kinship in this new refuge close to the main road and thus to barricades populated by "big Interahamwe."

No chronological precision is included in the text to indicate at what point the little girl found her mother again, having left her in their home region before following Kobizaba. Without a guide to follow the "side paths," the girl seems to have gone straight down that very dangerous highway. Reading the description of the mother's state, one understands that the girl had trouble repressing her sobs, though they would risk alerting the killers:

> My mother, too, left the place where I had left her. The way she left that place, it was very bad. They had looted her clothes, she was left with only a little pair of panties and a bra. I saw her with my own eyes, I wept, and when I wanted to approach her they refused. At that moment, the Hutu women and men were making fun of her, saying: "Ah, see what the figures of Tutsi women look like!" One man among all those I didn't know slapped my mother violently. She seemed to lose her mind. When he struck her, I saw it and I was frozen, but he struck her as though he didn't want to kill her right away. But she lost her mind. At that point it started to rain; they dragged my mother away and tossed her into the gutter. The water kept falling on her body. She spent the day and the night in there. The day before, in the evening, we had already gone to see her, the lady and I, so she would know I was still alive. She was with her baby. A soldier had slapped the baby, and my mother watched him cry without comforting him, without the will to quiet him.

In the morning, the little girl rushed toward her mother, still lying in the gutter, even interceding for her with one of the soldiers. An intervention like that immediately awakened suspicions, and the woman who was hiding her had to calm them with lies:

The lady was in the house, and when she found me again she saw me speaking for my mother to the soldiers. When she arrived, the soldiers began to ask me if she was really my mother. The lady arrived, took me by the arm, and drew me back. The soldiers then took the lady and asked her: "This child has just told us that she isn't yours." And Mukarubuga answered at once that I was her only child. The lady led me immediately back into the house and she went back, she found the soldiers and went into a long explanation with them.

Shortly after the long discussion with the militia men and the soldiers, the child, inseparable from her mother, mingled in with the crowd of onlookers heading off to witness her murder near the Nyabarongo River. This time her protector accompanied her. Here is the story of the *spectacle* with which she was confronted:

So an Interahamwe man whose name I didn't know said: "This woman is a filthy *inyenzi*," and he went on to say that they had taken photos of Papa and Mama practicing how to kill with a knife. . . . The boy called Mi also confirmed that he had seen those photos and added that she should be thrown in the river but that she should be finished off at once. . . . They took my mother down. The lady and I accompanied her. We arrived at another barricade, on the road, very close to the Nyabarongo. They made her sit down there, and a boy said: "Give me that *inyenzi* so I can kill her." The others answered: "We don't want her to die right away." And the boy said: "That too is something I can handle." The boy took her and kept her face in his hands so she looked him straight in the eyes. They looked at each other. And the boy said that those eyes should be taken out. He took her, took the knife he was carrying and stuck it in one of her eyes and the eye fell; he pulled it out. It was at this point that Mama cried out in pain. And they all spoke at the same time: "Take out the other one too!" And he took out the other eye while the other people held my mother. They let her go and right then she lost her mind, she lost her mind, she lost her mind. You understand, Mama lost her mind. They killed her cruelly. I cried so hard that the lady put her skirt over my mouth and brought me back where we lived. I was sick for days and days because of what I had seen.

A narrative gap separates this unbearable story from the description of the departure for Zaire, when the FPR was approaching. However, with her plan for leaving Rwanda the child's "second mother" was unknowingly prolonging the threat considerably. At every manifestation of danger on the long trajectory of the collective flight, they maintained the mother–daughter fiction. "My father is Zairian and my mother is that lady over there," was the girl's reply to the skeptical questions that were invariably asked at every barricade along the road leading toward Gisenyi and then Goma. In the chaos of the exodus of nearly 1.5 million people,[23] the woman maintained her protection, as attested by one gesture in particular:

> This good person I was with took her wrap skirt, put it around her waist, and then added another, attaching me to her belly with it so we wouldn't be separated and I wouldn't fall into the lake. And then we crossed the border and we went to Congo.

After finding her husband, the woman wanted to see her own mother, a refugee in one of the huge camps surrounding Goma. There the girl found some of her killer neighbors. "Even if I had changed my names, that didn't prevent all of them from recognizing me, and they hunted for me so relentlessly that every night I slept in a different place." In November 1996, APR troops attacked the refugee camps, which had effectively become fallback bases for the genocidal forces.[24] The woman, her new companion, and the little girl then plunged into the impenetrable Zairian forest. Lost, exhausted, parched, and starving, the group was beset by tension, and the woman's partner unloaded his anger on the child, while the adoptive "Mama," for her part, maintained her inviolable attachment to the girl:

> The man said: "Where we are now, it's everyone for their own family." He went on: "Let the husband take his wife, let children take their parents." He immediately said: "I'm taking my wife." Then the woman asked him: "What do you mean by that? That I should abandon *my* child?" And the man answered: "Is it you that brought her into the world?" The woman answered: "Thanks, but instead of abandoning this child, I'll let you go and we'll meet again when God wills it." The woman purchased the path of my survival because the man said: "I could have killed you so you would rejoin your people! What's more, what are you fleeing from, you filthy *inyenzi!*" I answered him that I was no longer *inyenzi.* . . . Then the woman told me to calm down, saying that she would not abandon me. We went to bed, and at dawn the woman got up and said

to her husband: "The only member of my family that I see is her. You, goodbye."[25]

This definitive break preceded the return to Rwanda, where once again the woman had to ward off threats against the girl.

> "What kind of question are you asking her when *her mother* is here? Why didn't you ask me what you wanted?" They let me go and we got back in the bus. They said what they had to say to one other, and when they came back, she brought me a Fanta, which I drank on the road.[26]

The thread of their connection broke in December 1996, when they got back to Rwanda, where the girl found a maternal aunt and uncle who took her in. Countless conflicts weighed upon the family relationships, however, and the girl decided to live with her maternal great-aunt, an old woman to whom she was attached by daughterly affection. But the years that had passed, those of an exhausting life, did not diminish the memory of her protector: The very first "wish" that she expressed to Avega, in concluding her notebook, was formulated in the following terms:

> So my wish, I beg you, help me visit that lady who hid me, who took me abroad, who brought me back to life. Since 1996 I haven't been able to visit her because I haven't had the means to do so.

PART THREE

The Life of an Orphan Has No End

Ubupfubyi ntibushira

8

"WE WENT BACK TO OUR RUINS"

The final sections of the texts recount "life after the genocide": It would be pointless, here, to hope for a heroic fresco of "resilience." Drafted in April 2006, the notebooks include invaluable testimony on the subjective experiences of survival by writers henceforth orphaned. The available statistics on the number of victims and survivors make clear the central place of children in the genocidal process: The youngest, on the same basis as their parents, were removed from the common world of humanity and taxed with animalizing nicknames such as "little snakes" (*utwinzoka*) or "snake eggs" (*amagi y'inzoka*). Thus it is hardly surprising to observe a massive presence of children among the victims—according to some reports, even a majority.[1] Children were found in huge numbers in the common graves exhumed for medical and legal purposes. Of nearly five hundred bodies examined, 66 percent were those of women and children under the age of fifteen; one-fourth of the victims were less than ten years old.[2] Conversely, the demographic structure of Rwandan society, marked by its youth, explains why children under age fifteen formed nearly 38 percent of the surviving population, and more than 50 percent if we include those between ages fifteen and twenty.[3] Finally, the radical destruction of families is evidenced by the very significant proportion of orphans who had lost both father and mother.

The immense family losses were compounded by total material devastation: The properties belonging to the Tutsi had also been erased from the landscape of the hills and the neighborhoods. In the case of one boy who had escaped at age twelve with two siblings, in a family that initially had nine members, the attacks on property were interpreted as an essential element of the extermination enterprise:

At the time when they killed Papa and Mama, their brothers and sisters along with their friends, they were not content to kill the people while leaving their property alone: They ate the cattle, they looted the harvests, they laid waste to the bananas and the other crops, they ravaged them. All that so that, if one survivor remained, he would die of hunger, of isolation, of the lack of a place to live, because the houses too had been destroyed, they were taken down to the ground.[4]

Similarly, at the end of her text, one girl cast a retrospective gaze tinged with irony on the destruction of property:

What astonished me is that they drove us away from our property, and I thought they were going to give it back to us. But as they are not very intelligent, they did not restore our possessions but destroyed them. They thought they were wiping out the name of the Tutsi. And what delights me is that even if they are now only ruins, these ruins are the traces of the Tutsi.[5]

Through these lines and so many others like them, we discover a landscape of devastation. Nothing remains of the familiar spaces; the hills are literally "overturned," as we learn from another boy, also twelve years old at the time. The only survivor of a family of eleven, he concludes his narrative of the "time of the genocide" in these terms: "Today I am alone, I am nothing but a single grain [*ndi imbuto rukumbi*]. . . . I have survived in our Rwanda."[6] To express this feeling of disconnection from the places "from before," several writers chose especially gripping terms. The first boy cited earlier describes the cradle of his childhood in these terms: "We came back to what was *once upon a time* our home [*Taragaruka* ahahoze ari iwacu*]."[7] The use of a temporal marker referring to a remote, irretrievable past is also a feature of some lines devoted to family losses in the text of one girl born in 1985: "Formerly [*kera*], we had an extended family; more than three hundred people with whom I had kinship ties died. When I look at my family, we were a real family, *pe*!"[8] Two factors seem to shed light on the link between the count of repeated losses and the material devastations. In Kinyarwanda, terms such as *iwacu* conflate a familial entity with a spatial entity. A variety of expressions used by the writers at this point in their testimony underlines the total abolition of the "world of yesterday."

More concrete descriptions of the upheaval affecting the totality of the spatial context punctuate the texts when the writers related their treks in search of food and water after they had been regrouped in displaced persons' camps. The first vision reported here deals with the invading presence of the corpses. Three girls who were eight or nine years old at the time remark on the state of streams and ponds:

> Life after the genocide was very bad. It was very different from the life before, which was better. It was hard for me to live in the damp. There was only bad food: corn paste, corn, and the water was dirty because they had thrown bodies in it. In the water there were many filthy things like hair, human fat, fingernails. So you find life very bad because of the diseases, because of the diseases produced by the life we were living.[9]

> They put us in another camp, at a place called mu Kizungu, and we lived there. We went to draw water from the pond in that place, which is called Kadirimba, a place full of corpses. I pushed the corpses aside and I drew water, and that was the water we drank and that we used for cooking. We continued to live like that. We had no clothes to wear. We lived that way.[10]

> Finding water was just as hard. Where I went to draw water, I had to push away the corpses that were floating. The water was full of human fat and hair. When I arrived in the camp I was very sick, and I kept on with that bad life.[11]

When the security conditions made it possible for the refugees to disperse, the writers described their return to the hills in quest of shelter: Here, too, bodies infiltrated the living spaces, as one young woman, a fifteen-year-old in 1994, reported in striking terms:

> When we thought we had a house, we found dead bodies, and we weren't able to remove them. At one point, because I had lost my sense of smell, I dragged them out with hoes, and when the bodies were outside, I didn't find anyplace to put them, so the horrible odor spread throughout the city. An *umukada* [a member of the FPR in charge of mobilization] came, he found us another house, and he arranged to bury the bodies I had taken out of the house. When we left that house, we lived in several places abandoned by their refugee owners [Hutu refugees in Tanzania].[12]

The landscapes that had been definitively disrupted by the massacres were now traversed by new figures: those of FPR soldiers, the Inkotanyi. One can understand why they were described in positive and complimentary terms by the children, who saw, with their arrival, the end of the murderous hunt: "They took away corpses for us": Statements like this punctuate most of the narratives, at the heart of which the writers described themselves as immersed in the depths of a common burial pit or blocked by piles of bodies, they themselves too seriously wounded to move. Thus the rare survivors of the massacre in the Kiziguro parish on April 11, 1994, were pulled out of a well nearly eighty feet deep; they had been tossed there after they had been forced by the killers to pile up hundreds of victims at the site.[13] One text written by a young man, a twenty-year-old at the time who had been in that handful of escapees, describes in detail the conditions under which he was extracted from the pit by FPR soldiers:

> We lived there and we were able to get out of that pit thanks to the Inkotanyi. The Inkotanyi and the Tutsi who were fleeing from Bicumbi, Gikoro, and Muhazi [communes neighboring Murambi] got us out of the pit by using ropes. They wove the ropes together before dropping them into the pit, we wrapped them around our waists, and the person who was above the pit pulled on the ropes the way one milks a cow. They continued that way to the eighth person. This last one, when she reached the edge of the pit the rope gave way; the person fell back into the pit, landing on the little hoe we had. She broke her back, she died afterward because she did not get good care. There were eleven of us who got out: Four died, seven survived, but they aren't living well. Example: They have endless illnesses, constant infirmities; in short, this is how things happened during the genocide.[14]

This almost clinical picture of one rescue operation was not accompanied by a general defense of the FPR. On the contrary, the lines that follow are far removed from any exaltation of heroism:

> Life after the genocide, what I can say about it is that I never laughed again; I became mute because I did not have a good life; I suffered from back pain and chest pain; I had heart problems; I lost my parents, whereas I needed to be trained like other children; I lost brothers and sisters, neighbors, friends, peers [*urungano*: people of the same age], classmates; I lost my patrimony and a lot of other things besides.[15]

In the vast majority of the notebooks, however, the young writers described the care received from the soldiers, who calmed them down; washed, fed, and clothed them; and bandaged their wounds. Powerful affective bonds sometimes linked the young escapees with particular FPR officers; these children became "orphans for the second time" when the officers were later killed in the fighting.[16] As a general rule, the return to humanity came by way of attention to the body, as the following excerpt attests (the text is by a girl who was about twelve at the time, but there are many similar statements):

> We left with those soldiers and went to the company store in Kibungo. There were lots of dead bodies and blood was still flowing. We stayed with the soldiers, they spoiled us. *They removed our lice and our fleas and we became human again. They gave us clothes because we no longer had any, they cared about us very much.* But we had to separate, and we went to an orphanage in Gahini. There, life was hard.[17]

While we still lack enough information to be able to describe with certainty the health measures mobilized by the FPR to look after the thousands of wounded people found over the course of its advance, the texts suggest that those measures were quite rudimentary. This is suggested by another young girl, about ten years old at the time, in the following excerpt:

> I left and went to an empty house; a soldier found me there and said to me: "Follow me out of here." We left, and when we reached the front of the house I saw the child who was just below me in age: They had just cut him on his head; they had cut his nose in two; they had cut off both ears. Since he wasn't dead yet, the soldier took him in his arms and carried him to the hospital in Kabgayi. He left him with me and he left without turning around [*arigendera*; this can also mean "to leave with regret," for he had been called back by his military duties]. The child deteriorated with me because he never had any medicine. I said to that child: "Follow me, come on, let's go." We went into a house we saw nearby to ask for water to drink. They told us to stay there, they heated water; they washed him, massaged his head. Then he began to recover some strength. Afterward, they placed us in the orphanage in the Kabgayi orphanage headed by Fred Nkunda.[18]

The children transferred to the Gahini health center also wrote about these hospitals bereft of everything, as in the following text by a girl aged nine in 1994:

As for me, a soldier carried me to Gahini. Then, along the way, he gave me to others before picking me up again and taking me to Gahini. They put me in the hospital with the others; they were all wounded. I continued to be in very bad shape. My remaining teeth were starting to rot, and I lost them. My swollen head had not gone down to normal size, and my legs couldn't touch the ground. I had been hit by many exploding grenades. In the places where the shards entered, water and blood were starting to come out along with the shards. But those that remained were much more numerous, and even today some are still coming out.[19]

Thanks to the care they provided, the Inkotanyi won the trust of the surviving children, although that trust was far from definitive. Many writers confessed the fear inspired by those unknown soldiers from far away, who had been depicted by extremist propaganda in animalistic terms. An excerpt from the text of a boy who was barely seven years old at the time renders the sensitivity of the youngest refugees to the terrifying portraits of the FPR in striking terms:

> After a few days, we learned that the Inkotanyi had arrived, but they were said to have *dangling ears*. . . . When I saw them, I was frightened and I thought that they were all Interahamwe. Since they had neither tails nor dangling ears I didn't recognize them. After three weeks [probably only a few days, in reality], we saw a vehicle transporting the Inkotanyi, who were looking for people in their hiding places in order to reassure them and move them. I went out hesitantly, I was walking slowly and they saw me. They called me over, saying: "Come on, don't be afraid." They brought me over, they reassured me along with my companions in misfortune. *They explained to me that they had neither dangling ears nor tails.* They told us that since we were with them, we would not run into any other problems.[20]

Older (about twelve) and thus less susceptible to being taken in by animalizing fables, one girl nevertheless confided her fear of the FPR, which was based on images distilled by the war propaganda:

> When the Inkotanyi arrived, we were still in the bush. You have to understand, no one knew the Inkotanyi. And because I was the oldest [child] of the second wife [of her father] and because I was the one with some intelligence. . . . But I didn't know what the Inkotanyi were. I remember

when I was in primary school, we were told that they were little insects [*udukoko*] that have tails. We didn't even know that they were coming to save those who were being killed. We kept on fleeing with the Hutu, and we went together into the bush. And that was when they observed that we were still living and they wanted to kill us.[21]

A third narrative features similarly terrifying visions of the FPR soldiers, attesting to the invasive presence of a war culture to which the children, it seems, were particularly exposed:

I was a child [an eleven-year-old girl], and they told me that the Inkotanyi had dangling ears and tails. I didn't think they were humans; I thought they were pigs, and I was very afraid of pigs. Then we started to run away.[22]

In this case, as in the previous one, the internalization of a system of representations mingling bestial characteristics with evil intentions prolonged the sense of living under a threat, delaying definitive rescues.

Other writers experienced the extension of the time of the genocide quite concretely, when they found themselves prisoners of the Hutu populations in their exodus toward Zaire, in Tanzania, or in the displaced persons camps of Kibeho. As we have seen, affective attachments and the desire for protectors led some children to cross the border into Zaire in the company of benevolent adults. But other motives, the opposite of helpful intentions, led some families to bring girls with them into exile in order to exploit them as domestic slaves. Still other children, lost and on their own, sometimes followed a crowd on the move and ended up becoming prisoners inside the refugee camps.

It is first in Burundi that we follow the exhausted steps of a little girl, seven years old at the time. Originally from the commune of Runyinya (Butare prefecture), first she reached the Cyahinda parish, located further south, in the neighboring locality of Nyakuzu. On April 15, the thousands of refugees faced repeated assaults and then a more extensive attack coordinated this time by the police.[23] The few survivors, hidden under the corpses, decided to join together to escape the *ibitero* who were coming back mercilessly to finish off those who were dying. They went back up toward the north in the hope of finding a refuge in another church. There too, they were told: "The people are done for." Clearly distraught, the little group got lost, passing by Gishamvu again before going back further south, to

Nyakizu, where they were exposed to the intimidating asphalt road leading to the border with Burundi. At that moment and in that particular place, the straggling column lost many of its members:

> On both sides of the road, there were killers, those who had machetes, bows, clubs, pruning knives, and other things as well; there were even soldiers. Whether they were behind us or along the sides, there were killers. And when we were walking, they killed those who were within reach. Sometimes they killed your companion in flight right beside you, and you remained. A parent carrying a child on his back, they fired on the child and the parent remained, and kept walking down the road with the dead child on his back. Sometimes the parents realized that they were carrying a dead child and they brought the corpse down carefully from their back because they themselves were dead. And you went on and when you got a little further ahead, they fired on a woman who was carrying an infant on her back. The Interahamwe finished off those who were not quite dead. They kept on walking, they were cutting us.[24]

When they reached a point a few meters from the Akanyaru, the river that constituted the border, the little girl and her companions in misfortune were attacked again. She finally managed to escape from the killers and reach Burundi.

The Burundian authorities then put the escapees in makeshift camps. As evoked by the same little girl, the conditions of life there were terrifying:

> In the morning, they brought us *sheetings* [tarps provided by NGOs], cooking pots, and blankets. They gave us corn and beans, but the people remained in bad shape because they were seriously wounded. Even in Burundi the bad life continued, children died, adults died because of hunger and what they had been through. They fed us with corn that was half raw, and those people who had been beaten or had gunshot wounds continued to die. And we kept on going in our *sheetings*. Every day, people got sicknesses caused by the bad living conditions and the place where we lived. Severe dysentery took many people from us.
>
> We arrived in Burundi in May, we kept on living in those bad conditions. The refugees' life was not good. But we heard people say that the Inkotanyi, the children of Rwanda, were looking for a way to get us back into our country, Rwanda. But I didn't want us to go back there because

I thought that the people who had killed us were still there and that they could still kill us. And this time not a single one would remain. But at the same time, my other heart was telling me that, maybe, if we went back, we would escape from this bad life in Burundi and that, maybe, we would find some brothers and sisters as well as our parents, especially those we hadn't seen die. I thought that I had been separated from mine at the moment we were being shot at in Cyahinda. I had hope that they were not dead and that we would find one another. I thought they might have found a hiding place and that, maybe, they had survived. We kept on living that life until July, and that is when they said that we were going to go back to Rwanda because the war had come to an end.[25]

The narrative continues, still tinged with the ambivalent recommendations of the writer's "two hearts," the first advising her to stay in Burundi to escape a terror that was locked into her soul, the second urging her to go back, in the hope of finding a relative alive:

At a certain point in time they came and told us to get into some cars, saying: "We're going back to Rwanda. Peace has returned." I didn't believe it; I thought they were going to kill us again, and I saw that it was a new way of getting us together so that we would all be finished off for good. I thought that if a Burundian ever agreed to keep me so as not to return to Rwanda it would be better. I preferred to stay and become Burundian because, always, I thought they would kill us again, that we would no longer find the means to come back to Burundi, and that the Burundians wouldn't accept us a second time.

The car brought us to the customs house and they said: "Leave on foot and go back home." Then I remembered what it was like on the road and how they killed us there, how the Interahamwe pursued us. I thought they were going to kill us again and that we wouldn't make it to where we were supposed to go. I saw soldiers who didn't look like the ones from Burundi, and I believed they were going to kill us. Moreover, I told my traveling companions: "Here are the killer soldiers, they're still there and they're going to kill us again." But they reassured me, saying: "Those ones don't kill, they're the Inkotanyi." But I thought they were lying. I heard the soldiers talking to us in gentle tones, and I thought it was a trick to bring us back together and kill us without leaving anybody behind. We continued on our way, on the road from Burundi toward the city of

Butare. Along the way, my feet got swollen from walking on the tarmac broiling in the sun. We spent nights in the forests, but the Inkotanyi protected us. But I thought they were going to take advantage of our sleeping to kill us, that we were going to be finished and that that was exactly what they wanted. Afterward, I saw that they cared about us; they were taking care of us. When we got to Rango (in the city of Butare), I saw that there were other people, and I began to understand that the Inkotanyi were going to protect us, that nothing bad could happen to us from now on. . . . Then we returned to the place where we were born. And when we got there, we saw that there was nothing left but bush and ruins, that everything was done for, so that you couldn't recognize the place.[26]

Once again, the text makes clear how very hard it was for the child to trust the soldiers she encountered, despite the difference in their uniforms and the reassuring comments of the adults accompanying her. Once back in "her" ruins, the little girl found no parents; she thus became "mother" to two of her young siblings. From a family of seven members, only three children survived.

By the time the girl returned to Rwanda in July 1994, the FPR had gradually taken control over the country as a whole: Kigali fell on July 4, and a transition government was put in place on July 19. Although as of July 4 the French soldiers with the Opération Turquoise had established a "secure humanitarian zone,"[27] part of the territory nevertheless remained out of the FPR's control for several more weeks. The region was "secure" especially for the killers, the leaders of the criminal government, and the extremist officers of the FAR. The handful of texts written by the children caught in the nets of the internal displaced persons camps in the Gikongoro prefecture attest to the ongoing threats to their lives.

The lot of one escapee from the huge massacres carried out in the Rukumberi sector (Sake commune), a second girl, twelve years old at the time, was to remain a prisoner of the fleeing crowd and cross through the Turquoise zone. Like many other young Tutsi girls, she owed her survival to her exploitation as a domestic slave. She reported the following words of the killers, pronounced at the very moment she had been flushed out, with others:

When you kill the children, be careful, because Hutu children have been mixed in helter-skelter with the Tutsi children. The girl children, take them with you and use them as servants. Since their brothers will soon be done for, they will be married to Hutu men.[28]

It seems that the girl was initially treated as a servant in a first *rugo* before leaving with "her" Hutu—as she herself put it—for Butare. Here is how she described setting out on an interminable trek punctuated with intimidating blockades:

Frankly, I had no more heart. I didn't know where I was. I was tortured by hunger because they used the same machetes to kill the Tutsi and to kill the cows to be eaten (the Tutsi's cows). The Hutu came to ogle us; they said they were coming to look for a Tutsi girl. When the time came I fled with the Hutu. All along the way, the Hutu killed women and girls especially, because the men were already dead. At the barricade, you had to show five people who knew you, especially when you didn't have an ID card. And if you didn't have those five people, you died.[29]

The inquisitorial interrogations were repeated at each barricade. One neighbor, whom the girl had come across in the mob, insisted on contradicting each of the lies the girl had concocted in responding to the killers, who were unfamiliar with her region of origin and thus had no way of verifying her status as "Hutu" or "Tutsi." The girl went into detail in describing such interactions, which blended suspicion on the part of the questioners and canny evasiveness on the child's part.

We kept on following the path and when we arrived at the blockade (that man was called Ep, the entrance to his *rugo* was just across from ours)[30] . . . Ep told the people who were holding the barricade: "Kill this child for us, because she's a Tutsi." The Hutu at the barricade replied: "She's from what region?" He answered them: "She's from Rukumberi at Kibungo." Then the Hutu at the barricade responded: "A Tutsi girl who has left Rukumberi and who has arrived here, it's not for us, people from Butare, to kill her. We're full to the brim of Tutsi blood! Go on with her, you who have brought her." Ep went on to say: "Lend us a machete, we'll kill her ourselves." The people at the barricade replied: "Our tools too are full up with Tutsi blood." As for me, I was already dead. The only word I repeated was this: "He's lying, I'm not Tutsi." They searched me, I don't know if they were trying to find out whether I was carrying a weapon, for I was young, I was only twelve years old. Ep, to show that he knew me, kept going by asking his own child: "She's from whose house?" And the child replied: "From Ruta's." Those wild beasts at the barricade asked me: "Do you hear that? What they're saying is true! Even the little child knows you!" Then I said to them: "Listen, I'm going to tell you the truth." (I was lying). "Mama was Tutsi but Papa was Hutu. Papa died a long time ago. That man killed my mother, so now he wants to kill me because he's afraid that when the Inkotanyi come I'll go tell them that he killed their sister." Then the people at the barricade said to me: "Oh, that's why?" And I answered: "Yes, just for that!" They said to Ep: "Take your person away, get her out of our sight!" We kept on going; they insulted me, and when we came across people, he told them constantly that I was a Tutsi; they slapped me and I saw fire sparkling [the equivalent of "I saw stars" after a blow to the head].[31]

Finally freed from grasp of that neighbor, the girl proceeded along the path from Butare to Gikongoro. Hidden in the "countryside" and carefully concealing her identity, she survived for nearly two years in a hostile environment, convinced that she was the sole Tutsi survivor in the country, as she herself explains:

We kept on going and we went with their families until Gikongoro. But I was still afraid; I thought that I would meet a (Hutu) person there who knew me and would kill me. The clothes I had were just dirty rags, and the lice were about to kill me. We were in the commune of Mudasomwa, in Gikongoro, in the Hutu camp located there. They kept on killing Tutsi women and children. As for me, I went to hide in the countryside. I didn't want them to discover that I was a Tutsi girl, and in the country nobody knew me.

In short, for me the genocide continued because in Gikongoro my life was very bad, terrifying. My work consisted in gathering wood for cooking at the tea factory in Kitabi and taking it to the Gasarenda market. That's where I sold it to buy food. That's how I fed myself. I kept on living in that place, I couldn't imagine that there was a single living Tutsi in Rwanda. To say that the Inkotanyi arrived in Rwanda, in Gikongoro, in any case I didn't see them. Where I was, I told myself that no one could help me because I was convinced that my parents were dead. I didn't imagine being able to make the trek in the reverse direction, the one I'd made on foot. For me, the genocide ended when I gave my photo to the

Red Cross, when I said where I had come from, and they went to see if there were any survivors. It was in 1996 that they told me that Papa and my next younger brother had survived. The Red Cross then turned me over to Papa.[32]

The terrible odyssey of that child, who had remained for a long time in very real danger because of the proximity of the internal displaced persons camps, was not unique. Other little girls were retained as hostages in the families of killers beyond Rwanda's borders, especially in Zaire. One girl who was six years old in 1994 found herself pulled out of the Kanzenze swamp to become the household slave of a family that took her with them in their flight. The description of the circumstances of their departure evokes a universe of ill will and menace:

> After several days, the Inkotanyi liberated the place. We fled immediately. They told me that I was going to live through a second war [a second genocide]. They made me carry pots and pans and plates. To be truthful, I didn't manage to carry them, but I did my best. Along the way, I thought about my parents, about how they had killed them and where they had killed them. We were fleeing toward Congo on foot. They directed me with a stick, like a cow. When I tried to walk on the side to escape the crowd, they hit me on the back with sticks. My back was ruined. We didn't eat often, and I shared the food with their children. I didn't know how to eat quickly, and when they put the food on the platter, the others took it and filled their clothing with it. I was truly going to die of hunger. My feet were swollen.[33]

The writer went into detail about the terrifying conditions of her domestic slavery and the racist mockery with which she was assailed once they had crossed the border:

> When we arrived in Congo, I led a miserable life. They treated me badly, and I didn't live like the other children. They made me work very hard; I did jobs that weren't appropriate for my age. I was actually very young. I learned to light a fire, which I hadn't known how to do before. I had become their servant. I cooked, even though I had never learned how and I didn't manage very well. They beat me. I went to get water with a big fifteen-liter can, and it often fell to the ground because I couldn't carry it. They said: "That's normal, since the Tutsi don't have any strength." They

said constantly: "Look how that filthy little Tutsi girl works." I never had the right to play with the other children; they had forbidden them to play with me. I was always alone. They had said that if they saw me laughing they would pull out my teeth. They constantly reminded me that I no longer had anyone to smile at. What really hurt was when they wanted to make me suffer and would ask me: "Do you know where your family is?"[34]

The writer confessed that, under the weight of the insults and the taxing work, as a six-year-old girl she wanted to put an end to her life:

> They began to make me truly suffer, to cause me pain, so much so that at one point I thought about suicide. There was a lake quite close to where we were, and I went there to drown myself. When I was on the verge of throwing myself into the water, a person came up and said: "Why do you want to drown yourself in the lake?" And I replied: "It's because of the suffering." But I didn't want to tell him about my life. He said to me: "Suicide is a bad thing." He also said that if I killed myself I would burn in the fires of hell. So I gave up and returned to that family, where they continued to persecute me. I prayed to God that a new war would start so I could go back home to Rwanda. I knew that I was the only one who remained from our whole family, that I was an orphan. God heard my prayers and sent war. I remember that it was in 1996. The Inkotanyi came to Congo.[35]

In the face of the APR troops' attack against the refugee camps in Zaire in November 1996, the family went deeper into the Congolese forest. In that environment supplies quickly became scarce, and the rigor of the trek quickly exhausted the strength of the very young child. Disoriented, crushed by exhaustion, starving and tormented by thirst, she retained a particularly vivid memory of her hallucinatory wanderings in the immense green forests of Zaire:

> We took the path into the forest. We left. The food I was carrying on my head had been eaten and hunger was beginning to kill us. We were walking in the forest and we had the feeling of going around in circles without getting anywhere. I was dying of hunger and thirst because there wasn't anywhere to find water in that forest. I began to eat grass, I also squeezed rotten trees to find water. I really can't say what became of me and how I changed. We kept on walking and, by luck, I came back to Rwanda. I found my home again.[36]

In reality, she did not reach "home" right away, contrary to what that last somewhat laconic statement indicates. Passing through a transit site located a few dozen kilometers from her commune of origin, she found her mother, who had never stopped looking for her over those two long years. Word of mouth probably guided the mother's steps toward the transit camp. But there is nothing effusive in the girl's story of their meeting, for at first the little girl failed to *see* her mother:

> When we got back to Rwanda, I went to Gitarama for I didn't think that even one person from my family had survived. At one point, Mama came to the place where I was living. In truth, I didn't imagine that she could be alive. She came with a man and his wife who were our neighbors. When I saw them, I didn't recognize Mama. I greeted her companions. Mama saw me, but I didn't pay attention to her. I was happy to meet our neighbors. I asked them: "Is Mama alive?" And they answered: "Here she is." Mama was frozen like a tree. I hugged her and I didn't want to leave her embrace. I hadn't recognized her because her whole face was striped with scars and I couldn't imagine that a single person from the family could have survived; I thought I was the only survivor.[37]

The rediscovery was deferred even longer, in a sense, for both mother and daughter remained unable to speak to each other, mute from grief in both cases:

> I started school in first grade, but I didn't speak, I didn't laugh because I remembered the life I had lived with the Hutu who had taken me away [to Congo]. Nothing could make me happy, and even at home I didn't talk. People tried to ask me what had happened to me, but I didn't answer. I would say that that state ended when I finished primary school [that is, six years later]. It was then that I managed to tell Mama everything that I had gone through. Mama was close to me, she took me everywhere she went. For her too, it was a great miracle to have found me alive. After all that time, I started to ask Mama how they had cut her. She told me that they had shot at her, at her cheek; they had sliced her arms with machetes; they had struck her with a spear. Then I remembered the dead people, and I started to cry, I cried and kept on crying. Mama said to me: "Go ahead and cry, that way your head will find a little rest." After a few days, my tears stopped.[38]

For the children who had remained in Rwanda, too, the genocide wasn't done with its killing. If the search for family members sometimes had good outcomes, the joy of finding a parent or a sibling alive was often quickly cut short. In fact, "deferred deaths"[39] increased the weight of the repeated losses. The lethality of rapes became the primary reason for the accumulating disappearances of family members in the immediate aftermath of the geno- cide: Mothers, sisters, and aunts succumbed to the brutality of sexual as- saults and even more often to AIDS.[40] For one girl who was eleven years old at the time and hidden by a friend of her father's during the massacres, the reasons for the illness of her only surviving sister remained obscure, for she could not conceive of the nature of the violence her sister had suffered:

> After the genocide, I learned that my older sister was alive but that she had been raped by an Interahamwe from Mabare. Only I didn't know that *kubohozwa* meant getting married by force. I thought that if the *umukiga* [in this context, a Hutu from the Northwest; this was the friend of her father's who had hidden her] had kept me to raise me, that he too had sub- jected me to rape [*kubohozwa*]. When I heard that they had "raped" my sister, I believed that she too had been brought up as I had been. I didn't understand that they had taken her as a wife. And my cousin who had also been raped brought my sister to me. She [the sister] was in very bad shape. When I saw her, I cried all day and all night. In the morning, I had lost my voice. But I was hopeful that she would get better, and in spite of every- thing I had just found a sister again. From where she was lying down, she told me things and she asked me questions about the deaths of the others. And she in turn told me about the deaths of others. She asked me to ac- company her back to our ruins, if she regained her strength. This was to visit the ruins where our parents were buried. During the days we spent together, she wasn't able to regain enough strength to go back to the ruins of our home as I had promised her. She died. She died in my arms. She asked me to recite a last prayer for her. When I finished, she began to rest for all eternity. The next morning we buried her, and I became *incike* [liter- ally, "amputated of the members of my family"].[41]

If all the expressions designating rape have been transcribed here in Kin- yarwanda, it is precisely to try to illustrate how difficult it is to name and then to understand the writer's sister's tragic fate. The incidents of sexual violence were in fact masked by a series of euphemisms, especially the one about which the little girl wondered: *kubuhoza* (*kubohozwa* in the passive form), which means "liberated." In the context of the genocide, it refers to the violent act of possessing the bodies of Tutsi women.[42] Other terms, tinged instead with respect for the victims, also referred to rape, for example *iby-amfurambi*, a term we have encountered elsewhere in these texts. Seeking to inscribe this crime in the postgenocide penal arsenal, Rwandan legislators had to resort to a semantics that did not reflect judicial orthodoxy, either. In this connection, it seemed difficult to settle for the definition of "rape" inscribed in the penal code of 1977: That code very euphemistically designated the act by the term *ubusambanyi*.[43] This word, which had its own particular history, weakened the dimension of constraint by referring to "adultery," probably under the influence of Catholic culture.[44] Unable to convey the brutality of rape in peacetime, the later texts proved even less able to express the specificity of the acts of sexual violence committed during the genocide. "Genocide rape" was thus specified in the aftermath, establishing the category of "sexual tortures" according to the terms of the law of August 30, 1996, the first law to govern the proceedings against the authors of the massacres. The parliamentary debates summarized the will to include this type of practice fully within the enterprise of extermination, emphasizing that the perpetrators had aimed at "the dehumanization of the victim, the humiliation of a category of the population, torture, and subjugation," noting in addition that "many victims died or contracted incurable sexual diseases as a result."[45] For these reasons, the definition of rape included in the 1996 law was deliberately extended to include "acts perpetrated by torturing or mutilating the sex organs."[46]

The language of children, like that of the law, struggles to convey the unheard-of radicality of rapes committed with the unquestionable aim of extermination. Thus the assaults inflicted on women in the spring of 1994 resulted in new losses within families already grieving the loss of most of their members. One boy's mother, suffering from AIDS, died in 2000, when the writer was about fourteen, six years after the genocide:

> When we arrived home, in the place where we had lived, the house had been destroyed, there wasn't anything left. Only the forest was left, and I'm going to tell you the story of the forest afterward. It's incomprehensible, I don't even know if anything remained. We looked for housing. Mama was constantly getting sick: diarrhea, coughing, constant

headaches, and still other illnesses one after another. Afterward, we learned that it was that calamity, AIDS. And that is what took her life later ... in April 2000. During her illness, she sold the forest and other property that could help the family (it was to get medical treatment). She left us that year, she left us when we were three orphan boys. She left us without anything, without land, without anyone.[47]

At first taken in by an "old Mama survivor" during their mother's illness, the brothers were separated after their mother died. The breakup of the sibling group, connected with the mother's death, compounded the shock of separation. It is hardly surprising, then, to find in the very first line of the young man's "concluding wishes" this statement: "If God wills, my brothers and I are going to find one another and live in solidarity as brothers, be happy together, be sad together, console one another, and rebuild ourselves together."[48]

To the "deferred mourning" of the genocide was added the weight of the grieving produced by war, for those who learned that a surviving brother had died in the fighting. While certain writers left alone in the world after the massacres joined the FPR and found a substitute family there, others saw their siblings disappear in the conflict between the APR and the remnants of the criminal army on the run. The military seizure of power by the FPR, symbolized by the fall of Kigali on July 4, 1994,[49] marked the defeat of those responsible for the genocide, to be sure, but the losers left behind a worn-out, drained country. The war did not come to a definitive end after the entire territory had been conquered, for members of the former government and the remnants of its army carried out a simple "strategic withdrawal" into the refugee camps in eastern Zaire. Assassinations, sometimes taking the form of veritable massacres targeting the survivors of the genocide, took on a disturbing scope, especially over the course of 1996.[50] At the same time, hostilities continued in Zaire, while the northwestern section of Rwanda remained subjected to a form of armed insurrection until 2002, which was also the year when the Rwandan troops withdrew from the Congo.

At the level of individual narratives, that *ongoing* war led to new family losses. Thus, two sisters lost two of their three surviving brothers, when one died in the northern part of the country in the struggles against the *abacengezi* (infiltrators) in 1998 and the other in a traffic accident as he was rushing back to bring the grim news.[51] Another young man, who had been eight years old in 1994, listed his repeated losses, each one further aggravating his material and emotional destitution:

> My older brother, named L., also got married, and then he came to get me from my sister's house [a sister who too had just married] and brought me to his home in Gi. After a while my other older brother came and he got married. But he died during the war in Congo in 2002. Even my older brother L. died right away, he followed my grandmother who had just died also. I didn't know what to do, where to go, what to take or leave behind, I lost hope. Then I said to myself that God didn't exist, because what He had done to me led me no matter what to suicide: I was left behind for nothing. All the more because we had learned that Papa had died and we weren't able to find his bones. We remained just the three of us, for the old woman was also gone, as I said.[52]

Within this already decimated sibling group another brother died later on, in combat. Similarly, it was the pursuit of the war that left another very young boy (age six in 1994) deprived of his only surviving brother, forcing him into an interminable wandering among multiple host families:

> It didn't stop there, because my older brother, with whom we had stayed, the Abacengezi shot him in the former commune of Cyabimgo. As for me, I became an orphan for the second time. Even the one who remained with me, they killed him, and I was left with that girl, my sister.[53]

9

ESCAPING FROM THE "TEETH OF THE MOCKERS"

Surviving in Hostile Surroundings

Four years after the genocide, on August 14, 1998, a letter signed by the head of Social Services in the prefecture of Ruhengeri was sent to Damas Gisimba, who was at the time the head of one of the largest orphanages in Kigali.[1] The local official wanted to ensure the transfer of a child taken in by a religious congregation, and he set forth with icy precision the reasons for such a request: *"Those who killed his parents* have continued to persecute him, until on August 1, 1998, they ended up entering the center, firing on him and wounding him. Because this child is still frightened, we beg you to take him in the center you direct, all the more because he no longer has any trust in the place where they shot at him."[2] To be sure, the northwestern part of the country was still subject at the time to intense fighting between the RPA and what was left of the defeated army, but in this case the assailants had chosen not just any anonymous target. More than four years after the end of the massacres, the child remained threatened by his family's murderers.

The fact that killers and victims remained neighbors after the genocide unquestionably represents one of the singular aspects of the social configuration in Rwanda. The demographic upheavals deriving from the genocide and the war considerably modified Rwandan society: Several hundred thousand Tutsi refugees returned from their long years of exile, while cases of vengeance and suicide multiplied in the ranks of the RPA.[3] When the vast majority of Hutu refugees were repatriated by force from the camps in Zaire and Tanzania, in November 1996, Rwandan society was a very diversified whole, bringing together communities whose historical experiences were not only different but opposed. These reminders serve to underline the false self-evidence of "national reconciliation," which stemmed from a political slogan rather than from simple necessity. Rwanda was thus facing an exceptional situation in which it was a matter of "remaking society" by unifying victims and killers in a single nation.[4] The genocide thus became something like the matrix event of a new concept of citizenship, requiring the rewriting of the national story. Presented as the ultimate consequence of a history based on discrimination, exclusion, and massacre, it *had* to give birth to a new epic celebrating Rwandan unity.

This newly defined political project presented a colossal challenge; it soon had to face the tests imposed by cohabitation between survivors and killers. The scope and nature of the fears weighing upon the security of the survivors were thus broadly documented by the Rwandan government. On several occasions, starting in 2003, public institutions ordered a series of investigations aimed at assessing the scope of manifestations of the "ideology of genocide." From a political standpoint, it was a matter of finding ways to suppress physical or verbal persecutions against the survivors but also of evaluating the degree of social cohesion at the heart of the "national reconciliation" project.[5] Strongly criticized, especially by international NGOs, owing to a definition of the infraction deemed too vague and penalties considered too heavy, the laws punishing the expression of the "ideology of genocide" were the legal result of the considerable information collected on the persistence of hostility toward the survivors.[6] Under the political and legal banner of the so-often deplored "ideology of genocide,"[7] one finds a series of behaviors itemized in detail in the institutional investigations— behaviors that it is impossible to set aside on principle if one seeks to grasp the survivors' experiences between 1994 and 2006, between the genocide and the moment when the orphans took up their pens.[8]

The individual narratives turn out to be largely in harmony with the data collected on a broader scale. Thus the young writers manifested an acute fear of the hostility manifested by their neighborhoods during precise moments when the official reports noted a resurgence of aggressions and killings committed against the survivors, in particular at the start of the *gacaca* trials in 2005–2006 and during the commemorative period in April. In contrast, one dimension of the subjective experience escaped the statistical apparatus: The powerful feeling of injustice felt in the face of the dissymmetry in material and emotional living conditions that existed between the decimated families and the families of the killers.

Returning to "their ruins" during 1994, children were confronted with the direct threat of neighbors who had nourished the hope of taking over lands that had belonged to the exterminated *ingo*. The sole survivor and sole heir to the paternal patrimony, one boy, seven years old at the time, thus barely escaped the murderous rage of a man whom he identified as one of his father's killers:

> I lived there [in a camp for returnees], but I remained isolated because they had finished off all my family and I knew it. I lived there and when the time came, when calm was restored to the country, we were told to go back to where we lived before to see if a scrap [of our families] had remained. I left, and when I got to the place where we used to live, I found Papa's killer on our lands. When he saw me, he said: "You, the little snake, where were you hiding?" He said to his son Mu: "Give me my machete so I can show you. I'm going to pull out this weed." Mu came into the house, and as for me I don't know how I used the wall of the house to jump into the sorghum field that was above. They looked for me, they passed right by me and I saw them. The man was saying: "That filthy snake child, where's he hiding?" When they went back to their house, I turned on my heels and went back to Rutare. There, I denounced him; they caught him and put him in prison. What astonished me is that they put him in prison and then freed him. Today, we cross paths on the road or in the market, whereas he exterminated and finished off my family, without even leaving a single person who could testify to what happened. And he took our patrimony for himself.[9]

The greed sharpened by the disappearance of the Tutsi appears as well in the text of another boy, age eleven at the time, who found himself deprived of the revenue from the crops of his father's fields by neighbors indifferent to his fate. Without seeking to kill him directly, these neighbors *dispossessed* him of his only means of subsistence, in the continuity of a social distance characteristic of the genocide itself:

> We returned to our fields, those that Papa had left us. But the Hutu made us die of hunger, for they stole all the harvests in the fields, the bananas and so on. You understand, you too, that the family was no longer respected

because it consisted only of orphans. God has protected us in this life that is not good up to now. . . . In truth, you understand that I had just remained alone and that I couldn't lead a good life. I was among the people that didn't have the same ethnic group [*ubwoko*] as I did, people who were my enemies. They said that I am a child of *inyenzi*, though they didn't hurt me. But I can't forget how they starved me, they stole everything that could have fed me.[10]

During the genocide, systematic looting had enriched most of the victims' neighbors, who henceforth took a dim view of the surviving heirs. The latter were all the more susceptible to the threat in that they were still very young when they came back, and they were made even more vulnerable by the absence of any family support.

But the fear of eventually having to restore stolen property was not the sole factor nourishing hatred against the survivors. In fact, at the heart of many of the texts, the fear connected with the discovery of bodies that could reveal participation in crime spurred and increased the hostile behaviors. In this respect, the story of the desperate search for the remains of family members occupies a central place in the account written by a young woman from the commune of Rukara, who had been eighteen years old at the time.[11] A survivor of the parish massacre, she found her mother, an older sister, and a brother at the Gahini hospital, all three seriously wounded. Another brother, who had hidden elsewhere during the killings, joined the ranks of the FPR, while a young cousin completed the meager count of family survivors. Since the security conditions did not permit a return to the sites where the survivors had lived before, the school adjacent to the hospital was transformed into a refugee camp. There, the writer's mother and sister met a neighbor, the "wife of an Interahamwe" from their home sector, who provided some information about the circumstances of the murder of another sister, married with several children, one of whom remained alive:

> At the Gahini school there were other people, then we lived with a woman called Muka, the wife of the president of the Interahamwe [in their sector]. She was taking care of the child of my married older sister, who was her neighbor. That woman said to Mama: "Don't cry any longer for your daughter, because I have already cried for her and then I buried her. In other words, I took your place. Look, she left me her child." Mama began to cry again. And that Muka said to her: "Why don't you calm down.

I buried your child well, in sheets. I did it the way you would have done it yourself." She left the child with us and she went back to her home.[12]

The seemingly charitable attitude of that woman led the surviving mother to turn to her again to ask where the remains could be found, so as to provide a decent tomb for them:

> Afterward, an officer [of the FPR] told us to gather all the people they had thrown out along the roads, in places where they never should have been, in order to bury them in a dignified manner. Those who were in pits or latrines were pulled out before being buried with dignity. And Mama had the idea of asking Muka where she had buried the children [the older sister and her children] so she could bury them on the family grounds. Mama left and then she asked that woman. The latter replied: "Why are you asking me that? Do you think I am the one who killed them?" She refused to show her the place and began to look at Mama as an enemy.[13]

During that first phase of collective burials that were supposed to remedy the offense of "bad death," the question of the hidden bodies arose within neighborhoods. Concealed from the survivors' ardent quests, the remains were even moved on several occasions, as the same young woman relates:

> Next, that woman dug up the bodies and moved them to another place. We then asked the authorities for help. And the residents of that place, who included some who had contributed to their deaths, also refused to show us the place. With those residents, we dug up the earth on all Muka's fields until the residents revolted, saying: "Why are you bothering us like this, asking us to dig up the earth of that person when she is here? Why not call her and have her show us where the bodies are?" They told the head of the cell and a resident to go ask that woman for explanations. She said to them: "Go ask R. to show you because he was there." R. is the child left to her by my sister, and he was only one year old. Whereas among her own children, the oldest was eighteen, and he said that he no longer remembered the place. The others were sixteen and fourteen, still others were younger. She said that that child R. was going to show us the place. The cell leader came back and told us that. Then everyone went back home.[14]

If the motives for such determination to hide the bodies are open to various interpretations—the desire to mask one's possible participation in the crime? a perverse intention to sharpen the pain?—one thing is sure: The neighbor was mocking the desperate efforts of the survivors. In the immediate aftermath, other neighbors also got involved, this time misdirecting the survivors who were trying to locate the grandparents' bodies, they too having been murdered somewhere in the neighborhood.

> The killings had decreased in intensity, and the people were able to return to their property. After the genocide, we met persons who told us how our family members had been killed. We met a man called A., he told us: "The old man and the old woman [grandfather and grandmother], I buried them well, like relatives. I sought people to help me and we buried them well. We dug a grave for each one." But we told ourselves that, perhaps, they too weren't there [that they had been moved, like the daughter and her children]. After a while, after recovering from that ordeal, we thought that we should bury grandpa and grandma with dignity. We asked that man A. to show us where they had been buried. He came and showed us the place. Then, when the time to dig up the remains had come, the man did not show up. How shameful! What he had told us wasn't true. As soon as we started to dig we found their bones almost on the surface. It was obvious that he had not dug graves for them. Something else, they had piled up their bodies: grandpa on top, grandma below. What hurt us also was that their bodies hadn't been covered by any mat or sheet. And they were still wearing their shoes. We took them out of there and buried them with dignity. We sought to find the other bodies.[15]

A similar lie having to do with supposed respect paid to remains had in fact been proffered in answering the questions of the two women by the man who didn't appear at the moment of exhumation, aware of the offense inflicted on two elders, ordinarily worthy of the greatest respect. In the present case, the grandparents were the only ones that could be buried "with dignity," for, with the exception of one paternal uncle, all the bodies remained prisoners of the neighbors' lies. Each of the searches, all of them fruitless, aroused hostility and provoked insults, as the passage directly following the preceding one attests; here we again find the wife of the Interahamwe leader cited earlier:

> We pursued the information concerning our paternal uncle and his nephew step by step. But in their case, even their slightest traces had

disappeared. We asked Muka once again to show us the place. She refused and said to us: "Show me where my husband is, and I'll give you the place where your dirty bones are!" We didn't know where her husband had fallen.[16]

The evolution of legal policy on the matter of setting into motion the *gacaca* trials led the government to decree the provisional liberation of sixty thousand detainees in two successive waves, in January 2003 and then in October 2005.[17] Having been arrested in massive numbers in 1994 and especially in 1996 after the dismantling of the refugee camps, prisoners who were elderly, ill, or had been involved in a procedure of confession benefited from a temporary extension of the wait for their trials before the *gacaca* courts. Less than ten years after the genocide, the survivors thus saw their neighbors/killers come back to the hills.[18] For the girl whose text we are following here, the return of those men and women who were supposed to have supplied detailed confessions of their crimes seemed like a new opportunity. Perhaps one of them would prove to be a person of good will and would designate the place where the family of her older sister was buried. But here again, her hope was disappointed:

> Afterward there came the project of freeing the people who had admitted their crimes. Among them there was a man who was called Bu. He had killed my older sister and her husband. When he came back to the hill, he acknowledged that he knew where the bodies were. We went down with him and he showed us the place. When he was finished showing us the place, he went back home and ran into Muka. She rushed to keep him from showing us the place. The next day, we went to dig up the bodies. We found two graves, but they were empty. Except in one, where we found a scrap of cloth from the maternity dress of my older sister. When they killed her, she was pregnant, her pregnancy was advanced. We told ourselves that he [Bu] had moved them. Even today, we don't know where they are.[19]

If the neighbors demonstrated their inventiveness and their energy to ensure the definitive disappearance of the bodies, they manifested unstoppable volubility when they related in detail the conditions under which the older sister was murdered:

And when you question the neighbors [of her older sister's family], they tell you how she was humiliated before so many spectators and how they trampled on her stomach, saying it was to see how a Tutsi gave birth. Two women, one called Mu and the other named Ka told my sister not to die before the arrival of the Inkotanyi. They told her: "Before you die, show us where to plant so that you can give us beans as usual." And the other one said: "Show us what the sex of a Tutsi woman looks like." They stomped on her stomach, saying: "You are pregnant with an Inkotanyi boy and he doesn't want to die." She died on April 9, 1994, whereas they started killing her on April 7, 1994.[20]

The young woman writer does not spell out the exact circumstances under which she gathered the terrible details, although it is probable that she heard the story during the "fact-finding sessions" that preceded the *gacaca* hearings. The legal narrative of the killers was awaited in ambivalence, dreaded as much as hoped for in view of the weight of violence it was hiding.

The violence inflicted by the neighborhood during this long aftermath made a lasting mark on the writer's memory. In concluding her testimony, she came back to dwell on the insults directed at the survivors:

When we say that those who had killed our loved ones spent their time calling out hurtful words, words that drove us crazy, while they were still in the process of killing our loved ones . . . the reason I am telling this is that when they wanted to make us lose our minds they would tell us: "Nothing has happened! You're going to see us once again!" Or they would say: "Come on, we're going to show you your dirty bones." They often wrote that on tracts, but we never discovered who the authors were. One other thing I would wish for is that our safety be assured, because the survivors are being persecuted.[21]

Unlike other writers who expressed the desire to have their identity masked for security reasons,[22] this young woman meant to inscribe her story within a *historical* legacy, at once public and familial. At the heart of that aspiration, she placed the memorials enclosing the bodies and bearing the names of the deceased:

If this testimony is appreciated, if that is possible, sell this book in a market stall. Perhaps it will be purchased, because what I am telling you took place in broad daylight. May it not be a secret, and may it constitute the history that our children will learn—the history of the Rwanda of former times. May it be a memory for our children. If the genocide is not yet in the time of history, we who are still living, I would wish that you help us at least to maintain the places where we have buried our loved ones so they are dignified, in such a way that our grandchildren and our great-grandchildren know where they are. I would wish that during the month of April in the years to come, these children commemorate these digni-fied places where their family is buried. . . . One more thing for which I would like to ask for your help would be to write the names of our loved ones on the memorials. The time will come when we will no longer be alive, and I would like our children to know where their family is.[23]

It is clear that, for the survivors, the effort to reestablish a national identity took on more complex and more painful contours than for the killers. Liv-ing in a nation shared by killers and their victims, certain young survivors were forced into internal exile. Since the immediate proximity of a neigh-borhood that they knew to be murderous was intolerable, they left the hills of their childhood behind for good. One boy who had survived the massa-cres in the Kanzenze swamps as a six-year-old thus tells how he was over-come by irrepressible terror when administrative measures opened the way to his "ruins":

Today I can't live in the region where I was born, in Bugesera. Living there is impossible. For example, when we go there to seek the attestations of the FARG [assistance funds for the genocide survivors] and when I spend the night there, among the people who were our neighbors, I don't get a wink of sleep. And yet I really love that place. But when I get there and I see our ruins, I don't spend the night there. I don't know what happens to me. I am thus asking for your advice. My remaining sister, when she goes there and spends the night, she comes back traumatized. That's why, when we left the orphanage, we didn't choose to go back home. In my case, when I arrive in Ntarama, where my parents' remains lie, I have no desire to see all those Hutu who have been liberated. I can't live in that place.[24]

Another young man, eight years old in 1994, similarly confessed his lasting abhorrence for the places where he spent his childhood; the sites are irremediably associated with the memory of the genocide and the picture of his neighbors exploiting the family lands:

> But I cannot forget the genocide that took place in Gitarama because it hurt me too much, so that since it ended, I refuse to acknowledge it. I've gone back there only twice. I don't want to hear the name of that place or hear people say that it's my home. The first thing that hurts me is that I don't know my Papa's killers. I hear people say that it was an Interahamwe woman who killed him; others say that it was the people who hid him who killed him. We didn't bury him; no member of the family was buried, moreover. The other thing that hurts me is that our patrimony is being degraded. Today the Hutu who were our neighbors profit from this patrimony because we for our part are afraid to go back there. No man of the family has survived; the only survivors are women, and they are vulnerable. Since the genocide was brought to an end, we have chosen not to go back; we have bought some land here. We have been helped by a benefactor and we have built [homes]. I see that it isn't sufficient in comparison with what we had before, but it's better than going back among the killers. I live with Mama and my sisters as well as my older brother.[25]

The two boys don't say this, but it is quite likely that the need or desire to help with the *gacaca* trials took them back, for a time, to their hills. At the end of April 2006, when the young survivors were invited by the Avega association to write their stories, the *gacaca* hearings began throughout the country. This singular judiciary system, set up by the government at the dawn of the twenty-first century, placed the responsibility for investigating and judging the crimes committed during the genocide in the hands of "ordinary" citizens: Everywhere on the hillsides, neighbors judged their neighbors. The implementation of the *gacaca* process was gradual and halting. At first limited to a few regions starting in June 2002, it spread throughout the territory in March 2005. In the meantime, the first law dating from January 26, 2001, was modified by a second, passed in June 2004, which was then significantly amended in March 2007 and again in May 2008.

These successive modifications give a clear picture of the hesitations involved in an unprecedented legal process. When the national phase was launched, more than 12,000 jurisdictions were set up.[26] Among them, the *gacaca* cells were charged with what could be compared to an "investigation," that is, with a public gathering of information related to the victims, the killing sites, the rescuers, the property looted, and the accused parties. The fact-finding process relied on the testimony of the population included in the jurisdiction. Thus the dossiers of the accused, for the judgment phase, were constituted according to the criminal category in which they had been placed. In 2006, most of the dossiers were ready, so the judgments could begin, managed by the *gacaca* tribunals of each sector. But the declarations gathered during the investigation phase led to a considerable inflation in the number of accusations: More than a million people were accused of having taken part in the massacres—thus vastly more than the 130,000 prisoners registered in 1999.[27] Those who participated in the collection of data and were trained to proceed with judging were ordinary citizens, elected from within their communities of residence, as *inyangamugayo* (honest, upright individuals). The elections, which began in October 2001, went on through November 2005, as the process extended to the entire territory. Nearly 150,000 men and women, for the most part neighbors of the accused or of the victims, conducted the trials on a voluntary basis.[28] As a direct result of this anchoring of the judges so close to the actors, in 2006 a third of them were removed from their positions after accusations were brought against them.[29] Survivors, witnesses, and sometimes killers, too, served as judges over their former neighbors, friends, colleagues, or classmates: The *gacaca* sessions eminently embodied the irreducible specificity of the Tutsi genocide, carried out at the heart of intimate social connections.

For the survivors, already skeptical of this new model of justice,[30] the trials further increased the neighborhood hostility toward them; they appeared henceforth as uncomfortable witnesses against the accused and their families. This powerful feeling of insecurity was not simply a matter of subjective perception; Rwandan police data confirm a significant increase in the number of survivors murdered in 2006.[31] In such a context, it is hardly surprising to find so many repeated expressions of *fear* in the notebooks. Here is one example, drafted by an adolescent (she had been five years old at the time of the genocide) whose mother was subjected to death threats in connection with her participation in the trials:

> We constantly saw their hostility, and they often said that they did not want us to be their neighbors. . . . They did not like Mama because she did not beg from them, and they saw clearly that she managed to help us in our studies. Mama has a lot of problems because she remains alone in

the house, among the enemies. Recently, Mama went to testify in the place where we lived before; she was also going to see the man who killed Papa. But because she couldn't return home directly afterward, she asked for local lodging. She did not sleep in the place where she was staying, for they spent the night throwing stones at the house; they also distributed tracts to scare her. On those tracts, it was written that if she spoke again, she would be killed. Mama informed the authorities about this, and they promised to ensure her safety. But that didn't prevent them from continuing to torment her. During the war [the genocide] they raped and beat her so badly that she is disabled today.[32]

For another young writer (a boy who was ten years old in 1994), the atmosphere of permanent fear prevented getting any rest at night: "I also request that it [the government] ensure safety, because today, there is no question of sleeping, we spend our nights uneasily, jumping up for any little thing."[33] In these texts, the initial confrontations with justice appear far removed from the calming effects that were vaunted on the advertising posters spread along the country's roads displaying the slogan "Truth heals" (*Ukuri kurakiza*). Thus it is anger, stirred up by the behavior of the accused, that dominates the following passage written by a young woman who had been about eight years old during the genocide:

> They should stop coming to the *gacaca* on the pretext that they're providing information about what they did, when they are deceiving us. This takes our information in a backward direction; we remember what they did to us and what we had to go through. It means that we have a heart that will never be able to forgive and this is because of the ill will they have in their own hearts. Something else, there are people who are accused in the *gacaca*, most notably those who have been provisionally liberated, they are outside and they live with those whom they have harmed. They boast, saying: "We did it and we will do it again if we get the chance." They say: "We have been accused but with what result?" This heightens the hatred between the survivors and the families of those who have harmed us.[34]

In this delicate period, marked by the beginning of the decentralized trials at the level of every hillside, the survivors again became the primary targets of neighborhood violence: They are thus in a position to describe its manifestations with precision. All report a worsening of social relations, moreover, during the commemorative period in the month of April. Here again, the investigations carried out on the national level confirm the intensity of the aggressive—sometimes homicidal—attacks on cattle and personal insults.[35] Generally accompanied by burials "with dignity" when victims' bodies have been found, the ceremonies took place on both the national and local levels starting on April 7. But the frenzied search for bodies unleashed mockery, as the following excerpt (by another girl born in 1986) attests:

> The reason that leads me to speak this way is that I have a deep sorrow [*intimba*] mingled with a great deal of pain [*agahinda kenshi*] and sadness [*umubabaro*]. All that because I have not been able to bury my loved ones and especially my Papa. Those liberated people whom I cited earlier and the others who have not been in prison, who were not hunted during the genocide, but who spend their time preying on our nerves, telling us that we love the bones as dogs do and that once we went to bury dog bones believing that they belonged to Tutsi, and who tell us, too, that they would prefer to go back to prison rather than to talk; you understand that they are playing with our nerves and that they rejoice in our unhappiness. In short, "the death that killed the cow is still there" [*urwishe ya nka ruracyayirimo*, signifying that the danger has not gone away].[36]

The same animal comparison ran through the statements of neighbors referring to the annual commemorative activities that took place on the hills, as one young woman born in 1976 noted:

> There is one other thing that causes me grief: When the month of April arrives and we begin the week of mourning, we go here and there and we find Hutu who say that we are resuscitating the evil spirits or that we are going to dig up the bones as dogs do. It still hurts me a lot when I see Hutu who carried out the genocide and who were liberated saying that they have confessed and who, when they arrive in their homes or in ours in the countryside, begin to mock us by saying that they have killed us and that they will kill us again. They say that cutting a Tutsi is like cutting the trunk of a banana tree; or that cutting the buttocks of a Tutsi woman is like cutting a squash.[37]

The persistence of hostility against the survivors, expressed with striking clarity by the young writers, attests to the long extension of the time of the genocide, something impossible to envision based on its "objective" chronology (April–July 1994). Long after the month of July 1994, the event was irradiating everyday social life as well as the psychic life of the survivors.

While the manifestations of violence were significantly decreased by the end of the *gacaca* process in 2012, common burial pits are being brought to light even today, restoring the memory of the massacres at the heart of life on the hills and in the neighborhoods. Thus in 2018 thousands of bodies were removed from a multitude of wells dug under the foundations of houses in Kabuga, a few kilometers from Kigali. For nearly twenty-five years, they had remained hidden owing to the *omerta* of the residents.[38]

Obsessive images of bodies "imprisoned" in hidden or inaccessible pits come up with insistence in the texts, and the silence of neighbors is repeatedly denounced. The bitter words of one young girl transcribe a profound feeling of impotence in the face of neighbors who remain stubbornly mute, refusing to reveal where the victims' remains are located:

> In addition to all that, they rejoice in our unhappiness, saying that we will always be orphans and widows, that we can do nothing for ourselves, that we are beggars forever. All this only reopens the wounds. Some of the members of my family are still prisoners of the latrines, others of the quarries, and still others, we don't even know where they tossed them. As for those in those pits, it is hard to get them out.[39]

10

"MY HOBBLED LIFE"
Writing Moral Pain

After the genocide, one young man born in 1987 wrote that "the Tutsi thought their lives had no more meaning: They had gone *beyond* despair."[1] What deep meaning lies behind that "beyond" for the young people who were writing in these notebooks? How are "expressions of suffering"[2] conveyed at the heart of an endless experience of catastrophe? With the intimacy of their wounds and the depths of their pain, the writers retained meticulous relationships.

Just as there was no word in the Rwandan language to designate genocide, no semantic resources were available to designate the brutal manifestations of the past that were springing back to life. Nor did recourse to Western nosology make it possible to render an accurate account. The inventiveness of the populace and mental health clinics in Rwanda filled that gap by forging two concepts: The first, *ihungabana*, refers to "the distress experienced by the subjects in their internal psychic space"; the second, *ihahamuka*—which means, literally, "to have one's lungs outside of oneself"—"conveys from the start the idea of an expulsion from the inside toward the outside, a process through which internal sufferings would be found in a public space."[3] The etiology of the *collective* crises of *ihahamuka* situates their appearance in secondary schools as early as 1996; they reached an unprecedented scope in April 2004 during the tenth commemoration of the genocide.[4] One mental health worker recalls adolescents who had been evacuated and hospitalized in 1999: "I remember that we had been sent several female students from Ririma by minibus; they were unconscious, in a sort of coma . . . they did not react. . . . It was really hard to bring them out of that state."[5]

On April 7, 2004, in Amahoro, the national stadium in Kigali, tens of thousands of persons were brought together to attend the official ceremony. From the very first words pronounced in Kinyarwanda, which recalled—in terms that were still very raw at the time—the conditions under which the victims of the genocide had been put to death, heart-rending cries arose from the stands, many women fainted, while the seats emptied little by little; soon only the officials remained.[6] While a "National Trauma Center" had existed since 1995 within the Ministry of Health, the manifestations of psychic suffering on the public stage fully broke out only in April 2004, leading to modifications of the commemorative rituals that euphemized overly direct reminders of the violence.

Among the populations most vulnerable to crises of *ihahamuka* were young adults and adolescents, those who had been children aged four to fifteen in 1994.[7] According to a remarkable study carried out by the Rwandan psychologist Darius Gishoma, the youngest among them suffered the first crises between 2006 and 2010, leading the clinician to conclude that these subjects had had a longer period of post-traumatic latency.[8] However, the extended time span between the genocide and the crisis experienced in recollecting it did nothing to diminish the pain. Gishoma's study offers another fruitful intuition: Psychic vulnerability cannot be conceptualized and understood without attention to the individual's social and economic vulnerability. "Existential difficulties," which in fact meant material hardships, reactivated for each of the victims the "total disappearance of the familial universe"[9] and the terrible conditions in which that universe was engulfed. For *all* the young writers, "the genocide endured in their daily lives,"[10] obstructing any approach to psychic pain that failed to situate it in the thickness of their personal experience and that did not take into account the very concrete dimensions of material and emotional destitution.

It is appropriate, then, to look closely at the processes of radical disconnection from the world of childhood—embodied in the disappearance of families, the decimation of sibling groups, and the eradication of familiar spaces—and then to evoke in as much detail as possible the attempts at reaffiliation through the creation of new figures of kinship. As we have noted, the family unit constituted the primary target of the genocidal policy: Thus it is hardly surprising to observe a profound upheaval in kinship structures in the aftermath. In addition to the texts we are examining, other types of archives offer striking pictures of the absolute disaffiliation produced by the extermination. Thus the records of "information about children separated from their parents" developed in the immediate aftermath by the Red Cross and other NGOs often bear a single word on the page that is supposed to mention the names and addresses of known adults: "None." On the record of one very young boy, a social worker slipped in the following note: "The child was taken in by another orphan boy fourteen years of age. The latter saw that the little boy remained alone and thought it was right to take that two-year-old child as his younger brother."[11]

The young writers, too, attest to these families reconfigured among survivors, sometimes without any prior kinship ties. One text in particular allows us a clear view of this double movement of disaffiliation followed by reaffiliation. At the end of a long year of mistreatment, probably between May 1994 and June 1995, a girl scarcely six years old at the time was taken in by a "Mama," a woman widowed during the genocide, four of whose six children had been murdered along with her husband. The girl described how she was welcomed and explained the ties that united her from then on to that woman:

> If you told me not to call her Mama, I would go denounce you to the police, because what she did for me is more than I can understand. Taking care of a child whose family you don't even know and doing it the way she did is really out of the ordinary. . . . When we arrived, we found them getting ready to eat, outside on some grills. They welcomed us and gave us places to sit. . . . When we arrived, they gave us something to eat, we ate and we talked. And when we had finished, we put on some cream. They gave us more to eat and we went to bed. The next morning, they woke me up so we could go off to pray. They gave me some clothes and I wore them. We left and when we came back we drank tea, ate bread, and then we went to play with other children. At noon they called us for lunch and afterward we took naps. As I was not used to so much attention, I felt as though I had arrived in paradise. I didn't manage to sleep. The children were sleeping but I stayed awake. They woke up too, to keep me company. Often we went out of our room, we sat outside and we talked during the night. And little by little I got used to a beautiful life.[12]

Here the girl describes a new time, the rediscovered time of childhood, punctuated no longer by exhausting domestic tasks and insults but by the generous care she was receiving. That she should go into detail, meticulously relating the forms of attention she received, is probably no accident, so striking is the contrast with the fate that had been hers before she became part of the new family. First hidden by one of her mother's friends, a woman whose husband was one of the most zealous members of the *ibitero*, she had witnessed her mother being raped multiple times and then saw her put to death under atrocious conditions. For a while, the woman did her best to work out a series of ploys to divert her husband's suspicions: "If I am alive today, it's thanks to her lies," the girl noted.[13] But an event soon overturned her protector's initial benevolent attitude: Her husband was killed, hit by a stone thrown by a persecuted Tutsi. Here is how the girl described this radical change:

> When her husband died, she stopped feeding me. She began to persecute me, she would insult me by saying: "You *inzoka*, I can turn you in today. You're worth no more than my husband." And the next day she said: "Hurry up and leave. I don't ever want to see you again!"[14]

Sent away from the protective *rugo*, the little girl tried to hide in the neighboring sorghum fields before hunger led her to go back in spite of everything. If the woman deigned to take her back, it was to reduce her to the state of a domestic slave, as is clear from a precise listing of the exhausting tasks required of a six-year-old girl:

> I kept on being persecuted. Then a woman came. She said . . . : "Why did you leave her alive? Won't she set our clothes on fire?" And the other one answered: "She'll draw water, she'll cook, she'll carry my child around and many other things. You don't know that I'm soon going to give birth?" And it was true, she was pregnant. As she had said, I became her all-around maid. The people had gone back to their property and I didn't know if I should return to mine. I accepted being her maid. It was the time for starting school but I didn't go because I had no one to send me. I did everything in the house, even what I didn't know how to do. I carried a jerry can [a five-gallon canister] even though I was small. For example, by eleven o'clock in the morning I was supposed to have finished drawing water, cleaning the house, doing the dishes, gathering the wood for cooking. And in the evening I did the washing, without a moment's rest. I cooked the beans with dry sorghum stalks and I stayed next to the fire until the beans were cooked.[15]

In addition to being exploited for her labors, she was constantly insulted. Thus when she was raped by an Interahamwe wandering through the countryside in the interstices of the postgenocide period, when security remained precarious, here is how she was received by her cruel foster mother:

> When I got back to the house, the woman greeted me by hitting me with a stick; she said: "Where have you been hanging out, little piece of shit?" I hadn't brought the sorghum back [as she had been told to do]. I know where that Interahamwe who took me by force lives but I don't know his name. When the woman saw me that way, she didn't offer any help at all. She sent me to fetch water. I left but this time I came back in peace and brought her the water. Then she sent me to get wood for the stove. I didn't have any more strength, but I went anyway, because in Kinyarwanda we say: "He who no longer has his paternal aunt to pray for him must pray for himself." I did everything she had asked me to do, and when I came back after going to get the wood for cooking, I saw that she had prepared manioc dough for herself alone, and she told me to prepare the dough for myself. But I was supposed to prepare sorghum dough and I didn't know how to cook it. I did the best I could. When I started to eat, it wasn't dough but flour. It wasn't properly cooked. I ate that dough with beans without oil, while she had eaten beans well cooked.[16]

In the face of the persecutions, the little girl thought she saw a promise of salvation in the proposal of a young woman from the parish who organized her "evasion" to take her into her own home. Unfortunately, there too she was treated like a domestic slave, assigned to an equally degrading task: keeping the pigs, creatures situated at the very bottom of the symbolic hierarchy of animals.[17]

> I lived with that girl and her whole family. They bought pigs, and I was the one who looked after them. You understand that I had fled the frying pan for the fire.[18] For days on end I kept the pigs: I fed them, I prepared their pens, I took them out to roll in the mud. And I did a lot of other things as well.[19]

Not able to go to school, she wandered from pasture to pasture to look after the family's cows. That was where she caught the attention of her future "Mama," the widowed survivor who worked out a stratagem for extricating her from the claws of that second abusive family, which didn't want to lose a profitable source of labor. The child, resisting intimidation and blows, *chose* to join the family of the widow, whom she called "Mama" from then on.

While that little girl managed to reestablish stable kinship relations within this parental arrangement, others escaped the mistreatment inflicted by their host families thanks to a different type of reaffiliation, which was initiated in 1996 by the Association of Student Survivors of the Genocide (AERG). To address both the psychological distress and the insurmountable socioeconomic problems that confronted the orphans, families were created at the initiative of young survivors who took on the responsibilities of parents and took the youngest, the most vulnerable, under their protection. The existence of such "families" twenty-five years after the genocide attests to the power of the bonds woven in that way.[20] The following narrative describes these unprecedented relations among children, which helped calm the disorder of lives undermined by family conflicts. Returning to his hills in the commune of Runyinya (Butare) after a long and perilous period of wandering in the neighboring region of Gikongoro, one boy born in 1981 noted the total disappearance of his first familial circle:

> On our lands, I went to verify whether there were any survivors. But I knew perfectly well that Papa and my brother were dead because I had seen their corpses. But I told myself that Mama, my little brothers and my little sister were alive. But as the woman had told me [a woman who accompanied him on the way back], I found that of my family of seven people I was the only survivor.[21]

Henceforth deprived of parents and siblings, he nevertheless found an uncle. And the first appearance of that individual, in principle very close in the order of kinship, bore the sign of emotional distance, for the boy described the latter as "the one who called himself my paternal uncle." The writer offered no details about the uncle, so we do not know whether he too was a survivor or if he had returned from exile. Between the orphan and his uncle, two objects of discord arose: the sale of a cow the child had found and the appropriation of the paternal lands. The situation rapidly deteriorated:

> He stopped buying me clothes. He began to mistreat me and I even spent nights without eating, whereas I was working. I started to pick ripe avocados and I ate them. He had forbidden his wife to give me anything to eat. I began to study, and to get money, I hunted moles in the fields and

people paid me a little. I went to look for sorghum leavings to sell them, and then I could buy clothes. And I saw that I was going to die of hunger, when I had been rejoicing that I had found family members and could live with them.[22]

Soon taken in by a benevolent cousin, his living conditions improved for a time. It was when he was rediscovering certain attentions on the part of adults, especially those having to do with food, that he *experienced* the overturning of—and his own absolute uprooting from—a world that had been populated with beloved beings:

> And when she [the cousin] observed the condition I was in, without clothes, they bought me some clothes and they fed me. At first I didn't manage to eat, because my paternal uncle and his wife had killed me with hunger. I refused milk, and they asked me why I didn't want to drink milk, then I answered: "My father's cows have been exterminated, I'll never drink milk again. And the cow that I found, my uncle sold it and took the calf, I won't drink milk again." Up to today, I've never drunk any more milk.[23]

Though he was well treated in his cousin's home, the orphan rebelled against the loss of his property and decided to "go back and confront [his relatives]." Having obtained the right to pass on to secondary school, he thought, no doubt naively, that he could win over his uncle thanks to his success in school. He met with another failure when the uncle retorted: "Do you think you're my son?" and categorically refused to buy his nephew what he would need for life in boarding school. Despite repeated notices by the local authorities, the uncle contested all the child's claims to the paternal lands. An interminable legal muddle ensued.[24] When the boy returned to his hillside during school vacations, his neighbors told him what the uncle had threatened to do to him should he be bold enough to come back: The definitive break was sealed. Rejected by the only surviving members of his family, the boy began to show signs of self-destructive behavior:

> Then I looked for a house to live in and I began to prepare a garden. I asked for sweet potatoes to eat and cuttings that I could plant. I was starving. But as I had already been waiting patiently for a long time, I kept on waiting. And when I was on the point of dying from hunger, I went into my uncle's sweet potato fields and I grilled them. I started to smoke and

I smoked so much that at my place there was the light of tobacco in place of the light of someone who cooks. We went back to school, I had so much anger inside. . . . Then the director asked me to bring my parents, I answered him that I had no parents, that I lived alone at home. The director didn't pay any attention to me. . . . I went to the parents' meeting, and as he had forbidden me to say a word I went just to listen. I accepted, but I escaped from his vigilance to go plant among the ruins. Because every time I was on vacation I was dying of hunger even though I possessed fertile lands and my relatives hadn't wanted to rent those lands to me and they had forbidden the others to rent them to anybody at all. He [the uncle] said that whoever cultivated those lands would have problems. Once the school proctor caught me when I was coming back from the fields because I used to go there on Saturday [whereas he was supposed to stay on the school grounds]. He denounced me to the director. The latter asked me if I was going back to cultivate the lands and I answered: "Yes, because during the vacations I don't find anything to eat." He was confused. I had often skipped school, but sometimes I studied and I succeeded.[25]

Later, enrolled in a new school too far away for him to return to his own lands to cultivate them aside from vacation periods, he suffered more than ever from hunger and with the feeling of solitude:

The semester ended and I didn't have a [bus] ticket to go home. So I had the idea of going back on foot as far as Butare. I went along a paved road, I walked, and I arrived at Butare at 6:30 PM. I spent the night under a tree. Daylight came and I went back [to his administrative sector]. I saw that the grass had grown a lot and the house was carpeted with spider webs. The sons of those spider webs welcomed me on my return. Children who were members of the AERG helped me clean up and then I could go into the house. At school I don't smoke and I don't drink beer because I'm not worried, I have food. I'm worried when I don't have any more pens, any more soap; I no longer use skin cream because I can't afford to. When I find a pen, I'm happy.[26]

For the first time, the boy mentioned the gestures of solidarity on the part of the AERG students he had met in his new school. These children deployed their energy and their ingenuity to come to his aid despite an increasingly desperate situation. For the gnawing hunger and despair were soon accompanied by alcohol consumption, including *kanyanga*, an adulterated and sometimes toxic drink.

> Then I became a vagabond; I didn't plant anything that year because I was despondent. I died of hunger. I caught malaria and couldn't leave the house. Where I was staying, no one came to see me except the children and students on vacation. A young man from the neighborhood came. . . . But when he saw that it wasn't locked, he pushed the door open and found me in bed. I looked like a corpse. Hunger and malaria were going to kill me. He sought people to carry me on a stretcher made of branches and they took me to the hospital. I had a card from FARG [funds to assist the victims of the genocide]. I was hospitalized, and that young man stayed with me. It was the children who had just finished school who brought me food. I recovered from malaria and right away I bought a hoe and began to cultivate the land. . . . Then I became like a crazy person because of some problems, because of hunger, tobacco, and beer. But I didn't smoke any hemp. Since they had hit my head with a club, I had constant headaches. So at one point I stopped *kanyanga*. But I was like a child of the streets. The people living around me were confused, the students were confused. . . . I became like a crazy person because of the beers I was drinking without eating.[27]

Describing himself at this point in the story as "a child who had no one to continue his life," he was again helped by the young people of the AERG, who decided to plead his cause before the local agents of the FARG. Created in October 1998, that fund received an amount equivalent to 5 percent of the nation's annual budget; it developed several programs to support survivors of the genocide in the areas of schooling, health, and housing.[28] Commitment to this policy entailed a considerable budgetary effort for a country whose economy had been bled dry. Still, successive audits—confirmed by the narratives in our corpus in which many of the writers told of exhausting and fruitless undertakings—reveal incompetence and corruption at the level of the lower administrative agencies.[29]

Supported by the encouragements of the AERG families, the young boy armed himself with courage and patience to demand the help he was owed, going so far as to assail the FARG office with a determination tinged with revolt, as he put it himself:

The latter [members of the AERG] went to tell my story to the person in charge of the FARG of the district [a new administrative entity created after the reform of 2006].[30] He couldn't do anything, and I was in conflict with him because every time we told him about the problems we were having, he answered that he was not a solution for the orphans. We went to see him with a young girl and he responded the same way. So we remained right by his office, and, when he went out, he found the girl in tears. I myself was sitting calmly beside her, because I was used to the problems. The manager of the bank asked why he wasn't giving the money to the children when the funds had been transferred to the account. He found us sitting there and he chased us away, then a policeman asked him the same question: Why doesn't he give us the money, when the funds had been deposited? Then he gave us 400 FRW [Rwandan francs, the equivalent of 40 cents in euros]. I refused to sign and I forbade the young girl to sign as well. Then he scolded us and gave us 3,000 FRW [about 3 euros]. And since that money could not be of much use to me in the face of my problems, I swallowed it and I went on with my life.[31]

This description of the rather tense exchange with the FARG administrative agent attests to the boy's determination in the face of an adult perpetuating an injustice that had become intolerable. With each difficulty he encountered, though, representatives of the boy's new "kin" from the AERG turned up, in particular an orphan girl he depicted this way:

She didn't abandon me. It was a girl I loved and whom I viewed as a relative because she gave me advice even though we had no real family connections. She told me that God loved me. The people from the AERG told the students that they would look for solutions to my problems and that I would continue to study.[32]

The AERG members convinced the child, who had been out of school for a while, to resume his secondary education. Like real parents, they followed his results assiduously:

I went back during the school vacation, they asked me for the report card, and it was the first time anyone had asked me for my report card. I gave it to them and they thanked me, and that boosted my morale.[33]

That last comment is not insignificant. Indeed, in many of the texts, one of the markers of the profound solitude linked to the disappearance of fore-bears was the absence of a satisfied or disapproving response to school re-sults. The AERG families helped fill that void. School thus occupied a central place in the narration of the postgenocide ordeals. Sometimes a source of anguish, sometimes a place where new kinship ties were forged, schools were described with ambivalence, as we can see especially clearly in this orphan girl's account:

> The children of the FARG fail in large numbers; many people call them dunces. Let us be dunces, you who don't know what you're saying. Who can tell you whether so-and-so is a dunce if you don't know him. The night is described by the one who has lived through it and "he who suf-fers closes the door" [*ubabaye niwe ubanda urugi*]. We run into a lot of problems in school, yet we hold on. That is why you hear it said that the FARG children are failing. It's because of the problems they find them-selves in. . . . The problems are submerging us. Someone else asks: "Am I going to open up my own house of solitude? How am I going to grow food? Will I go back to school?" Everything eludes you, you don't know how to do anything. You're in the grip of despair and you wonder about a lot of things. Then you look back, you remember your parents and your relatives, wondering what your life would be like, where we would be in our studies if we were being brought up by our own loved ones, in a big family? All that is the cause of our failure in school. From now on, let no one say that the FARG children fail, for "the pain of the hen is known only in the spot where she has pecked." Concerning my social relations with my schoolmates, we get along well, but you are friends with people who want to be friends, for some refuse even to speak to us, they have their reasons. When you talk to someone who listens to you, you're not wasting your time. Normally, we're friends with the schoolmates with whom we share the same problems, especially those of the AERG, for most of the time these are the people we meet and chat with, the ones we talk with about our respective problems. They're the ones we prefer to live with.[34]

Boarding school life accentuated the hardships, partly because the students had to pay fees for bedding and hygiene; it also sharpened the deep sense of solitude felt by students who had no visitors. Thus the joy of being admitted to secondary school, expressed a few lines earlier, cruelly disappeared when it came time for the monthly visits between parents and children:

> Once I arrived at the secondary school, I found other children there who had their brothers who came to visit. The cars and motorcycles came, parked in the parking lot. And when I thought that I had no one at all, I was overcome with sadness, I shut myself off and I cried. I had other problems and I ended up failing in class, because of the bad life I had lived as a result of the genocide. I continued to live with my mom [*muke-curu*, an affectionate term the girl used to designate her foster mother]; she encouraged me to pray, saying that God was the father of orphans and the spouse of widows. That gave me some moral strength, and we were able to face up to other problems that arose. We couldn't do anything to resolve them because of the destitution in which we lived.[35]

The exhaustion and despair provoked by an extremely fragile material existence grew even more in the case of families managed by children. In all the texts, the "life afterward" was punctuated by an agonizing quest for lodging, food, and clothing and by the need to cover various expenses associated with schooling (bus or train tickets, personal hygiene supplies). But the worries were doubled for the "orphan heads of household" obliged to take care not only of their own needs but also of the children in their charge. A social innovation born of the catastrophe, these "families of orphans" disrupted kinship relations, deprived as they were henceforth of adults. The emergence of these new family entities doubtless stemmed from two factors: on the one hand, the government policy aiming to encourage *national* adoptions, and, on the other, the desire of the orphans themselves to group together so as to escape mistreatment by foster families. In addition, the orphanages were overcrowded,[36] inadequate in number, and unevenly distributed throughout the country;[37] they were perceived by the authorities as a colonial legacy destined to give way to an ancient cultural practice of adoption by extended families.[38] According to an investigation carried out by UNICEF in 2004, more than one hundred thousand children were living in 42,000 households headed by an older orphan.[39] If the "heads of the household" were often young people, they nevertheless remained the "children of their vanished parents,"[40] and at the time they took on the status of "precocious parenthood,"[41] they were for the most part still minors before the law; the age of majority in Rwanda was twenty-one.

Several orphans wrote about these "maternities" and "paternities" imposed by the genocide, their accounts always studded with painful glitches, as in the following excerpt in which a young girl described how she became "mother" to seven children:

> The genocide of the Tutsi ended when the Inkotanyi saved *those who were not dead.* After what had just happened, I had a bad life. I stayed with two children and a baby, so there were three of us. We had no roof, so we wandered here and there. But I tried to gather together those who had been born of the same womb. Peace wasn't yet ensured, but people were moving around anyway. There were four children from my maternal uncle's home; the oldest was fourteen, and the Interahamwe had raped her when she was still just a child. They said that they were going to train her to become their wife. When the Inkotanyi found out who had done that, they went looking for her [where the Interahamwe were holding her as a sex slave]. These children [the children of the maternal uncle] no longer had anyone to look after them, for their entire family had been exterminated. They were entrusted to me so I could live with them. Among them was a three-year-old child. I brought them up even though I myself needed to be brought up. And I began to take on responsibilities that weren't appropriate for my age: teaching those children. I had no place to live, and that is still true today, at the moment when I'm speaking to you. We lived without having anything to eat. All that fell on my shoulders, whereas I too needed to be brought up like the others. I was only nineteen years old.[42]

This girl endured this precarious life in a state of constant worry about what would become of *her* children, fully assuming—and with what courage!—the "maternity" that fell to her owing to the disappearance of the adults. All the more so in that the destitution was compounded by fears for the life of one of the little girls:

> We could go a year without paying [the rent]. They [the local FARG agents] lied all the time, saying that they were going to build houses for us. And up to now we have been renting a house with all these children. We are eight in a small house. This is how we have continued to move

through life. What is worse is that among the children one girl was infected by the AIDS virus, transmitted by the man who had raped her. I was feeding all those children. . . . Because we had no roof, because we had no food, and because we spent so many days at the hospital with the child who had been infected, I wasn't able to study. I studied one year and then the next year I was in all that: Either I was at the hospital, or else they were driving us out of the house because we didn't have the means to pay. And when I was at school, I worried about the children, I wondered if they had spent the night without eating, if they had been driven out of the house or if they had been attacked and killed. Because the Hutu continued to say that those who were left were going to denounce them, my heart was not at ease. I was afraid they had been attacked. I couldn't study. Instead of concentrating on my studies, I was constantly thinking about the lives of those children whom I had left alone. The courses slipped out of my brain, vanishing at the very moment in which the situation of *my* children was imprinting itself on my mind. Even though I have never given birth, they are my children.[43]

Under such conditions, it was impossible for her to pursue an education, even though that would offer her the promise of a job and thus a more secure economic existence for her family. And it is between the lines devoted to the description of her distress as a mother powerless to feed and care for her children that the first utterances of psychic suffering appear:

Instead of advancing, I was going backward. I was studying, I was trying to figure out how to feed the children during the vacations, and because of the need to take care of everything, nothing succeeded: my studies, finding food for the children. It was hard, it was *making me crazy.* The genocide had taken away my own family and I had not had a life. . . . I didn't even know where my family members were buried, and that also *affected our brains.* . . . The life we lived was living without a home, having no one who could become a parent in the place of my father and Mama, not to have any food or any material goods for all the children I am raising.[44]

Material and affective destitution were experienced profoundly and intimately; the cruel lack of basic necessities kindled the memory of her parents' disappearance. This violent feeling of solitude and lack of comprehension no doubt inspired the final lines of this girl's notebook, written as a sort of poem punctuated by interrogative anaphora. Drafted as an address to an absent party, this conclusion, nourished by the personal experience of its writer, sketches an omniscient portrait of the fate of the "orphan heads of household":

> Seeing a child who becomes a parent of children almost of the same age and who carries their problems, do you believe she doesn't need a confidant?
>
> Seeing a child who has to know how to feed her brothers and sisters when she was supposed to receive that from her parents or from those who might have replaced them, do you think she doesn't need people close to her who take care of her?!
>
> Seeing a child who takes another to the doctor when she too needs to be guided, don't both of them need people close to them who take care of them?!
>
> Seeing a child who spends a night without sleeping because those she is bringing up are ill and she doesn't have the means to get treatment for them; she spends the night wondering how she is going to get them treatment. Shouldn't there be someone to help her and share her thoughts?
>
> Seeing a child who thinks about the days to come for the other children, doesn't she need someone close to her? The child who has to look after the other children when they are on vacation, who has to supervise their behavior, doesn't she need someone close who can watch over her studies, make sure she is really keeping up with her coursework, watch over her success or her failures! Isn't such a person indispensable?
>
> Seeing the children who always have tangles in their hair whereas those who have come back from their exile have the power to find their houses clean again, whereas we, the children of the country, who need our future, we don't stop being homeless; and yet our parents had solid houses that have been destroyed by Rwandans. In this life, don't they need a person who comforts them?!
>
> Seeing a Rwandan who kills another because of how she was created, or because of the family into which she was born, a child who has no idea where all that came from or where it is leading and who nevertheless falls into it, doesn't she need a person who can get her out of it?![45]

Another text attests to the same relationship between a "debilitating life" and brutal manifestations of psychic pain, mentioned here as crises of *ihahamuka*. The author is a girl who was seven years old in 1994 and who became the head of a family composed of the last remaining members of her sibling group: a younger brother and sister. Suffering was experienced *through the body*, as she describes with great delicacy:

At that time, even if we went to school, we didn't succeed, because you can't be at school and wondering how the little sister whom you left alone in the house is doing, the sister who is perhaps going to die of hunger or will perhaps be killed alone in the house. . . . The place where we lived was very close to where we used to live and the Interahamwe who were our neighbors were still there.

You can't live that life and succeed in school. Yes, people say that the children who survived are dunces, but I would say that we are intelligent because to study with all the problems we bear and to succeed in getting the grades we have is a big mark of heroism. As I see it, we do what we can. During the time when we're studying while thinking about our little sister, left alone without food or clothing; we ourselves are studying without any school materials, without shoes, without clothes, without wraps against the cold, you study even though you often get sick; and especially *sicknesses from problems* in your stomach, your back, and other places. This life continued to submerge me. I saw that not a single person in life loved us. And I left school for a long time, during a semester. I don't know how it happened, but I felt great fear, as much as the fear I felt during the genocide. My heart was pounding very fast, as if I had a *heart malady* (hypertension). I shouted out a lot of calls for help, and every little thing made me jump. I suffered a lot. And later God had pity on me and I met a doctor named Munyandamutsa Naason.[46] People took care of me and talked with me about what I had undergone and what had hurt me. All that meant that I didn't succeed the way I should have. During the time we were in school, I was often thinking about my little sister whom I had left at home. Sometimes study time was over and I was still caught up in those things, or else at night I didn't sleep; I spent the night crying sometimes and I was cradled by sadness.[47]

The "sicknesses from problems" evoked in this text constituted a real public health issue in postgenocide Rwanda. According to a study dating from 2008 and carried out under the auspices of the Rwandan Ministry of Health and the World Health Organization, more than 30 percent of the population presented symptoms of post-traumatic stress disorder (PTSD).[48] If the overall data document the health challenges of the time, we must nevertheless take care not to read the subjective descriptions of psychological pain in the light of that single grid of nosological interpretation. To be sure, the terminology of "trauma" has gradually been incorporated into common usage to designate a phenomenon distinct from "madness" (*ibisazi*), which was not only deemed inappropriate in the clinical context but also tainted by negative value judgments. As Darius Gishoma has written: "It became less acceptable, even degrading, to call someone 'mad' or 'possessed,' whereas everyone around knew for sure that all that stuff was due to the genocide."[49] Several young writers thus used a "Kinyarwandized" form of the term "trauma," while resorting nevertheless in a more current fashion to the designations *ihahamuka* and *ihungabana*. One young orphan, a girl born in 1986, wrote a striking account of the intensity of the crises that led to her successive hospitalizations:

> When I reached the fourth grade in primary school [in 2000], I became like a crazy person, I screamed and I ran. People caught me. I finished the sixth grade without any change. I started the first year of secondary school and I still had crises of *ihahamuka* every week. I had no peace. And I prayed to God to let me die and rejoin Papa. In the first year of secondary school, I studied but I had constant headaches and I didn't manage to study. I went into the second year of secondary school and I couldn't get through a week without getting sick from the trauma at least three times. When I got sick, I would spend at least a week in bed. When I got my strength back, I would spend a month without being able to say a word, I became a deaf-mute. And I contaminated other children who shared my problems. I couldn't be taken back home because there was no one to hold me down [during the crises] and I could cause problems at home. It still isn't over even now, because I have a lot of memories. They gave us counselors at school, but for me, in spite of everything they could do, the things never left me. Perhaps those things will never leave me, until the day when I see Papa because I loved him so much and because I no longer have anyone among my brothers and sisters. I think this will be my death because all that has already outstripped me. It will never

leave my heart. For example, at school sometimes I take up a notebook and write, but when these things come back I feel like a crazy person. I didn't know that one could live alone, without a family. I'll die with it. Where I'm going, I'll never forget those things. That has left me with a deep pain that will never go away. If I die, if I stay alive, if I become rich or poor, I will always remember that terrible misfortune that fell upon me, while I was still a child. What I am saying is an indelible memory. That is why I can never forget Papa, not ever in my life.[50]

Reliving traumatic scenes, loss of speech, fear, and panic are all symptoms of the manifestations of psychic pain described by the young girl. Another orphan, a boy born in 1982, adds a form of catalepsy to the clinical picture: "My true nature then showed itself (I'm speaking of *guhahamuka*). I found myself on a hospital bed and I was told that I had just spent three days sleeping."[51] The delayed appearance of *ihahamuka* crises, several years after 1994, thus stretched the subjectivized time of the genocide to infinity. Several writers expressed this clearly, like another boy, born in 1987, who also gave a precise account of the symptoms of his "sickness":

> So, I'm suffering. As the years pass, these years increase my suffering. For me, the training offered by SURF and Avega was very useful, because I met trauma counselors and I am going to be able to show them the symptoms of my sickness. Among these sicknesses, there is anxiety [the writer used the French word], sorrow, anger, incidental mistreatment, crying every time something bothers me, for example when I'm hungry or when someone is mistreating me or when I don't have the resources to go back to school. The trauma counselors are going to help me find a way to behave in this situation. They're going to try to find out what sickness I'm suffering from and what I can do so that my life will be better in general.[52]

The psychic and somatic presence of the experience of the genocide also manifested in the return of obsessional images that break into daily life. Thus one orphan, a girl born in 1987, describes the precise contours of the atrocious visions that haunt her henceforth:

> Instead of advancing, I'm regressing in school, and if there are people who can help a person not to despair, I would like them to help me; because everywhere I am, I see corpses before my eyes. They're the corpses

among which I was lying, and among these corpses I always see Mama cut in half. That image never leaves me and it increases my despair. I see my father in the wheelbarrow, as if he were no longer anything but a crude bunch of bananas. I still see the image of my maternal uncle as his blood flows out, rain falling on him, without being buried with the honors due to a human being, as if he had never had either a family or children. All that comes back before my eyes and it makes me remain closed in on myself.[53]

For another boy, born in 1981, reexperiencing the scenes he has lived through completes the demolition of any self-esteem:

When the war [the genocide] began, I was studying in the fifth grade of primary school. I started over in the fourth grade, but with the consequences of the genocide. Sometimes the teacher would explain the lessons and I would be rewatching the film of the war [the genocide] in my mind. Once the teacher was explaining a lesson and I was in the process of escaping the machetes because I saw the people who wanted to hit me with machetes. When the teacher asked me a question, I would answer like a person who has just woken up. Look, today, I'm a twenty-five-year-old young man, five feet tall; I'm a young man finished off by thinking.[54]

Images like these, evoking a life without value, devoid of any meaning, often accompany the expression of a desire to die. While to my knowledge there have been no long-term epidemiological studies on the prevalence of suicide among survivors of the genocide, the study cited earlier points to depression as the principal "factor of comorbidity" in PTSD that correlates with the high proportion of symptoms of a "major depressive state" within the population studied.[55] Described with the intensity of the orphans' words, the nosological categories are translated into powerful feelings of solitude or into a series of somatic metaphors expressing disgust with oneself and with life, as in this statement by a boy born in 1988:

For example, when you get sick at school, they bring you dough [from manioc or corn], and, when another student who still has his family also gets sick, his family brings him good things. That makes me feel different from the others, I feel cursed.[56] It's too much for me, I'm desperate. I feel it would be better for me to die rather than remain on this earth.[57]

And another made by a boy born in 1984:

> The genocide has left me with a lot of after-effects. When you see my face, you think I am healthy, yet my heart is a stinking piece of rotting rubbish and my head is like dead.[58]

Like that boy, other writers stress the gulf separating the social mask from the psychic distress inside:

> Up to now, I am alive and I'm fine, but that's only in appearance. I'm talking about what there is in the depth of my heart: I can't get away from the sorrow of the loss of my parents, my brothers and sisters, my friends carried off like innocents. I also suffer from other problems that I encounter in my everyday life. I suffer from the consequences of the wickedness of those Hutu who killed us for no reason.[59]

Reading these lines by another boy born in 1981, one cannot help but note the rich vocabulary mobilized to designate the moral affliction. Nuances of intensity and duration mark each of these terms, even if they are sometimes used strictly as synonyms: *umubabaro*, *agahinda*, *intimba*, and *ishavu* are the words for sorrow, composing a refined semantic cameo to describe an infinite dereliction.[60]

The orphans' voices continue to prolong the echoes of that social and affective disaffiliation. One such echo, from a boy born in 1986, comes with the features of a being existing apart from the world, *uprooted*:

> I live the way the enemies want, like a bird from branch to branch, even though I wasn't born on a tree and even though we had property. In short, I don't know what I am among men. I consider every person I see before me as an unknown thing. Even if they could help me, even you, if you wanted to help me, it would be hard, because I am like a wild animal.[61]

From another orphan, a girl born the same year, this final word: "I have no relation to the world, even though Rwanda is full of people."[62]

ACKNOWLEDGMENTS

For the completion of this work, I owe a great deal to the public and private institutions that welcomed me into their archives. In Rwanda, the National Commission for the Fight against Genocide (CNLG) was where I found the precious notebooks, and I want to thank in particular its executive secretary, Jean-Damascène Bizimana, along with his invaluable colleagues Jean-Damascène Gasanabo, Martin Muhoza, Devota Gacenderi, and Rose Karigirwa. At the Ministry of Local Administration, Assumpta Ingabire allowed me access to the archives of the "policies of the disaster" that were established immediately after the coup. Without the welcome offered by Brother Benjamin Ngororabanga and Jean-Népomuscène Ntambara at the Dominican Center for Research and Gospel Study, I could not have learned what I needed to know about Rwandan botany, zoology, and popular medicine. In Nyamirambo, Damas Gisimba also opened the doors to the archives of his orphanage with trust and warmth. I also want to thank my very dear friends from Ibuka: Naphtal Ahishakiye, Olivier Ngabo, and Égide Nkuranga. In Paris, the Shoah Memorial is a welcoming site for all those concerned with the history of the genocide of the Tutsi: I thank its director, Jacques Fredj, along with my friends Sophie Nagiscarde, Bruno Boyer, and Iannis Roder. I should also like to address my thanks to Delphine Pagès-El Karoui for her help. Finally, I want to stress that the entire project would have been impossible without the support of the National Center for Scientific Research (CNRS).

Without the patience and tenacity of Clémentine Vidal-Naquet, who was kind enough to welcome me into the collection she heads, this book would simply never have seen the light of day.

After the devastation, Rwanda has had the mysterious power to bring new families into being. It is to my little Rwandan family that these modest words are addressed, in the hope of conveying to them my infinite gratitude and unfailing affection.

My first thought is for Pierre Galinier and Yvonne Mutimura, whose generosity toward me has always been fraternal. And I shall not forget Snave Imanzi, without whom this first familial circle would not be complete.

For over fifteen years, one woman in particular has accompanied me in Rwanda in my contacts with the *imbabura*, in intimate murmurings about the wickedness of men or sinuous stories about court intrigues: Marguerite Mukagakwaya has been *maman wa batisimu*, my godmother. Without her, I would not be able to hear Kinyarwanda in its full beauty. Without her, I would never have approached the experience of the survivors' solitude. And I would not have grasped the intimacy of their wounds without the presence in my life, over the years, of Alain Ngirinshuti.

In the larger family of the *"datawacu"* I must mention Jean Ruzindaza and Jean-François Dupaquier—without forgetting Eugénie—when the silhouette of the wise *sogokuru* (grandfather) takes on the features of Jean-Pierre Chrétien. Among the clan, the Abavandimwe, there is also Émilienne Mukansoro, whose sensitive intelligence gave such depth to the exercise of translation; then, too, my friends Ariane Mathieu, Cloé Drieu, Anouche Kunth, Béata Umubyeyi Mairesse, Louisa Lombard, Rana El-Diab, Yvonne Uwanyirigira, Julien Seroussi, Monia Dridi, Christian Ingrao, Henry Rousso, Nicola Werth, and Jean-Paul Kimonyo; finally, since childhood, Flore, Marion, Héloïse, and Yvan.

Stéphane Audoin-Rouzeau is the *imfura*, this very strong Kinyarwanda term that characterizes someone with nobility of mind and heart; his support has been unflagging during all these years.

As the *amashami*, the branches of the family, grow and strengthen, I would like to express my gratitude here to the students who have been accompanying me: Timothée Brunet-Lefèvre, Juliette Bour, Léonard Arnould, Léa Druesne, Nathan Ingrao, and all the Science Po students, all those born after 1994.

I cannot speak of the family without going back to the most essential members of all: my parents, my sister, and her children: Flore (*in memoriam*), Camille, Sasha, and Ana.

GLOSSARY

Grammar note: in Kinyarwanda, singular and plural forms are marked differently according to the class to which the substantive belongs, following a system common to all Bantu languages.

datawacu: my paternal uncle

gacaca: a tribunal inspired by earlier forms of justice set up in Rwanda between 2002 and 2012 to prosecute and try those accused of having taken part in the genocide against the Tutsi

icyitso (pl. *ibyitso*): accomplice

igitero (pl. *ibitero*): an attack, a murderous band

ihahamuka: literally, "to have one's lungs outside of oneself"; a traumatic breakdown, a breakthrough of repressed memories leading to an uncontrollable outburst

induru: war cries, screams

Inkotanyi: a popular name for the Rwandan Patriotic Front (FPR)

Interahamwe: a Hutu extremist paramilitary organization

inyenzi: cockroach; a dehumanizing nickname for FPR fighters and, by extension, Tutsi

inzoka: snake, a dehumanizing nickname for Tutsi

kera: once, formerly

mamanwacu: my maternal aunt

muzehe: literally "old man," father or grandfather

rugo (spelled *urugo* in certain contexts; pl. *ingo*): home, household, family, courtyard

NOTES

FOREWORD BY LOUISA LOMBARD

1. Dogs had been beloved companions for many Rwandan children, making their turn to violence all the more painful. Christopher Taylor met a young survivor in Nairobi just after the genocide whose family had been killed but who desperately sought news of his dog, the one creature he alone had been responsible to protect. Christopher C. Taylor, *Sacrifice as Terror: The Rwandan Genocide of 1994* (New York: Routledge, 1999).

2. See Aalyia Sadruddin, "After-Afterlives: Aging, Care, and Dignity in Postgenocide Rwanda" (PhD diss., Yale University, 2020).

3. Aalyia F. A. Sadruddin, "Death in an Ordinary Time: Reflections from Rwanda," *Medical Anthropology Quarterly* 36, no. 2 (2022): 198–216.

4. This is a generalization, of course. There were areas within the territory now delineated as Rwanda that did not fit these patterns—areas where people cultivated absent a lot of centralized control and also areas where herders lived more nomadically. Gérard Prunier, *The Rwanda Crisis: History of a Genocide* (New York: Columbia University Press, 1996).

5. Charles Mironko, "Social and Political Mechanisms of Mass Murder: An Analysis of Perpetrators in the Rwandan Genocide" (PhD diss., Yale University, 2004), 37–42.

6. Cattle keeping was higher status than farming, but this demonstrates that herders and farmers shared a symbolic repertoire that prized cows and, for instance, taking nourishment from milk rather than solid foods.

7. The highest-status things to consume were milk, beer, and honey. Drinking could be done publicly, but not eating. Christopher C. Taylor, "Mutton, Mud, and Runny Noses: A Hierarchy of Distaste in Early Rwanda," *Social Analysis* 49, no. 2 (2005): 213–30.

8. Jean-Paul Kimonyo, *Rwanda's Popular Genocide: A Perfect Storm* (Boulder, CO: Lynne Rienner, 2016).

9. Frank Rusagara, *Resilience of a Nation: A History of the Military in Rwanda* (Kigali: Fountain Publishers Rwanda, 2009).

10. Kimonyo, *Rwanda's Popular Genocide*, 29.

11. The government justified its policy of discrimination on behalf of the majority on the grounds that it was a necessary means of making up for the ways Hutu had historically been treated as subservient and denied opportunities.

12. Peter Uvin, *Aiding Violence: The Development Enterprise in Rwanda* (West Hartford, CT: Kumarian, 1998).

13. Mironko, "Social and Political Mechanisms."

14. Rwanda's economy nosedived from the mid-1980s to 1993, when it had the highest percentage of people living in poverty (86 percent) in the world, the result of falling export prices, structural adjustment, repeated currency devaluation, drought, population growth, and violence. Jean-Paul Kimonyo, *Transforming Rwanda: Challenges on the Road to Reconstruction* (Boulder, CO: Lynne Rienner, 2019), 58.

15. Kimonyo, *Transforming Rwanda*.

16. For a detailed explanation of the densely polyvalent symbolism of those cartoons, see Taylor, *Sacrifice as Terror*.

17. Michela Wrong, *Do Not Disturb: The Story of a Political Murder and an African Regime Gone Bad* (New York: Hachette, 2021), 365.

18. The report was not made public, but its findings were publicized. See, e.g., "Report: Rebels Cleared in Plane Crash That Sparked Rwandan Genocide," CNN, January 11, 2012, https://edition.cnn.com/2012/01/11/world/africa/rwanda-president -plane/index.html.

19. Other books that help explain the interactional dynamics of the genocide include Taylor, *Sacrifice as Terror*; Lee Ann Fujii, *Killing Neighbors: Webs of Violence in Rwanda* (Ithaca, NY: Cornell University Press, 2011); Hélène Dumas, *Le génocide au village: Le massacre des Tutsis au Rwanda* (Paris: Seuil, 2014); Kimonyo, *Rwanda's Popular Genocide*; Omar McDoom, *The Path to Genocide in Rwanda: Security, Opportunity, and Authority in an Ethnocratic State* (Cambridge: Cambridge University Press, 2021).

20. Kimonyo, *Transforming Rwanda*, 98.

21. For a firsthand account of the Kibeho Massacre from the perspective of an Australian peacekeeper, see Terry Pickard, *Combat Medic: An Australian's Eyewitness Account of the Kibeho Massacre* (Newport: Big Sky, 2008).

22. Kimonyo, *Transforming Rwanda*, carefully presents the evidence for killings and their extent.

23. For a discussion of how humanitarians could be so blind to the ways their aid was supporting genocidal actors, see Fiona Terry, *Condemned to Repeat? The Paradox of Humanitarian Action* (Ithaca, NY: Cornell University Press, 2002).

24. Rick Orth, "Rwanda's Hutu Extremist Genocidal Insurgency: An Eyewitness Perspective," *Small Wars and Insurgencies* 12, no. 1 (2001): 85.

25. Orth, "Rwanda's Hutu Extremist Genocidal Insurgency," 90.

26. One early task was creating a new national military. RPA formed the backbone, but already by the end of 1994 some two thousand members of the defunct Rwandan Armed Forces had returned from Zaire and were undergoing training and reeducation at the Gako military base. More returned in the following years, and the military became the first new national institution, one based on an ideology of Rwandan unity and a disavowal of the old racial/ethnic labels.

27. *The Mercy of the Jungle*, dir. Joel Karekezi (2018).

28. In 2012, a new rebel group calling itself M23 emerged in eastern Congo. The Rwandan government was widely criticized for supporting M23. Western donors pulled aid from Rwanda to protest what they saw as Rwandan warmongering. A combat unit of the UN peacekeeping forces in the Congo, with backup from the Congolese armed forces, fought M23 and pushed them into a defensive position, from which they agreed to a peace settlement. M23 fighters mostly moved to camps in Uganda, where they awaited return to their home country and the terms of their integration into the armed forces. They waited until late 2021, when they began attacking villages in Congo's North Kivu province. They claimed they had taken up arms again because the peace agreement's terms had been ignored and in order to protect Tutsis in the Kivus in the context of rising anti-Tutsi hate speech. The Rwandan military has again been accused of supporting M23. For a helpful overview of the actors and interests involved in the M23 conflagration, see Judith Verweijen and Christoph Vogel, "Why Congo's M23 Crisis Lingers On," International Peace Institute: The Global Observatory, May 30, 2023, https://theglobalobservatory.org/2023/05/why-congos-m23-crisis-lingers-on/.

29. As I observed on several occasions in 2002.

30. Kimonyo, *Transforming Rwanda*, 138.

31. Phil Clark, *The Gacaca Courts, Post-Genocide Justice, and Reconciliation in Rwanda: Justice Without Lawyers* (Cambridge: Cambridge University Press, 2010).

32. Another critique of *gacaca* was that it tried only people accused of genocide and not RPA or others who killed in retaliation. The government's rationale was that those other crimes should be heard in regular or military courts and not the genocide-specific forum of *gacaca*.

33. Letter from Alison Des Forges to David Rawson, November 19, 1998, https://digitalcommons.georgefox.edu/cgi/viewcontent.cgi?article=1098&context=rawson_rwanda.

34. RPF dominance has been clear since the end of the genocide, but it was not clear how long it would hold; one critical argument has long been that, absent political liberalism, Rwanda will devolve into war. See, for example, International Crisis Group, *Rwanda at the End of the Transition: A Necessary Political Liberalization*

(Nairobi/Brussels, 2002). So far that has not happened, but, as noted in what follows, some of Rwanda's political tensions have been pushed into the diaspora and the Congo.

35. Kagame won elections in 2003, 2010, and 2017. He was permitted to stand in the last of these only after a constitutional amendment abolished the earlier term limits.

36. Reasons for this shift included that the RPF elites who had been educated in English during their exile were more comfortable with it; they saw French as a dying language on the world stage and were angry at French support for the genocidal government even after the extent of the genocide was known.

37. For moving portraits of Rwandan elders, see Aalyia Feroz Ali Sadruddin, "The Care of 'Small Things': Aging and Dignity in Rwanda," *Medical Anthropology* 39, no. 1 (2020): 83–95.

38. For instance, the musician Michael Makembe travels the country to record traditional songs and then remixes them, using a blend of acoustic and electronic instruments.

39. Briefly, their false claim is that while there was a genocide against Tutsi of short duration, there was a much longer genocide against Hutu, perpetrated by Tutsi.

40. André Sibomana, *Hope for Rwanda: Conversations with Laure Guilbert and Hervé Deguine* (London: Pluto, 1999), 139.

41. Sibomana, *Hope for Rwanda*, 129. He thought Catholic clergy made the best shepherds; their complicity in genocide meant that many Rwandans disagreed.

42. *Ejo* means both yesterday and tomorrow in Kinyarwanda; this term was coined by Chaste Niwe for a forthcoming article.

43. Jean Hatzfeld, *Blood Papa*, trans. Joshua David Gordon (New York: Farrar, Straus, and Giroux, 2018), 14, 77.

44. With thanks to Thierry Cruvellier for the conversation that elicited these statements.

45. Beata Umubyeyi Mairesse, *All Your Children Scattered* (Europa Editions, 2022), 221.

INTRODUCTION: GENOCIDE THROUGH THE EYES OF CHILDREN

1. Archives de la commission nationale de lutte contre le génocide (ACNLG), C421E (birth date not indicated).

2. According to the United Nations' statistics, there were eight hundred thousand victims, while the Rwandan government estimates 1,300,000. In the absence of a more precise count, I am adopting an intermediate figure, while recognizing the unpleasant and even indecent aspect of such a discrepancy between the two counts.

3. One illustration of this type of representation can be found in a series of "reports" published by Jean d'Ormesson in the French daily newspaper *Le Figaro* on July 19, 20, and 21, 1994. Moreover, on November 8, 1994, thus a few months after the massacres ended, France's President François Mitterrand made the following declaration during a Franco-African summit held in Biarritz: "One cannot ask the impossible of the international community, and still less of France . . . when local leaders decide deliberately . . . to settle their accounts with machetes." François Mitterrand, "Discours," https://www.vie-publique.fr/discours/128703-discours-de-m-francois-mitterrand-president-de-la-republique-sur-la-d.

4. For example, on October 25, 2018, in an article by a journalist writing for a major national weekly magazine, killers and victims were reversed, in a reference to "the genocide of the Hutus by the Tutsis." Can one imagine for a moment the scandal that would have been provoked by published assertions such as "the genocide of the Ottomans by the Armenians" or "the genocide of the Nazis by the Jews"? For the genocide of the Tutsi, a simple "tweet" was enough to appease the few protests. "A mistake," the journalist claimed, in what constituted an epilogue to the "affair."

5. The corpus includes a total of 2,011 pages in Kinyarwanda.

6. This institution, created in 2008, is charged with addressing all questions relating to the history and memory of the genocide.

7. From the 105 notebooks preserved in this archive, forty-six have been published, in a very small number of copies, by the CNLG. Transcribed in Kinyarwanda, they nevertheless do not appear in their original form, as they were subjected to substantial cuts. CNLG, *Ribara uwariraye: Igitabo gikubiyemo ubuhamya bw'abana barokotse Jenoside yakorewe Abatutsi* [The horror that can only be recounted by someone who lived through it: a work bringing together the testimonies of child survivors of the genocide perpetrated against the Tutsi], 2 vols. (Kigali, 2017).

8. Atle Dyregrov, Leila Gupta, Rolf Gjestad, and Eugénie Mukanoheli, "Trauma Exposure and Psychological Reactions to Genocide among Rwandan Children," *Journal of Traumatic Stress* 13, no. 1 (2000): 14.

9. Psychotherapists who have been trained in Rwanda to support survivors of the genocide are called trauma counselors. Generally speaking, they are salaried employees of associations or decentralized services operating under the Health Ministry's Department of Mental Health.

10. On the history of this association, see Esther Mujawayo and Souâd Belhaddad, *SurVivantes: Rwanda, histoire d'un génocide* (Paris: Éditions de l'Aube, 2004).

11. Among the bundles, three notebooks whose authors came from the commune of Runyinya (Butare prefecture) thus did not belong to the writing project organized by Avega, giving rise to the supposition that similar collective workshops may have taken place elsewhere. I sought but failed to find a complete

collection of these other stories, which were most likely solicited by the Association des étudiants et élèves rescapés du génocide (AERG: Association of Students and Schoolchildren Survivors of the Genocide).

12. Judith Lyon-Caen and Dinah Ribard, *L'historien et la littérature* (Paris: La Découverte, 2010).

13. Ibuka ("Remember," in Kinyarwanda) is one of the principal associations representing the survivors of the genocide, along with Avega and the AERG.

14. Dukundane Family, *Ishavu ry'Abato: Ubuhamya kuri Jenoside yakorewe abatutsi mu Rwanda* [The sorrows of the children: testimonies on the genocide perpetrated against the Tutsi in Rwanda] (Kigali, April 2009); Florence Prud'homme, ed., *Cahiers de mémoire, Kigali, 2014* (Paris: Classique Garnier, 2017); Prud'homme, ed., *Cahiers de mémoire, Kigali, 2019* (Paris: Classique Garnier, 2019). For the most part, these last two works, translated from the Kinyarwanda, present the testimony of survivors who were adults at the time of the genocide.

15. For an analysis that is necessarily partial, given the burgeoning corpus, see Remi Korman, "Indirimbo z'icyunamo: Chanter la mémoire du génocide," *Les Temps Modernes*, nos. 680–81 (October–November 2014): 350–61; and Paul Kerstens, "Amahoro: Chanter après le génocide," in *Les langages de la mémoire: Littérature, médias et génocide au Rwanda*, ed. Pierre Halen and Jacques Walter (Metz: Université Paul Verlaine, 2007), 99–103.

16. The two youngest were born in 1989 and the oldest in 1973.

17. Sixty-two of the 105 were girls; forty-three were boys. According to the census of the Rwandan government, 56.4 percent of the victims were male, 43.3 percent female. République du Rwanda, *Dénombrement des victimes du génocide: Rapport final* (Kigali, April 2004), 25, MINALOC archives.

18. ACNLG, C67MMGC.

19. I also recall Gervais's exasperation with the sometimes undecipherable handwriting in the texts and the often clumsy spellings of the "children," as he never failed to designate the writers.

20. The "hypermnesia of childhood" is evoked in an entirely different configuration by Manon Pignot, *Allons enfants de la patrie: Génération Grande Guerre* (Paris: Seuil, 2012), 386.

21. Throughout this text I shall privilege the use of the term "genocide" in its substantive form in order to retain the full specificity of the term, which the adjectival form seems to me to attenuate.

22. If we refer to the Rwandan government's count of victims in the Kibungo and Kigali-Ngali prefectures, the place of origin of most of the writers, the numbers are these: a total of 88,612 in Kibungo, which represents the sixth prefecture most affected by the massacres (out of eleven); in the Kigali-Ngali prefecture, the communes of Bicumbi (15,352 dead) and especially Kanzenze (50,035 dead) record the largest numbers of victims. République du Rwanda, MINALOC archives, *Dénombrement*

des victimes du génocide, Annexes préfecture de Kibungo et préfecture de Kigali-Ngali.

23. André Guichaoua, "'Vérité judiciaire' et 'vérité du chercheur': Témoins et témoignages devant le tribunal pénal international," in *Crises extrêmes: Face au massacres, aux guerres civiles et aux génocides*, ed. Marc Le Pape, Johanna Siméant, and Claudine Vidal (Paris: La Découverte, 2007), 119–35.

24. It suffices to have been present in a Paris *cour d'assises* (a civil court where serious crimes are addressed) during the trials of persons indicted in France for their participation in the genocide to have witnessed the way the testimony of the survivors was undermined by the accused and their defense teams. This was especially the case during the trials of Octavien Ngenzi and Tito Barahira in their first trial (May–July 2016) and their appeal (May–July 2018).

25. Thus in November 2007 the International Penal Court accepted five hundred drawings as "circumstantial evidence" of the conflict in Darfur. Zérane Girardeau, *Déflagrations: Dessins d'enfants, guerres d'adultes* (Paris: Anamosa, 2017), 258.

26. If we limit ourselves (prudently) to the figures provided by the Service national des juridictions *gacaca* (SNJG: National Service of Gacaca Jurisdictions) during the closure of the judicial process in June 2012, 415,016 persons were condemned for crimes connected with the genocide, while 1,266,632 were penalized for their participation in the looting. We should note that a given individual could be found guilty for participation both in the massacres and in the looting, which makes the manipulation of these statistics particularly delicate; see République du Rwanda, Service national des juridictions *gacaca, Résumé du support présenté à la clôture des activités des juridictions* gacaca (Kigali, June 2012), 55. Moreover, according to figures from February 2008, women represented 5.7 percent of the population of people in prison for crimes related to the genocide (2,133 women out of 37,213 in all). Nicole Hogg, "Women's Participation in the Rwandan Genocide: Mothers or Monsters?," *International Review of the Red Cross* 92, no. 877 (March 2010): 70.

1. THE WORLDS OF CHILDHOOD: FAMILY AND SCHOOL

1. If we use the figures from the general census of the population carried out in 1991, the synthetic index of fertility comes to 6.9 children per woman of childbearing age (ages 15–49). République du Rwanda, *Recensement général de la population et de l'habitat au 15 août 1991* (Kigali: Service national de recensement, April 1994), 235.

2. For example, maternal uncles are designated by the term *marume*, while paternal aunts are designated as *masenge*. Moreover, to refer to the brothers and sisters born to one's own parents, a term that comes up consistently is *abo tuvukana*, which means literally "those who have come from the same womb."

3. In 1991, 94.4 percent of the Rwandan population lived in rural areas. République du Rwanda, *Recensement général*, 32.

4. On the relative socioeconomic distribution in the prefecture of Kibungo, see Paul Rutayisire and Privat Rutazibwa, *Génocide à Nyarubuye* (Kigali: Éditions rwandaises, 2007), 27–28.

5. ACNLG, C3WNJC (birth date not indicated).

6. ACNLG, C24GI.

7. According to an investigation published by the Rwandan government in 2004, "the proportion of victims of the masculine sex (56.4%) is higher than that of females (43.4%)." République du Rwanda, *Dénombrement des victimes du génocide: Rapport final* (Kigali, April 2004), 25, MINALOC archives.

8. The actual proverb (*umugani*) reads, rather, "*Utaganiriye na se ngo ntamenya icyo sekuru yasize avuze*": "He who does not talk with his father cannot know what his grandfather said before he died."

9. ACNLG, C731VC.

10. ACNLG, C11RMM.

11. ACNLG, C66KFC.

12. ACNLG, C58NAC.

13. ACNLG, C87MFC.

14. One boy born in 1981 displays strikingly detailed topographical knowledge in his account of his life as a young herder, traipsing throughout the woods surrounding his *rugo* in search of the most satisfying pastures and waterholes for his cows. ACNLG, C82BO.

15. ACNLG, C86UA. In the countryside, it was customary for little girls to "play Mama" with the flower of a banana plant carried on their backs like a baby.

16. ACNLG, C84NP.

17. ACNLG, C23MSC

18. ACNLG, République du Rwanda, *Dynamiques des équilibres ethnique et régional dans l'enseignement secondaire rwandais: Fondements, évolution et perspectives d'avenir* (Kigali: Ministère de l'Enseignement primaire et secondaire, May 1986), 88. An illustration of this "ethnic census" can be found in the archive presented in the central notebook for the Centre d'enseignement rural et artisanal intégré (Integrated Center for Rural and Artisanal Instruction) of Zaza for the start of the school year 1989–1990.

19. Antoine Mugesera, *Les conditions de vie des Tutsi au Rwanda de 1959 à 1990: Persécutions et massacres antérieurs au génocide de 1990–1994* (Kigali/Miélan: Dialogue/Izuba, 2014 [2004 for the version in Kinyarwanda]), 261.

20. On the long history of racism and its inscription at the heart of the postcolonial political systems between 1962 and 1994, one book is indispensable: Jean-Pierre Chrétien and Marcel Kabanda, *Rwanda, racisme et génocide: L'idéologie hamitique* (Paris: Belin, 2013).

21. On the violence of the early months of 1973, see Chrétien and Kabanda, *Rwanda, racisme et génocide*, 153–54, and Mugesera, *Conditions de vie*, 192–97.

22. These figures, which are supposed to reflect the "ethnic proportions" of the population, are defined in an arbitrary way; the most recent census had taken place in 1956. It was nevertheless on the basis of that census that Grégoire Kayibanda decreed the following quotas: 85 percent Hutu, 14 percent Tutsi, and 1 percent Twa. We should note in passing that, under the new requirements of the Habyarimana regime, the Twa disappeared from the "efforts toward equilibrium." The example of these statistics offers a first demonstration of the political manipulation of Hutu and Tutsi as ethnoracial categories. See Mugesera, *Conditions de vie des Tutsi*; and Raphaël Nkaka, "L'emprise d'une logique raciale sur la société rwandaise (1894–1994)," doctoral thesis, Université Paris-1, 2013, 279.

23. Founded in 1975, the MRND remained the sole political party authorized in Rwanda until June 1991, when the constitution allowed the expression of diverse partisan inclinations. On April 10, 1986, the central committee of the MRND was charged in particular with examining the question of schools: Bonaventure Habimana addressing the "Militants Préfets": "Examen des documents relatifs aux admissions scolaires par les comités préfectoraux," April 29, 1986, ACNLG, Présidence du MRND.

24. "Examen des documents relatifs aux admissions scolaires par les comités préfectoraux."

25. République du Rwanda, *Dynamiques des équilibres ethnique et régional*, 252; italics original.

26. I am borrowing this expression from Arjun Appadurai, whose reflection on the obsession with "small numbers" and the construction of political legitimacy by reliance on statistical mechanisms is very clarifying in the Rwandan case. Arjun Appadurai, *Géographie de la colère: La violence à l'âge de la globalisation* (Paris: Payot, 2009), 89–90.

27. These terms refer to couples living as concubines, on the one hand, and couples who had managed to make their union "official" in the eyes of the civil state, on the other.

28. Thus, in 1987, an agent of the prefectoral intelligence services in Kibungo informed his superiors of a suspicion concerning a man who indeed possessed a "Hutu" identity card but whose "outward appearance" showed a "Tutsi aspect," adding that "some say that the family is Tutsi. These [people] having changed [their] ethnic group in 1973." The conclusion: "His ethnicity is dubious, as is that of his whole family. In-depth verifications to follow." Behind the words of a local official one can clearly see the influence of a mental universe dominated by racial differentiations, focused here on the *body* of the Other. The phenomenon is hardly limited to this case alone; local archives contain a number of communications of this type. République du Rwanda, "Formule message," ACNLG, AAPK 159.87.

29. République du Rwanda, ministre de l'Éducation nationale, Pierre-Claver Mutemberezi au président de la République, au ministre de l'Intérieur et au

directeur général du Service central de renseignements, "Contrôle des identités des élèves," Kigali, February 17, 1978, ACNLG document no. 07.04/706.

30. ACNLG, C30NB.

31. ACNLG, C53RAC.

32. ACNLG, C59NJDC.

33. ACNLG, C10RGC.

34. ACNLG, C35IP.

35. This decision led to an attack on Ms. Uwilingiyimana in her home the following month. Jordane Bertrand, *Rwanda, le piège de l'histoire: L'opposition démocratique avant le génocide (1990–1994)* (Paris: Karthala, 2000), 195.

36. ACNLG, C8RNEC.

37. ACNLG, C2WMA.

38. ACNLG, C81MI.

39. ACNLG, C13RKVC.

40. ACNLG, C57RFR.

41. ACNLG, C71MA.

42. See Chrétien and Kabana, *Rwanda, racisme et génocide*, 135–36; and Mugesera, *Conditions de vie*, 68–71.

43. Figures cited in Mugesera, *Conditions de vie*, 69.

44. In the words of the visiting Belgian colonial official in Kibungo: "The visit gives a rather bad impression: certain families linger in the large central camp, others are found in huts around which the bush is growing back wildly. . . . The visitor has the impression that these refugees are abandoned, left to their own devices, even though it all costs an enormous amount of money." Administrateur, Territoire de Kibungu, "Rapport de visite, installation réfugiés à Rubago (Bwiriri)," au Résident du Ruanda à Kigali, July 1, 1961, ACNLG, AARK. Concerning this internal banishment that had become a general policy extended to the entire territory by the Belgian colonial authorities, see also Chrétien and Kabanda, *Rwanda, racisme et génocide*, 137.

45. In the exact terms of the report: "*Ceux qui sont mal intentionnés, la faim les contraindra bien*" (Those who have bad intentions will be decisively constrained by hunger).

46. ACNLG, C61HIC.

47. ACNLG, C8RNEC.

2. CHILDHOODS AT WAR

1. ACNLG, C46NSC.

2. On the intellectual and political history of the FPR, see especially Jean-Paul Kimonyo, *Rwanda: Demain! Une longue marche vers la transformation* (Paris: Karthala, 2017).

3. For an account of this initial offensive, see Kimonyo, *Rwanda: Demain!*, 118–19.

4. Launched on October 4, 1990, by President François Mitterrand of France at the request of Juvénal Habyarimana, the Noroît Operation was officially intended to ensure the security of French and other foreign citizens. In fact, France maintained and reinforced its military cooperation with the regime until the end of 1993.

5. An eloquent illustration can be found in the speech given by Juvénal Habyarimana on December 7, 1990, to the FAR members stationed in the Mutara region, in what was the first theater of confrontations with the FPR: see ICTR (International Criminal Tribunal for Rwanda) Exhibits, Bagosora trial ICTR-98-41-T. See also Jean-Pierre Chrétien, ed., *Rwanda: Les médias du génocide* (Paris: Karthala, 1995), 142. Charles Mironko reproduces excerpts of programs broadcast by the RTLM (Radio Télévision Libre des Mille Collines) developing the theme of a struggle between "monarchists" and "farmers' sons" (*sebahinzi*) liberated by the "revolution" of 1959: Charles Mironko, "Social and Political Mechanisms of Mass Murder: An Analysis of Perpetrators in the Rwandan Genocide," (PhD diss., Yale University, 2004), 155–56. Also worth reading is the very enlightening document produced by the general staff of the Rwandan army defining the "enemy" at a meeting held in December 1991: General Staff G2, Rwandan Army, Ministry of National Defense, "Extraits du rapport de la Commission chargée de la définition de l'ennemi," Kigali, September 21, 1992.

6. The administrative archives of the Kibungo prefecture shed valuable light, owing to their concreteness, on civilian involvement in the war operations. For example, one prefectural account from March 1991 refers to a meeting held with mayors on the question of maintaining "security" by a new, very localized structure (the *nyumbakumi*, people put in charge of ten households). In the commune of Rukara, setting up such a structure was rejected on the grounds that there were too many Tutsi inhabitants in certain administrative cells. See "Avis des conseillers communaux sur la nouvelle structure dans le maintien de la sécurité," "*Nyumabakumi*" (ACNLG, AAPK). Similarly, the services of the subprefecture of Rwamagana reported on the direct participation in the war of civilian populations, again in the commune of Rukara. See "Sous-préfet de Rwamagana au préfet de Kibungo," January 31, 1991, ACNLG, AAPK. Moreover, a declassified French archive in the context of the work of the Mission of Parliamentary Information on the "military operations conducted by France and other countries and the U.N. in Rwanda between 1990 and 1994" provides detailed information about the distribution of weapons to civilians—and on what the French ambassador and the French defense attaché knew about this: "300 weapons (MAS 36 for the most part) will be distributed in the sector of Ruhengeri and Byumba and 76 in the Mutara [combat zones]. The persons constituted in self-defense militias who will receive these weapons will be chosen by virtue of their 'honorability' and 'counseled' by the staff of the FARs." Excerpt from a message from the defense

attaché in Kigali, Colonel Bernard Cussac, January 22, 1992; the text is included in annexes from the report of the mission of parliamentary information, made public on December 15, 1998; see Bernard Cussac, "Message de l'attaché de défense à Kigali," December 15, 1998, 165.

7. On this racist vision, one key text was prepared by Théoneste Bagosora, subprefect of Rwamagana, for his own defense shortly before he was arrested in Cameroon on March 6, 1996: "L'assassinat du président Habyarimana ou l'ultime operation tutsi pour sa reconquête du pouvoir par la force," Yaoundé, October 30, 1995. Considered one of the principal activists in the genocide, Bagosora was tried by the International Criminal Tribunal for Rwanda (ICTR) and sentenced to life in prison, then, on appeal, to thirty-five years in prison in the context of the trial targeting the officers of the Rwandan army, called "Militaires I." See *Jugement portant condemnation*, December 18, 2008 (ICTR-98-41-T), and *Arrêt*, December 14, 2011 (ICTR-98-41-T).

8. If we credit the census figures for the victims of the genocide, of the ten communes of the new Mutara prefecture, the commune of Muvumba was the most affected by the massacres in 1990 and 1991 and the least affected by the killings of 1994 (1990, 15 percent; 1991, 16.7 percent; 1994, 61 percent, whereas the 1994 death rates in the other communes were close to 100 percent). République du Rwanda, *Dénombrement des victimes du génocide: Rapport final* (Kigali, April 2004), Table 5, annex "Préfecture du Mutara," MINALOC archives.

9. A Belgian military journal also mentions the attack on refugees by helicopters: "In the north, the battle is raging. On October 10, in Kiziguro, I met the first dead and the first wounded; the latter are civilians who were fleeing from the combat zone, more to the north, and who were shot down by machine guns from the Rwandan army's Écureuil helicopters. Among them, women and children. The helicopters appeared, two of them, and opened fire on the column of refugees." Thierry Charlier, "Octobre rouge au Rwanda," *Armée et Défense: Air, Terre, Mer* 12 (December 1990): 25.

10. ACNLG, C64NSC.

11. ACNLG, C9RMC.

12. In French in the text.

13. ACNLG, C64NSC; emphasis added.

14. The FPR army was called Inyenzi-Inkotanyi by the extremists, with reference to the Inyenzi fighters in the 1960s. Before 1966, these exiles attempted several armed incursions into Rwanda that turned into immense massacres in the interior of the country, especially in the Gikongoro region around Christmas in 1963.

15. ACNLG, C90NJCC.

16. République du Rwanda, Ministère de la Justice, "Liste des personnes arrêtées suite à l'attaque des Inkotanyi du 1er octobre 1990, du 1er octobre au 31 mars 1991," ICTR, public database. The exact number given is 6,477 persons. In March 1991,

143 persons were still incarcerated, according to this report. Apart from the official sources, which may be suspected of undercounting the abuses, one can refer to the invaluable detailed compilation of the acts of persecution drawn up by the Committee for the Respect for Human Rights and Democracy in Rwanda: "Victims of Political Repression since October 1st 1990 in Rwanda," Kigali, December 1991. The report presents 973 individual cases into which an investigation had been carried out. It provides information not only about the arbitrary arrests but also about the assassinations of Tutsi from the northwest region (Ruhengeri and Gisenyi), the Abagogwe, victims of several waves of massacres in October 1990, in February 1991, and again in January 1993. On these killings of the Abagogwe, see also International Federation for Human Rights (FIDH), Africa Watch, "Rapport de la Commission internationale d'enquête sur les violations des droits de l'homme au Rwanda depuis le 1er octobre 1990," *Rapport final*, March 1993, 18–42.

17. ACNLG, C10KF.

18. ACNLG, C62MO.

19. ACNLG, C57RFR. This dialogue echoes to some extent the one reported by Jan Gross: "Joseph's wife looked at my feet: 'Honestly, you could leave me your boots, Madam.' 'But, Madam Joseph, I am still alive.' 'Fine, I didn't say anything, I just said that you had really nice boots.'" Jan Gross, *La peur: L'antisémitisme en Pologne après Auschwitz* (Paris: Calmann-Lévy/Mémorial de la Shoah, 2010), 82.

20. As of June 1991, multipartyism was authorized in the constitution. This measure led quickly to the rapid development of a series of political parties that competed on the local level, often with violence. In April 1992 and again in July 1993, two multiparty administrations ruled the country. This political recomposition explains why Agathe Uwilingiyimana, a female Democrat favorable to sharing power with the FPR, became prime minister in July 1993; she was still in that role in April 1994. She was among the first victims of the Hutu extremists, on April 7. On the political history of the country between 1990 and 1994, see Jordane Bertrand, *Rwanda, le piège de l'histoire: L'opposition démocratique avant le génocide (1990–1994)* (Paris: Karthala, 2000), and Jean-Paul Kimonyo, *Rwanda, un génocide populaire* (Paris: Karthala, 2008).

21. ACNLG, C81MI.

22. ACNLG, C81MI. The "Renewed Movement" refers to the MRND. On April 28, 1991, the party held an exceptional meeting for the purpose of adapting to the new partisan competition that was taking shape. It changed its name, becoming the National Republican Movement for Development and Democracy (MRNDD).

23. ACNLG, C77ME. Too young to be in school in October 1990, this writer is probably reporting the recollections that had circulated among his siblings. We find the metaphor of "banana tree trunk" for Tutsi in many other texts, often in connection with parodies of Fred Rwigema's burial.

24. Jean-Pierre Chrétien and Marcel Kabanda, *Rwanda, racisme et génocide: L'idéologie hamitique* (Paris: Belin, 2013), 193–95. Moreover, in the wake of multipartyism, a large number of organizations for the defense of human rights emerged in Rwanda. On September 11, 1991, some of these groups came together as a collective, the Rwandan Association for the Defense of Human Rights and Public Liberties (ADL). The voluminous reports produced by this association document the abuses of the Habyarimana regime courageously and in detail. The report on the massacres in the Bugesera region challenges the official figures (182 dead, 15,000 displaced, 1,500 houses burned, and 1,200 domestic animals killed) as significant undercounts; the ADL reports more than 300 victims, 774 refugees in the Catholic parishes of Ruhuha and the Pentecostal parishes of Rango in the commune of Ngenda, 460 refugees in the Rilima parish in the commune of Gashora, and more than 3,600 refugees in the Nyamata parish in the commune of Kanzenze. See ADL, *Rapport sur les droits de l'homme au Rwanda: Septembre 1991–septembre 1992* (Kigali, December 1992), 207–27.

25. A lay worker with the Soeurs hospitalières congregation, Antonia Locatelli arrived in Rwanda on December 16, 1970. After she denounced the massacres of the Tutsi in the Bugesera region on international radio, she was shot and killed by members of the armed forces during the night of March 9–10, 1992.

26. ACNLG, C76RP.

27. ACNLG, C38RSH.

28. ACNLG, AAPK, Service du renseignement préfectoral au Service central de renseignements, March 9, 1992: "letting you know that rumors have circulated in the Sake commune according to which Bugesera situation was going to be repeated in Sake because there are many refugees from Gashora and because Sake population (Rukumberi and Gituza) are going to cut and burn." And in another message dated March 16, 1992: "Moreover flow [*sic*] of words is circulating in Kibungo according to which 'the Hutu want to cut the Tutsi.'" ACNLG, AAPK.

29. In French in the text.

30. ACNLG, C71MA; emphasis added.

31. Prefect of Kibungo to the Ministry of the Interior and Communal Development, "Compte rendu du comité préfectoral de sécurité tenu le 11 mars 1992," transmitted March 20, 1992 (ACNLG, AAPK). The report mentions several cattle slaughtered and houses burned, people drowned in the Akagera River, and several murders and beatings, in the Sake commune as well as in Mugesera.

32. In French in the text. This expression, which was used for a long time, is hardly appropriate on the historical level, since it suggests an interethnic brawl among Rwandans. There is no such thing as a "Rwandan genocide" any more than there is an "Ottoman genocide" or a "German genocide."

33. In French in the text.

34. ACNLG, C10RGC.

35. "Rapport de la mission d'enquête sur le bourgmestre Gatete Jean-Baptiste de la commune de Murambi," Kigali, June 23, 1993, 2. According to this report, fifteen of the sixteen men arrested were killed by soldiers when they arrived at the Byumba prison. According to the ADL report, eighteen men "disappeared," two of whom were alleged to have died in the communal dungeon at the hands of Jean-Baptiste Gatete himself. In addition, in November 1991, in his own sector of origin, Rwankuba, Gatete orchestrated a series of very violent attacks on the Tutsi and on his own political opponents. ADL, *Rapport sur les droits de l'homme au Rwanda*, 148–58. Jean-Baptiste Gatete was sentenced to life in prison by the ICTR in 2011; the term was reduced on appeal a year later to forty years in prison. See especially the sentencing statement, "Le procureur contre Jean-Baptiste Gatete," March 11, 2011 (ICTR-2000-61-T).

36. Kigeri was the name of the reign of the last king (*mwami*) before the installation of the republican regime on January 28, 1961. Such accusations, which were supposed to demonstrate the Tutsi attachment to the despised monarchy, were not new. In 1985, an agent of the intelligence services of the Kibungo prefecture alerted his superiors to the fact that he had apprehended a potential "instrument of subversion" who had come from Tanzania and who bore on his arm the inscription "Vive Kigeri et Hitler [Long live Kigeri and Hitler]." ACNLG, AAPK, SPR of Kibungo to SCR, February 14, 1985.

37. ACNLG, C27RJB.

3. SEPARATIONS

1. ACNLG, C13RKVC.

2. In a speech given in Butare, broadcast April 22, 1994, on Radio Rwanda, Jean Kambanda, then prime minister of the interim government, hurled out these words: "This war in which we are is the last, the final war" (translated from a transcription of the broadcast, recorded in ICTR, public database).

3. ACNLG, C87MFC (female, born in 1985).

4. ACNLG, CC31UM.

5. ACNLG, C568HC.

6. ACNLG, C30BD. The young writer misremembered his age at the time of the events related.

7. ACNLG, C58NAC.

8. ACNLG, C11RMM.

9. On this point, see Élisabeth Claverie, "Techniques de la menace," *Terrain*, no. 43 (September 2004): 15–30.

10. ACNLG, C67MFC.

11. ACNLG, C82BO.

12. ACNLG, C75NE.

13. ACNLG, C75NE.

14. ACNLG, C79NC.

15. ACNLG, C56MY.

16. ACNLG, C74RM.

17. During the appeals trial of the Kabarondo town supervisors Tito Barahira and Octavien Ngenzi, several witnesses reported the existence of a militia whose membership started with a group of former hunters, the Abarinda (hearing notes, testimony of Anaclet Ruhumuliza, June 8, 2018).

18. ACNLG, C6MF; ACNLG, C14UC.

19. ACNLG, C87MFC.

20. ACNLG, C8RNEC.

21. ACNLG, C50RJ.

22. ACNLG, C27 JB.

23. ACNLG, C37BCC.

24. Paul Rutayisire and Privat Rutazibwa, *Génocide à Nyarubuye* (Kigali: Éditions rwandaises, 2007), 53.

25. Rutayisire and Rutazibwa, *Génocide à Nyarubuye*, 84.

26. ACNLG, CC23MSC. The narrative corresponds point for point with the one presented in Rutayisire and Rutazibwa, *Génocide à Nyarubuye*, 84–85, except for the bond of kinship between Vincent Hakizamungu and Laurent Bahutu. The former seems to have been Vincent Hakizamungu's father, not his paternal uncle, but given the role paternal uncles played in the culture, the confusion is understandable.

4. "THEIR GOD IS DEAD"

1. République du Rwanda, Service national du recensement, *Recensement général de la population et de l'habitat au 15 août 1991* (Kigali, April 1994), 126. The proportions indicated are the following: 89.8 percent Christian (62.6 percent Catholic, 18.8 percent Protestant, and 8.45 percent Adventist). According to the census of the victims of the genocide carried out by the Rwandan government and published in 2004, churches represented the second most important sites of massacre (11.6 percent of the victims), after the hill regions (59.3 percent). République du Rwanda, *Dénombrement des victimes du génocide: Rapport final* (Kigali, April 1994), 33, MINALOC archives.

2. ACNLG, CW2MA.

3. The estimates of the number of victims of the massacre in the Nyarubuye church oscillate around 26,000 dead. It is thus impossible that there could have been as many refugees as the boy indicated. Paul Rutayisire and Privat Rutazibwa, *Génocide à Nyarubuye* (Kigali: Éditions rwandaises, 2007), 91.

4. ACNLG, C87MFC.

5. ACNLG, CW4MA. The "white priest" is the Spanish priest of the parish, Father Santos (Ganuza Lasa Santos). "Le procureur contre Jean Mpambara," September 11, 2006 (ICTR-01-65-T). According to Father Santos's declarations to ICTR investigators in 2004, more than three thousand people had taken shelter in the parish before the massacre. ICTR-ol-65-T, item P16A, ICTR public database.

6. ACNLG, C46HY. Regarding the author's estimate of five thousand, according to Oreste Incimatata, the priest of the Kabarondo parish, between 2,500 and 3,000 people were sheltering in the church and its surroundings on April 12. For the entire diocese of Kibungo, the overall estimates of the victims are as high as fifty thousand. *Stella Matutina, Bulletin du diocèse de Kibungo*, no. 112 (June 1995): 7

7. ACNLG, C667MMGC.

8. ACNLG, C87MFC.

9. ACNLG, C87MFC.

10. ACNLG, C38RSH.

11. ACNLG, CW4MA.

12. ACNLG, CW4MA.

13. ACNLG, C46HY.

14. ACNLG, C46HY.

15. ACNLG, C87MFC.

16. ACNLG, C2WMA.

17. These are the words we chose to translate a common expression in Kinyarwanda, "*Imana ikinja akaboko*," which means literally, "God interposes his arm."

18. ACNLG, C45UAC.

19. ACNLG, C31UM.

20. ACNLG, C55NJCC.

21. ACNLG, C41HS.

22. ACNLG, C77ME.

23. ACNLG, C71MA.

24. ACNLG, C71MA.

25. ACNLG, CW4MA.

26. Judith Lyon-Caen and Dinah Ribard, *L'historien et la littérature* (Paris: La Découverte, 2010).

5. THEATERS OF CRUELTY

1. I have borrowed the expression "theaters of cruelty" from Denis Crouzet, "Les guerres de religion entre fin des temps et théâtres de la cruauté," *Revue des deux mondes* (February–March 2017): 87–102.

2. François Lebigot, *Le trauma psychique* (Brussels: Yapaka.be, "Temps d'arrêt," 2006), 7.

3. ACNLG, C52NAMC.

4. ACNLG, C3WNJC (birth date not indicated).

5. I have borrowed this expression from Véronique Nahoum-Grappe, "L'usage politique de la cruauté: L'épuration ethnique (ex-Yougoslavie, 1991–1995)," in *De la violence*, ed. Françoise Héritier (Paris: Odile Jacob, 2005), 280–81.

6. The child uses the verb *gujinka*, which in principle designates exclusively the fact of slitting an animal's throat.

7. She insists on their very young age with the use of redundancy: literally, "*utwana tw'impinja*" means "the young children babies."

8. ACNLG, C88MVC.

9. Atle Dyregrov, Leila Gupta, Rolf Gjestad, and Eugénie Mukanoheli, "Trauma Exposure and Psychological Reactions to Genocide among Rwandan Children," *Journal of Traumatic Stress* 13, no. 1 (2000): 6.

10. ACNLG, C5WUCC.

11. Here the class reserved for the designation of inanimate beings is used rather than the one used for humans, translating an instance of "thingification."

12. ACNLG, C90NJCC.

13. ACNLG, C30BD.

14. The specificity offered here by the young writer is not insignificant, since the designation of elderly persons by the term "old man" or "old woman" (*abasaza* or *abakecuru*) stems from basic politeness in Kinyarwanda. The fact that the killers did not use it themselves attests to the scorn with which they regard their victim.

15. ACNLG, C18TO.

16. In a study published in 1999, the AVEGA Association (Association of the Widows of the April Genocide, known as Avega) notes that around 66 percent of the rapes took place in public. Avega-agahozo, *Survey on Violence against Women in Rwanda* (Kigali, December 1999), 19. The percentage is based on putting together the various categories of actors counted as inciters or direct authors of the rapes (men, men and women together, adolescents, and children).

17. If only the men of the family are cited, it is clearly to emphasize the offense.

18. ACNLG, C13RKVC.

19. ACNLG, C13RKVC.

20. ACNLG, C18TO; emphasis added.

21. ACNLG, C10KF.

22. ACNLG, C50RJ.

23. ACNLG, CC21NCC; emphasis added.

24. ACNLG, C83MV (birth date not indicated).

25. In the obsessively maintained statistics that characterized Grégoire Kayibanda's First Republic and especially Juvénal Habyarimana's Second Republic, children were enrolled in the civil registries with the "ethnic status" of their father. The absurdity and fragility of the system became clear, nevertheless, when children born to unknown fathers were listed, for their part, under the ethnic rubric of their mother.

26. ACNLG, C55NJCC; emphasis added.

27. Cited in Frédéric Baillette, "Figures du corps, ethnicité et génocide au Rwanda," *Quasimodo* 6 (Spring 2000): 9.

28. ACNLG, CC27RJB.

29. ACNLG, CC61HIC.

30. In Kinyarwanda, the expression stresses the very young age of the little girl.

31. ACNLG, C45UAC.

32. ACNLG, C68UHC.

33. ACNLG, C79NC; emphasis added.

34. République du Rwanda, Service national de recensement (National Census Service), *Recensement général de la population et de l'habitat au 15 août 1991* (Kigali: Service national de recensement, April 1994), 74, 271. The exact age of life expectancy in 1991 was 53.7 years. According to that year's census, the average age of the population was 15.2 years.

35. République du Rwanda, *Dénombrement des victimes du génocide: Rapport final* (Kigali, April 1994), 24, MINALOC archives. The report notes, moreover, that "the elderly, for the most part, were abandoned in their homes, where they died of hunger" (31).

36. ACNLG, C68UHC and C37BCC.

37. ACNLG, C15UV.

38. ACNLG, C79NC.

39. ACNLG, C40MBC.

40. ACNLG, C41HS.

41. ACNLG, C1postUA.

42. The snake in question was a puff adder (French *vipère heurtante*, or "colliding snake"), a particularly dangerous venomous snake. See the children's book by Father Thomas Bazarusanga, *Inzoka n'Abagombozi* [Snakes and healers of venom] (Kigali: Éditions Rwabato, n.d.). The book lists the main species of snakes found in the country.

43. ACNLG, C38RSH.

44. ACNLG, C15UV.

45. ACNLG, C25KRC.

46. The common expression is, rather, "*ijoro ribana uwariraye*": "only the one who has traversed the night can tell its story."

47. ACNLG, C92KB.

6. ECOSYSTEMS OF SURVIVAL

1. République du Rwanda, *Dénombrement des victimes du génocide: Rapport final* (Kigali, April 1994), 33, MINALOC archives. According to this report, 59.3 percent of the victims were murdered on the hills.

2. See, for example, ACNLG, C6MF (male, born in 1987): "The State had changed, the dugout canoeists had been informed that they must not help any Tutsi to cross the water." On the control of the border with Burundi, see Jean-Paul Kimonyo, *Rwanda: Demain! Une longue marche vers la transformation* (Paris: Karthala, 2017), 316.

3. One can trace the itineraries described by the young writers with the help of the twenty-seven topographical charts at a scale of 1:50,000 produced between 1987 and 1989 by the National Geographic Institute of Belgium in collaboration with Rwanda's cartographic service.

4. ACNLG, C14RUC (birth date not indicated); emphasis added.

5. ACNLG, C14RUC.

6. ACNLG, CC8RNED; emphasis added.

7. ACNLG, C34IC.

8. ACNLG, C48NEC.

9. ACNLG, C34IC.

10. ACNLG, C45UAC.

11. ACNLG, C43IC.

12. The Bugesera region was taken by the FPR between May 12 and May 14.

13. ACNLG, C34IC.

14. ACNLG, C38RSH.

15. République du Rwanda, *Dénombrement*, cited in Antoine Mugesera, "Les noyés du génocide," *Dialogue* 190 (March 2010): 54.

16. ACNLG, C40MBC.

17. As attested by the itinerary traced on the 1:50,000 scale maps.

18. ACNLG, C58NAC. The toad (*Gikeri*) is a recurring figure in Rwandan fairy tales. See "Igikeri cyaciriye iteka umwana w'imfubyi" [A toad who rendered justice to an orphan], in *Imigani "timangiro" yu Rwanda: Les contes moraux du Rwanda*, ed. Aloys Bigirumwami and Bernardin Muzungu (Butare: Éditions de l'Université nationale du Rwanda, 1989), 60–61; Pierre Smith, *Le récit populaire au Rwanda* (Paris: Armand Colin, 1985), 168–69.

19. ACNLG, C70NB.

20. ACNLG, C8WUA. Literally, the expression means "Humans like ourselves withdrew their arms [from] around us," referring to the fact of abandonment.

21. ACNLG, C68UHC.

22. On the resistance of the Muslim populations and the Tutsi refugees in the Mabare mosque, see especially Emmanuel Viret, "Les musulmans de Mabare

pendant le génocide rwandais," in *La résistance au génocide*, ed. Jacques Sémelin (Paris: Presses de Sciences Po, 2008), 491–504.

23. ACNLG, C6MF.

24. ACNLG, C68UHC.

25. ACNLG, C77ME.

26. ACNLG, CC31UM.

27. ACNLG, C41HS.

28. ACNLG, C6MF.

29. ACNLG, C8RNEC.

30. See Jean-Baptiste Nkulikiyinka, *La chasse Umuhigo: Spectacle et informations sur la chasse dans l'ancien Rwanda* (Nyabisindu, published with support from the Mission française de coopération et d'action culturelle à Kigali, 1993), 12.

31. Nkulikiyinka, *La chasse Umuhigo*, 47.

32. Jean-Baptiste Nkulikiyinka, *Les chants du grelot et de l'arc au pays des esprits chasseurs: Chants et poésie de chasse au Rwanda* (Tervuren: Musée royal d'Afrique centrale, 2013).

33. The political scientist Charles Mironko has noted the reference to that quite particular "bellowing" (indoors) in the stories he transmits from the killers, associating it with the register of hunting and for traditional calls for help. Charles Mironko, "Ibitero: Means and Motives in the Rwandan Genocide," in *Genocide in Cambodia and Rwanda: New Perspectives*, ed. Susan E. Cook (New Brunswick, NJ: Transaction, 2006), 163–89. In a note to a passage about these traditions, Mironko characterizes the shout for help as "the 'whooping' or traditional distress signal that implied a responsibility to help" (174n8). He also refers to "whistles (*induru*) previously used to call for help (*gutabaza*) from neighbors [that] were transformed into harbingers of impending destruction" (175).

34. Alexis Kagame, *L'histoire des armées-bovines dans l'ancien Rwanda* (Paris: IRSAC, 1960).

35. Here I wish to thank Pierre Galinier, who graciously made available to me his collection of old photographs of Rwanda, especially those taken by Joseph Dardenne dating from the 1920s.

36. *Kangura* 40 (March 1993): 17–18: "Un cancrelat ne peut donner naissance à un papillon," cited in Jean-Pierre Chrétien, ed., *Rwanda, les médias du génocide* (Paris: Karthala, 1995), 155–56. The term *ikizungerezi* (plural *ibizungerezi*) means "a woman who makes one lose one's head." The "qualities" of beguilement were attributed to Tutsi women by Hutu propaganda.

37. ACNLG, C69UL.

38. ACNLG, C68UHC; emphasis added.

39. ACNLG, C79NC.

40. ACNLG, C82BO.

41. ACNLG, C8RNEC (male, born in 1972).

7. RESCUES

1. See, for example, African Rights, *Rwanda: Tribute to Courage* (London, 2002); Ibuka, *Les justes rwandais "Indakemwa"* (Kigali, December 2010); and Jean d'Amour Dusengumuremuyi, *Félicitée Niyitegeka: Une lumière dans la nuit rwandaise: Agir face à l'inacceptable* (Brussels, 2019). See also Charles Kabwete Mulinda, "Le sauvetage dans la zone frontalière de Gishamvu et Kigembe au Rwanda," in *La résistance aux génocides*, ed. Jacques Sémelin, Claire Andrieu, and Sarah Gensburger (Paris: Presses de Sciences Po, 2008), 361–75. In addition, the report produced by Ibuka identified more than four hundred rescuers in the territory as a whole.

2. ACNLG, C36UJ.

3. ACNLG, C36UJ.

4. King (*mwami*) Rwabugiri reigned over Rwanda from 1867 to 1895. He was the last *mwami* before the arrival of the missionaries and colonizers. His reign was marked by incessant rivalries at court and by a major territorial expansion, the annexation of the Gisaka region, located on the eastern borders of the central kingdom. His succession was accompanied by a violent struggle for power, which ended in the Rucunshu coup d'état in December 1896, sealing the victory of the Ega clan, to which the queen mother Kanjogera belonged (Rucunshu is a locality in what is now the Southern Province of Rwanda). See Jan Vansina, *Le Rwanda ancien, le royaume nyiginya* (Paris: Karthala, 2001).

5. This verb designates the fact of bringing food to a hospital patient or a prisoner. It also refers to the act of providing food to herders in the high pasture lands. More generally, it is used to define the action of bringing food to people physically unable to procure food for themselves.

6. ACNLG, C8RNEC.

7. ACNLG, C59NJDC.

8. ACNLG, C59NJDC.

9. ACNLG, CC31UM.

10. ACNLG, C40MBC.

11. ACNLG, C40MBC.

12. ACNLG, C31UM.

13. ACNLG, C31UM.

14. ACNLG, C12RUC (no birth date indicated).

15. ACNLG, C12RUC; emphasis added.

16. ACNLG, C12RUC.

17. ACNLG, C12RUC.

18. ACNLG, C32NL.

19. ACNLG, C32NL. All the excerpts that follow are from this text.

20. ACNLG, C32NL; emphasis added.

21. Here are the girl's words translated literally: "That boy took me to his house to hide me there because we were not very close neighbors."

22. This explains why the little girl would write "my names" in the plural, for both her names had been given to her by her parents.

23. Although the figures are the object of political manipulations, the estimate of 1.5 million persons in the refugee camps of Zaire and Tanzania is widely accepted.

24. An eloquent example of the pursuit of political and military mobilization inside the refugee camps can be found in "Compte rendu de la réunion des officiers du Haut Commandement des Forces armées rwandaises tenue à Gooma du 2 au 9 septembre 1994," signed by Major General Augustin Bizimungu in Goma on September 19, 1994: a piece of evidence labeled P45JA and presented in ICTR-98-41-T on February 12, 2006, accessible in the ICTR public database. This document, some fifty pages long, pays emphatic homage in particular to the members of the Interahamwe and the "recruits from civil self-defense" who "did their best to help the Rwandan Armed Forces [FAR]" (20).

25. Emphasis added.

26. Emphasis added.

8. "WE WENT BACK TO OUR RUINS"

1. République du Rwanda, *Dénombrement des victimes du génocide: Rapport final* (Kigali, April 1994), 22, 24, MINALOC archives. According to this report, children from birth to age fourteen represent 50.1 percent of the victims of the genocide. The youngest, from birth to age nine, represent 53 percent of the total number of victims from birth to age nineteen.

2. William Haglund (a legal anthropologist) and Robert H. Kirschner (a forensic anthropologist), *Investigations at Kibuye Roman Catholic Church: Kibuye, Rwanda* (Boston: Physicians for Human Rights, 1997), 1:40.

3. Republika yu Rwanda, Minisiteri y'Imibereho Myiza y'Abaturage, *Raporo y'imirimo y'ibarura ry'abacitse ku icumu ry'Itsembabwoko n'Itsembatsemba hagati ya tarikiy 01 Ukwakira 1990 na tariki y 30 Ukoboza 1994* (Kigali: MINALOC archives, 1998), 12.

4. ACNLG, C8RNEC.

5. ACNLG, C42IE.

6. ACNLG, C58NJDC.

7. ACNLG, C8RNEC; emphasis added.

8. ACNLG, C87MFC.

9. ACNLG, C69UL.

10. ACNLG, C69UJ (female, born in 1986).

11. ACNLG, C66KFC (female, born in 1981).

12. ACNLG, C13RKVC (female, born in 1979).

13. I thank Father Laurent Rutinduka for providing this information. A priest in the Kiziguro parish, his own birthplace, he has undertaken detailed investigations into the history of the genocide of the Tutsi in that region. See Padiri Laurent Rutinduka, *Uko jnoside yakorewe abatutsi yagenze mu cyajoze ari komini Murambi mu Buganza* [How the genocide perpetrated against the Tutsis unfolded in the former commune of Murambi in the Buganza region] (Kigali: CNLG, March 2011).

14. ACNLG, C27RJB (male, born in 1973).

15. ACNLG, C27RJB.

16. ACNLG, C70MB (male, born in 1982).

17. ACNLG, C25KRG (female, born in 1982); emphasis added.

18. ACNLG, C50RJ (female, born in 1984).

19. ACNLG, C4WMA (female, born in 1985). See also the indispensable narrative by Annie Faure, *Blessures d'humanitaire* (Paris: Balland, 1995). Serving as a pneumologist with Médecins du Monde (Doctors without Borders) from April 27 to July 17, 1994, she relates the terrifying conditions under which she practiced medicine in the Gahini hospital.

20. ACNLG, C6MF (male, born in 1987).

21. ACNLG, C23MSC (female, born in 1982).

22. ACNLG, C11RMM (female, born in 1983).

23. A detailed account of the massacre in the Cyahinda parish is available in a reference book edited by the historian Alison Des Forges for Human Rights Watch and Fédération Internationale des Ligues des Droits de l'Homme, *Aucun témoin ne doit survivre: Le génocide au Rwanda* (Paris: Karthala, 1999), 436–44.

24. ACNLG, C91KB (female, born in 1987).

25. ACNLG, C91KB.

26. ACNLG, C91KB.

27. Instituted by the French troops in the Opération Turquoise (June 22–August, 1994) on July 1, 1994, and lasting until the troops gradually withdrew from the region at the end of July, the "secure humanitarian zone" adopted the borders of the prefectures of Cyangugu, Kibuye, and Gikongoro in the southwestern part of the country.

28. ACNLG, C10RGC (female, born in 1982).

29. ACNLG, C10RGC.

30. This detail is not insignificant, since families in homes (*ingo*) whose entrances face each other are connected by reciprocal obligations and special bonds as neighbors. Thus when one family runs into any sort of problem, the first to come to their aid are supposed to be the neighbors whose *rugo* entrance faces theirs.

31. ACNLG, C10RGC (female, born in 1982).

32. ACNLG, C10RGC.

33. ACNLG, C45UAC (female, born in 1988).

34. ACNLG, C45UAC.

35. ACNLG, C45UAC.

36. ACNLG, C45UAC.

37. ACNLG, C45UAC.

38. ACNLG, C45UAC.

39. I am borrowing this very apt concept from the historian Anouche Kunth, who uses it in the work she has devoted to the survivors of the Armenian genocide. See Anouche Kunth, *Au bord de l'effacement: Sur les pas d'exilés arméniens dans l'entre-deux-guerres* (Paris: La Découverte, 2003), 157.

40. According to the report published by the Avega-Agahozo Association following an investigation carried out in 1998 among 951 women survivors of the genocide who had been raped, 66.7 percent of these women were HIV-positive or already suffering from AIDS. Avega-Agahozo, *Survey on Violence against Women in Rwanda* (Kigali, December 1999), 24.

41. ACNLG, C11RMM (female, born in 1983). The term *incike* is used in principle to designate adults who have lost all their descendants to the genocide.

42. The verbe *kubohoza* was also integrated into the everyday language of partisan violence between 1991 and 1994. For a political party, to "liberate" a commune meant the seizure of power to the detriment of a rival group. The word was used particularly often during local partisan competitions between the MRND and the MDR.

43. République du Rwanda, 1977 code pénal, articles 358–62. The term is sometimes used in a more general expression, marking constraint (*ku gahato*). Let us note, moreover, that the provisions related to sanctions against adultery designate that act by the term *ubusambanyi*, revealing the homology established between rape and adultery.

44. In precolonial Rwanda, the term referred to the consummation of a sexual relation deemed illicit, while under the influence of Christianity it took on a sense close to an act of adultery, or a sin. In the early years of the independent Republic of Rwanda, marked by the Parmehutu ideology, a song promised action: "Their women [those of the Tutsi], we shall make concubines, and their daughters, we shall make our wives." We are thus confronted by a semantics that is not only euphemistic but also imbued with the history of banalizing the rape of Tutsi women.

45. Excerpts from parliamentary documents, cited by Daniel de Beer in *Loi rwandaise du 30 août 1996 sur l'organisation des poursuites des infractions constitutives du crime de génocide ou de crime contre l'humanité: Commentaire et jurisprudence* (Kigali/Brussels: Éditions Alter Égaux, 1999), 48.

46. De Beer, *Loi rwandaise du 30 août 1996.*

47. ACNLG, C90NJCC (male, born in 1986).

48. ACNLG, C90NJCC.

49. The western part of the territory was still under the control of the "secure humanitarian zone" set up by France's Opération Turquoise. The FPR imposed its authority on the whole of the country on July 18, 1994, and declared a unilateral ceasefire.

50. On this point, see the detailed reports provided by the High Commission on Human Rights/Operation on Rwanda's Territory, available for the months January through September 1996, ICTR-96019-I, received on December 13, 1996 (ICTR, public database). These reports gave rise to decisions relating to the protection of witnesses who came to testify before the ICTR. On this question, see also African Rights, *La preuve assassinée: Meurtres, attaques, arrestation et intimidation des survivants et témoins* (London, 1996).

51. ACNLG, C85MNJC (female, born in 1985) and C7WNA (female, born in 1981).

52. ACNLG, C59NC (male, born in 1986).

53. ACNLG, C48NEC (male, born in 1988).

9. ESCAPING FROM THE "TEETH OF THE MOCKERS": SURVIVING IN HOSTILE SURROUNDINGS

1. With the help of his wife and his brother, Damas Gisimba managed to save nearly 325 children and eighty adults in the orphanage he ran in the Nyakabanda neighborhood in Kigali, where numerous Interahamwe militiamen were cracking down. See esp. African Rights, *The Gisimba Memorial Center: No Place for* Fear, a *Tribute to Damas Mutezintware Gisimba* (Kigali: African Rights, 2003); and James Karuhanga, "Kwibuka 25: Gisimba on Managing Largest Orphanage during Genocide," *New Times*, April 23, 2019, https://www.newtimes.co.rw/article/165933 /News/kwibuka25-gisimba-on-managing-largest-orphanage-during-genocide.

2. Archives of the Gisimba Memorial Center (ACMG); emphasis added. I thank Damas Gisimba for allowing me access to the invaluable archives of his orphanage, along with everyone who helped me organize them and put them in a safe place in June 2019.

3. According to the estimate supplied by the minister of rehabilitation to the journalist Philip Gourevitch, 70 percent of the residents of Kigali in 1995–1996 came from Tutsi communities who had returned from exile. See Philip Gourevitch, "After Genocide: A Conversation with Paul Kagame," *Transition* 72 (1997): 185.

4. The top leaders of the country were well aware that such a project was a tall order. Paul Kagame did not hide the challenges that awaited him. Gourevitch, "After Genocide," 177.

5. On this question, see Jean-Paul Kimonyo, *Rwanda: Demain! Une longue marche vers la transformation* (Paris: Karthala, 2017), 290–94.

6. A first law against the "ideology of genocide" was passed on July 23, 2008. In the face of criticism, especially from foreign NGOs, it was revised on September 11, 2013, by a second text in which the infraction was defined with more precision and the penalties indicated were weakened.

7. A summary of the set of critiques formulated against the law is available in Lars Waldorf, "Instrumentalizing Genocide: The RPF's Campaign against 'Genocide Ideology,'" in *Remaking Rwanda: State Building and Human Rights after Mass Violence*, ed. Scott Straus and Lars Waldorf (Madison: University of Wisconsin Press, 2011), 48–66.

8. Among the investigations produced on the question by Rwandan public institutions, see Republika yu Rwanda, Inteko ishinga amategeko, Inteko ishinga amateget, Umutwe w'abadepite [Republic of Rwanda, Parliament], *Raporo ya komisiyo idasanzwe gucukubura ubwicanyi bwabereye ku Gikongoro igengabiteker-ezo ya jenoside, n'abayihembera mu Rwanda hose* [Report of the special commission charged with shedding light on the killings perpetrated in Gikongoro, on the ideology of genocide and those who promoted it throughout Rwanda] (Kigali, January 20, 2004); Republique du Rwanda, Senate, *Idéologie du génocide et stratégie de son éradication* (Kigali, 2006); Republika yu Rwanda, Inteko ishinga amategeko, Umutwe w'abadepite [Republic of Rwanda, Parliament], *Raporo ya kimisiyo idasanzwe ishinzwe gucukumbura ikibazo cy'igengabitekerezo ya jenoside ivugwa mu bigo by'amashuri* [Report of the special commission charged with inquiring into the problem of the ideology of genocide in educational establish-ments] (Kigali, November 23, 2007); République du Rwanda, CNLG, *État de l'idéologie du génocide au Rwanda: 1995–2015* (Kigali, 2016).

9. ACNLG, C6MF.

10. ACNLG, C33KTC.

11. ACNLG, C62MO.

12. ACNLG, C62MO.

13. ACNLG, C62MO.

14. ACNLG, C62MO.

15. ACNLG, C62MO.

16. ACNLG, C62MO.

17. These provisional liberations occurred by presidential decree in January 2003 and October 2005. Sixty thousand prisoners were freed for humanitarian reasons in the cases of ill or elderly detainees but also in order to manifest the good will of the government toward those who had given confessions.

18. In 1998, around 124,000 people were incarcerated in Rwandan prisons, under the predictable conditions of promiscuity and poor hygiene. The figure was reported by the NGO Lawyers without Borders in its 1999 report. At the time, Rwanda had the largest incarcerated population per capita in the world.

19. ACNLG, C62MO.

20. ACNLG, C62MO.

21. ACNLG, C62MO.

22. On this point, another girl's statement is exemplary: "Since I am speaking of people who have been freed, who have all their children, who have their families, they are my neighbors, and if ever a book comes out in which my identity and my photo appear while these are my neighbors and there remain to me no more than three people in my family, that can only cause problems for me." ACNLG, C23MSC.

23. ACNLG, C62MO.

24. ACNLG, CC48NEC.

25. ACNLG, C74RM.

26. More precisely, 12,103 *gacaca* jurisdictions.

27. Republic of Rwanda, National Service of *Gacaca* Jurisdictions, *Final Report* (Kigali, June 2012), 88–89.

28. Seventy percent of the judges questioned in the 2002 Rwandan National Unity and Reconciliation Commission (NURC) survey had lived for more than five years in their respective provinces. Republic of Rwanda, NURC, *Survey of Opinion on the Participation in the* Gacaca *and National Reconciliation* (Kigali, 2003), 8.

29. In 2006, 45,396 *inyangamugayo* were replaced owing to accusations of participation in the genocide that had been drawn up against them. See République du Rwanda, Service national des juridictions *gacaca, Résumé du support présenté à la clôture des activités des juridictions* gacaca (Kigali, June 2012), 182.

30. According to the figures supplied by the NURC survey, 60 percent of the survivors questioned in 2002 asserted that the *gacaca* were only "another way of granting amnesty to the guilty parties"; 90 percent expressed their worry about their own security; 60 percent deemed that such trials would be "sources of new traumas"; Republic of Rwanda, NURC, *Survey of Opinion*, 14, 18, 21.

31. According to the Rwandan police, 156 survivors were murdered between 1995 and 2008, forty such cases during 2006 alone—the year that registered the greatest number of homicides. CNLG, *État de l'idéologie du génocide au Rwanda*, 169.

32. ACNLG, C21NCC.

33. ACNLG, C89MG.

34. ACNLG, C36UJ.

35. République du Rwanda, CNLG, *État de l'idéologie du génocide*, 164.

36. ACNLG, C69UL.

37. ACNLG, CC63NJ.

38. I was able to go to that vast mass grave following the confession of a young man in April 2018, thanks to two Ibuka leaders, Égide Nkuranga and Naphtal Ahishakiye, who served as intermediaries. See also Jean d'Amour Mbonyinshuti,

"Genocide: Over 18,000 Victims Exhumed in Kigali Mass Graves," *New Times*, September 18, 2018, https://survivors-fund.org.uk/news/over-18000-victims -exhumed-in-kigali-mass-graves/; Emmanuel Ntirenganya, "Remains of Genocide Victims Retrieved from Kabuga to Be Buried Next Month," *New Times,* April 17, 2019, https://www.newtimes.co.rw/article/165837/News/remains-of -genocide-victims-retrieved-from-kabuga-to-be-buried-next-month.

    39. ACNLG, C421E.

10. "MY HOBBLED LIFE": WRITING MORAL PAIN

    1. ACNLG, C1WMP; emphasis added.

    2. Translator's note: In the French original, the author notes that she has borrowed the term "*les dits de souffrance*," translated here as "expressions of suffering," from Arlette Farge, *Des lieux pour l'histoire* (Paris: Seuil, 1997), 16–17.

    3. On this topic, the work of Darius Gishoma, from whom I am borrowing these definitions, is indispensable: "Crises traumatiques collectives d'*ihahamuka* lors des commémorations du génocide des Tutsi: Aspects cliniques et perspectives thérapeutiques," doctoral thesis in psychology, Université catholique de Louvain, 2014, 167.

    4. Gishoma, "Crises traumatiques collectives," 156, 160.

    5. Gishoma, "Crises traumatiques collectives," 156.

    6. These are personal observations; I was present at the ceremony. In its report for the year 2005, the Health Ministry's National Program for Mental Health noted "a tendency toward increasing growth in the phenomenon." See Darius Gishoma and Jean-Luc Brackelaire, "Quand le corps abrite l'inconcevable: Comment dire le bouleversement dont témoignent les corps au Rwanda?," *Cahiers de psychologie clinique* 30, no. 1 (2008): 168.

    7. Gishoma, "Crises traumatiques collectives," 211, 279.

    8. Gishoma, "Crises traumatiques collectives," 259.

    9. Gishoma, "Crises traumatiques collectives," 311.

    10. Gishoma, "Crises traumatiques collectives," 311.

    11. ACMG, "Fiche de renseignements des enfants séparés de leurs parents," February 22, 1995.

    12. ACNLG, C5WUCC.

    13. ACNLG, C5WUCC.

    14. ACNLG, C5WUCC.

    15. ACNLG, C5WUCC.

    16. ACNLG, C5WUCC.

    17. Cultural repugnance meant that consumption of pork remained relatively rare in Rwanda, despite recent developments that had gradually made its consumption more acceptable.

18. The girl used an expression in Kinyarwanda, *"guhungira ubwayi mu kigunda,"* that means, literally: "When you have felt the irritating dust of sorghum, you find it again in even larger quantities in the bush where you have taken refuge."

19. ACNLG, C5WUCC.

20. In 2003, the AERG morphed into the GAERG: "Groupe des anciens élèves et étudiants rescapés du génocide" [Group of former students who survived the genocide]. See Kelly Rwamapera, "GAERG's Contribution to Restoring the Life of Genocide Survivors," in "Rescapés du génocide: 25 ans après: Bilan des interventions d'appui," special issue, *Dialogue* 210 (November 2019): 129–37. See also Claudine Uwera Kanyamanza and Jean-Luc Brackelaire, "Ménages d'enfants sans parents au Rwanda: (Re-)création d'une structure familiale après le génocide perpétré contre les Tutsi?," *Cahiers de psychologie clinique* 37, no. 2 (2011): 38.

21. ACNLG, C61HIC.

22. ACNLG, C61HIC.

23. ACNLG, C61HIC.

24. We find traces of such conflicts related to the seizing of orphans' lands in the archives of the Gisimba Memorial Center, where a number of court decisions relating to such matters are preserved.

25. ACNLG, C61HIC.

26. ACNLG, C61HIC.

27. ACNLG, C61HIC.

28. According to a count established on October 22, 2019, nearly two million people benefited from the "health program": The secondary school expenses of 107,489 students were covered, 39,000 university students received financial support, and nearly thirty thousand housing units were built with the help of the FARG. Antoine Mugesera, "Observations préliminaires sur les données chiffrées," *Dialogue* 210 (November 2019): 69.

29. Mugesera, "Observations préliminaires sur les données chiffrées," 60–65. See also Jean-Paul Kimonyo, *Rwanda: Demain! Une longue marche vers la transformation* (Paris: Karthala, 2017), 256. Let us recall that after the census undertaken by the Rwandan government in 1998, nearly half of the survivors had no roof over their heads. Minisiteri y'Imibereho Myiza y'Abaturage, *Raporo y'imirimo y'ibarura ry'abacitse ku icumu ry'Itsembabwoko n'Itsembatsemba hagati ya tariki ya 01 Ukwakira 1990 na tariki ya 31 Ukuboza 1994*, 25, MINALOC archives.

30. In 2006, the Rwandan government undertook a vast administrative reorganization of the country. Former entities such as communes and prefectures disappeared, replaced by districts and provinces. The law framing this reconstruction dates from December 31, 2005.

31. ACNLG, C61HIC.

32. ACNLG, C61HIC.

33. ACNLG, C61HIC.

34. ACNLG, C56MY.

35. ACNLG, C14RUC (no birth date indicated).

36. Republic of Rwanda, Ministry of Rehabilitation and Social Integration, UNICEF, *Évaluation des besoins des centres d'accueil pour enfants non accompagnés* (Kigali, January 1995), 7, MINALOC archives, box 56.

37. If we are to believe a study conducted in November 1994 by the Rwandan authorities and UNICEF, there were forty-nine centers in all, spread very unevenly throughout the territory; more than half were concentrated in Butare and Kigali. If we limit ourselves (prudently) to the figures available, the number of orphanages dropped from forty-nine to twenty-five between 1994 and 2003, when the number of children they sheltered dropped from 10,000 to 3,600 during the same period. See the January 1995 report just cited and Republic of Rwanda, Ministry of Local Government, Information and Social Affairs, *National Policy for Orphans and Other Vulnerable Children* (Kigali, 2003). The last orphanages closed their doors in 2015.

38. Kanyamanza and Brackelaire, "Ménages d'enfants sans parents," 14.

39. Kanyamanza and Brackelaire, "Ménages d'enfants sans parents," 19.

40. Kanyamanza and Brackelaire, "Ménages d'enfants sans parents," 18.

41. Kanyamanza and Brackelaire, "Ménages d'enfants sans parents," 18.

42. ACNLG, C31UM; emphasis added.

43. ACNLG, C31UM.

44. ACNLG, C31UM; emphasis added.

45. ACNLG, C31UM.

46. The first (and only) Rwandan psychiatrist after the genocide, Naason Munyandamutsa returned to Rwanda in 1996 after completing several years of training in Geneva. He initiated the creation of a system of psychiatric care for the survivors of the genocide. See Marie-Odile Godard, *Docteur Naason Munyandamutsa: L'umpfumu, un psychiatre à l'épreuve du génocide* (Paris: L'Harmattan, 2019).

47. ACNLG, C91KB; emphasis added.

48. Republic of Rwanda, Health Ministry, National Program of Mental Health, WHO, Dr. Naason Munyandamutsa and Dr. Paul Mahoro Nkubamugisha, *Prévalence de l'état de stress post-traumatique dans la population rwandaise: Diversité de figures cliniques, abus de drogues et autres co-morbidités* (Kigali, 2009), 25. The study is based on the definition of PTSD in the *Diagnostic and Statistical Manual of Mental Disorders*, 4th ed. (DSM 4). For a historical and anthropological reading of this nosographic category, see Didier Fassin and Richard Rechtman, *L'empire du traumatisme: Enquête sur la condition de victime* (Paris: Flammarion, 2011 [2007]).

49. Gishoma, *Crises traumatiques collectives*, 165. One orphan expressed the difference between "madness" and "trauma" in these terms: "When you turn your eyes toward the past and you remember 1994, the way our parents and our

brothers and sisters died with humiliation and cruelty, I feel that that's too much to grasp; and then anyone can be overtaken by *ihahamuka* and go crazy [*umusazi*], whereas he isn't really crazy; it's the problems that are too much for him." ACNLG, C89MG (male, born in 1984).

50. ACNLG, C4MCC.

51. ACNLG, CC70NB.

52. ACNLG, C47NTA. A similar formula can be found in another text in which it is the absence of the disappeared bodies that prolonged the time of the genocide: "As for me, I didn't bury any of my loved ones, I didn't find anyone's bones, and that hurts me badly. Because of all that, the more time passes the more I am afflicted with *ihahamuka*." ACNLG, C6MF.

53. ACNLG, C72RUC.

54. ACNLG, C41HS.

55. Munyandamutsa and Nkubamugisha, *Prévalence de l'état de stress post-traumatique*, 31. According to this study, among the population suffering from PTSD, 53.93 percent suffer from problems of depression, while 20.49 percent show signs of a major depressive state. On February 3, 2020, the Ibuka association presented the results of a study dealing with "problems of mental health" in the general population and among the survivors. The figures relating to suicide and risky behaviors reach 1.7 percent among the survivors, whereas the total is only 0.6 percent in the population at large. I should make it clear, however, that these phenomena are marginal in relation to the various "problems of mental health" mentioned during the presentation of the study. I thank Alain Ngirinshuti for acquainting me with this study.

56. The exact expression used in Kinyarwanda is *"agahita amfata nk'umuntu w'ikibwa."* According the French–Kinyarwanda dictionary, the root "-*cibwa*" refers to "a person [who is] hunted, shamed, cursed, damned. Used with [words of] classes 1 and 2, as in the following expression: *umuzimu w'umuntu wavumwe*, it designates the spirit of a person doomed to unhappiness and to life as a social outcast." The dictionary was established by André Coupez and Thomas Kamanzi (Butare: IRST / Tervuren, Belgium: MRAC, 2005).

57. ACNLG, C48NEC.

58. ACNLG, C2BJB.

59. ACNLG, C57RFR.

60. The dictionary offers no information that could differentiate these terms; they are presented as synonyms. I thank Jean Ruzindaza for his valuable indications about the nuances of words for sorrow.

61. ACNLG, C52NAMC.

62. ACNLG, C67MMGC.

BIBLIOGRAPHY

This bibliography, by no means exhaustive, presents a personal selection of books and other print materials that are directly linked to the issues raised by the orphans' texts. It is meant to offer essential material to readers seeking further information about a history that is still too often unknown.

HISTORY OF THE GENOCIDE AGAINST THE TUTSI

GENERAL HISTORY

Chrétien, Jean-Pierre. *L'Afrique des Grands Lacs: Deux mille ans d'histoire*. Paris: Flammarion, 2003 (2000).

———. *L'invention de l'Afrique des Grands Lacs: Une histoire du XXe siècle*. Paris: Karthala, 2010.

Chrétien, Jean-Pierre, and Marcel Kabanda. *Rwanda: Racisme et génocide, l'idéologie hamitique*. Paris: Belin, 2013.

Human Rights Watch, Fédération internationale des droits de l'homme. *Aucun témoin ne doit survivre: Le génocide au Rwanda*. Paris: Karthala, 1999.

Kimonyo, Jean-Paul. *Rwanda: Un génocide populaire*. Paris: Karthala, 2008.

Mugesera, Antoine. *Les conditions de vie des Tutsi au Rwanda de 1959 à 1990: Persécutions et massacres antérieurs au génocide de 1990 à 1994*. Kigali/Miélan: Dialogue/Izuba, 2014 (2004).

Rutazibwa, Privat, and Paul Rutayisire. *Génocide à Nyarubuye*. Kigali: Éditions rwandaises, 2007.

SCHOOL

Gasanabo, Jean-Damascène. "Mémoires et histoire scolaire: Le cas du Rwanda de 1962–1994." Doctoral thesis, Science of Education, University of Geneva, 2004.

République Rwandaise, Ministère de l'Enseignement Primaire et Secondaire. *Dynamiques des équilibres ethnique et régional dans l'enseignement secondaire rwandais: Fondements, évolution et perspectives d'avenir.* Kigali: May 1986.

RELIGION

Brunet-Lefèvre, Timothée. "Le Père Seromba et la destruction de l'église de Nyange, 6 avril 1994–17 avril 1994: Le génocide des Tutsi de la paroisse de Nyange à travers l'étude du procès d'Athanase Seromba devant le Tribunal pénal international pour le Rwanda, Février 2002–Novembre 2008." Masters thesis, Political Science, École des Hautes Études en Sciences Sociales, dir. Stéphane Audoin-Rouzeau. Paris, 2019.
Loumakis, Spyridon. "Genocide and Religion in Rwanda in the 1990s." In *The Global Impact of Religious Violence*, ed. André Gagné, Spyridon Loumakis, and Calogero A. Miceli, 47–83. Montreal: Wipf and Stock, 2016.
Rutayisire, Paul. *Christianisation du Rwanda (1900–1945): Méthode missionnaire et politique selon Mgr Léon Classe.* Fribourg: Éditions Universitaires, 1986.

WAR, POLITICS, AND VIOLENCE

Africa Watch, Rapport de la Commission internationale d'enquête sur les violations des droits de l'homme au Rwanda depuis le 1er octobre 1990. *Rapport final.* March 1993.
Association for the Defense of Human Rights and Public Liberties. *Rapport sur les droits de l'homme au Rwanda, Septembre 1991–Septembre 1992.* Kigali, December 1992.
———. *Rapport sur les droits de l'homme au Rwanda, Octobre 1992–Octobre 1993.* Kigali, December 1993.
Bertrand, Jordane. *Rwanda, le piège de l'histoire: L'opposition démocratique avant le génocide (1990–1994).* Paris: Karthala, 2000.
Chrétien, Jean-Pierre, ed. *Rwanda, les médias du génocide.* Paris: Karthala, 1995.
Comité pour le respect des droits de l'homme et la démocratie au Rwanda. *Victims of Political Repression since October 1 1990 in Rwanda.* Kigali, December 1991.
Nsengiyumva, François. *Ingoma y'amaraso* [The regime of blood]. Kigali: CLADHO, 1995.

PUBLISHED TESTIMONY

TESTIMONY OF CHILD SURVIVORS DURING THE GENOCIDE

Dukundane Family. *Ishavu ry'Abato, Ubuhamya kuri jenoside yakorewe Abatutsi mu Rwanda.* Kigali: Dukundane Family, 2009.

Habonimana, Charles. *Moi, le dernier Tutsi.* Paris: Plon, 2019.

Kabarari, Valens, and Élise Delage. *Vivant.* Saint Étienne: Utopia, 2019.

Kayitare, Pauline. *Tu leur diras que tu es hutue: À 13 ans, une Tutsie au cœur du génocide rwandais.* Brussels: Éditions André Versaille, 2011.

Kayitesi, Annick. *Nous existons encore: Ils ont massacré sa famille au Rwanda, elle se bat pour qu'on n'oublie pas.* Paris: Michel Lafont, 2004.

Kayitesi, Berthe. *Demain ma vie: Enfants chefs de famille dans le Rwanda d'après.* Paris: Editions Laurence Teper, 2009.

Kubana, Aimable. *Tu es Tutsi mon fils!* Nantes: Éditions Amalthée, 2014.

Lyamukuru, Félicitée. *L'ouragan a frappé Nyundo.* Mons: Éditions du Cerisier, 2018.

Murangira, César. *Un sachet d'hosties pour cinq: Récit d'un rescapé du génocide des Tutsi commis en 1994 au Rwanda.* Nantes: Éditions Amalthée, 2016.

Muzima, Philibert. *Imbibé de leur sang, gravé de leurs noms.* Miélan: Izuba, 2016.

Nsengimana, Albert. *Ma mère m'a tué: Survivre au génocide des Tutsi au Rwanda.* Paris: Hugo Doc, 2019.

Rida Musomandera, Élise. *Le livre d'Élise.* Paris: Les Belles Lettres, 2014.

Rurangwa, Révérien. *Génocidé.* Paris: Presses de la Renaissance, 2006.

Uwineza, Céline. *Untamed: Beyond Freedom, Based on a True Story of an African Child, a Rwanda Daughter.* Kigali, 2019.

CHILDREN'S DRAWINGS

Baqué, Serge. *Dessins et destins d'enfants: Jours après nuit.* Paris: Hommes et Perspectives, 2000.

Salem, Richard A., ed. *Witness to Genocide: The Children of Rwanda. Drawings by Child Survivors of the Rwandan Genocide of 1994.* New York: National Council of the Churches of Christ in USA, 2000.

Woodi Oosterom, Wiljo, ed. *Inyenyeri z'u Rwanda: Abana barandika bakanashushanya ibyabayeho mu gihe cy'itsembabwoko ryo muli 1994* [The stars of Rwanda: children write and describe what happened during the period of the 1994 genocide]. Kigali: Silent Work Foundation, 2004.

THE RESCUERS

African Rights. *Le Centre Mémorial Gisimba: Pas de place pour la peur, un hommage à Damas Mutezintare Gisimba*. London, 2003.

———. *Hommage au courage*. London, 2002.

Dusengumuremyi, Jean d'Amour. *Félicitée Niyitegeka: Une lumière dans la nuit rwandaise, agir face à l'inacceptable*. Brussels: Édition à compte d'auteur, 2019.

Ibuka. *Les justes rwandais "Indakemwa."* Kigali, December 2010.

Kagoyire, Yvonne-Solange, François-Xavier Ngarambe, and Jean-Marie Twambazemungu. *Rescapés de Kigali*. Paris: Éditions de l'Emmanuel, 2014.

Mulinda, Charles Kabwete. "Le sauvetage dans la zone frontalière de Gishamvu et Kigembe au Rwanda." In *La résistance aux génocides*, ed. Jacques Sémelin et al., 361–75. Paris: Presses de Sciences Po, 2008.

Seminega, Tharcisse. *L'amour qui enraya la haine: Comment ma famille survécut au génocide au Rwanda*. Esch-sur-Alzette: Schortgen, 2019.

Wilkens, Carl. *I'm Not Leaving*. Brooke Schlange, 2018.

SEXUAL VIOLENCE

African Rights. *Rwanda: Death, Despair, and Defiance*. London, 1995 (1994).

Avega-Agahozo. *Survey on Violence against Women in Rwanda*. Kigali, December 1999.

Bonnet, Catherine. "Le viol des femmes survivantes du génocide du Rwanda." In *Rwanda: Un génocide du vingtième siècle*, ed. Raymond Verdier, Emmanuel Decaux, and Jean-Pierre Chrétien, 17–29. Paris: L'Harmattan, 1995.

Brouwer, Anne-Marie de, and Sandra Ka Hon Chu, eds. *The Men Who Killed Me: Rwandan Survivors of Sexual Violence*. Vancouver/Toronto/Berkeley: Douglas & McIntyre, 2009.

Human Rights Watch. *Shattered Lives: Sexual Violence during the Rwandan Genocide and Its Aftermath*. New York, September 1996.

Mujawayo, Esther, and Souad Belhaddad. *La fleur de Stéphanie: Rwanda entre réconciliation et déni*. Paris: Flammarion, 2006.

———. *SurVivantes: Rwanda dix ans après le génocide*. Paris: Édition de l'Aube, 2004.

TESTIMONY FROM HUMANITARIAN SOURCES

Faure, Annie. *Blessures d'humanitaire*. Paris: Balland, 1995.

Gaillard, Philippe. "On peut tuer autant de gens qu'on veut, on ne peut pas tuer leur mémoire." *Revue internationale de la Croix rouge* 86, no. 855 (September 2004): 611–27.

TESTIMONY FROM JOURNALISTS

Gourevitch, Philip. *Nous avons le plaisir de vous informer que, demain, nous serons tués avec nos familles: Chroniques rwandaises.* Paris: Denoël, 1999 (1998).
Keane, Fergal. *Season of Blood: A Rwandan Journey.* London: Penguin, 1996 (1995).

THE AFTERMATH

Godard, Marie-Odile. *Docteur Naason Munyandamutsa, l'*umupfumu*: Un psychiatre à l'épreuve du génocide.* Paris: L'Harmattan, 2019.
Kimonyo, Jean-Paul. *Rwanda, demain! Une longue marche vers la transformation.* Paris: Karthala, 2017.
Republika yu Rwanda, Inteko ishinga amategeko, Umutwe w'abadepite [Republic of Rwanda, Parliament]. *Raporo ya komisiyo idasanzwe gucukubura ubwicanyi bwabereye ku Gikongoro, igengabitekerezo ya jenoside, n'abayihembera mu Rwanda hose* [Report of the special commission charged with shedding light on the killings perpetrated in Gikongoro, on the ideology of genocide and those who promoted it throughout Rwanda]. Kigali, January 20, 2004.
———. *Raporo ya komisiyo idasanzwe ishinzwe gucukumbura ikibazo cy'igengabitekerezo ya jenoside ivugwa mu bigo by'amashuri* [Report of the special commission charged with investigating the problem of the ideology of genocide in educational establishments]. Kigali, November 23, 2007.
République du Rwanda, Commission nationale de lutte contre le génocide. *État de l'idéologie du génocide au Rwanda: 1995–2015.* Kigali, 2016.
République du Rwanda, MINALOC. *Dénombrement des victimes du génocide: Rapport final.* Kigali, 2004.
République du Rwanda, Sénat, *Idéologie du génocide et stratégie de son éradication.* Kigali, 2006.

Hélène Dumas is a research fellow in history at the National Centre for Scientific Research (CNRS), affiliated with the Raymond Aron Center for sociological and political studies at the EHESS, Paris. She is the author of *Le Génocide au village: Le massacre des Tutsi au Rwanda.*

Louisa Lombard is Associate Professor of Anthropology at Yale University. She is the author of *State of Rebellion: Violence and Intervention in the Central African Republic.*

Catherine Porter is Professor of French Emerita at the State University of New York at Cortland and former president of the Modern Language Association. She has translated more than fifty books, including Bruno Latour's *Down to Earth* and Elisabeth Roudinesco's *The Sovereign Self.*

Robert Desjarlais, *The Blind Man: A Phantasmography*

Sarah Pinto, *The Doctor and Mrs. A.: Ethics and Counter-Ethics in an Indian Dream Analysis*

Veena Das, *Textures of the Ordinary: Doing Anthropology after Wittgenstein*

Clara Han, *Seeing Like a Child: Inheriting the Korean War*

Vaibhav Saria, *Hijras, Lovers, Brothers: Surviving Sex and Poverty in Rural India*

Richard Rechtman, *Living in Death: Genocide and Its Functionaries.* Translated by Lindsay Turner, Foreword by Veena Das

Jérôme Tournadre, *The Politics of the Near: On the Edges of Protest in South Africa*. Translated by Andrew Brown

Cheryl Mattingly and Lone Grøn, *Imagistic Care: Growing Old in a Precarious World*

Heonik Kwon and Jun Hwan Park, *Spirit Power: Politics and Religion in Korea's American Century*

Mayur R. Suresh, *Terror Trials: Life and Law in Delhi's Courts*

Thomas Cousins, *The Work of Repair: Capacity after Colonialism in the Timber Plantations of South Africa*

Hélène Dumas, *Beyond Despair: The Rwanda Genocide against the Tutsi through the Eyes of Children*. Translated by Catherine Porter. Foreword by Louisa Lombard

Printed in the USA
CPSIA information can be obtained
at www.ICGtesting.com
JSHW082243300424
62221JS00002B/25